MIXED METHODS
RESEARCH
for Social Work

Related books of interest

Using Statistical Methods in Social Science Research with a Complete SPSS Guide, Second Edition
Soleman H. Abu-Bader

Advanced and Multivariate Statistical Methods for Social Science Research
Soleman H. Abu-Bader

Research Methods for Social Workers: A Practice-Based Approach, Second Edition
Samuel S. Faulkner and Cynthia A. Faulkner

Social Work Evaluation: Enhancing What We Do, Second Edition
James R. Dudley

A Practical Guide to Evaluation, Second Edition
Carl F. Brun

The Community Needs Assessment Workbook
Rodney A. Wambeam

Clinical Assessment for Social Workers: Quantitative and Qualitative Methods, Fourth Edition
Catheleen Jordan and Cynthia Franklin

Evidence-Based Practices for Social Workers: An Interdisciplinary Approach, Second Edition
Thomas O'Hare

Using Evidence to Inform Practice for Community and Organizational Change
Maria Roberts-DeGennaro and Sondra J. Fogel

MIXED METHODS RESEARCH
for Social Work

Integrating Methodologies

to Strengthen

Practice and Policy

WENDY L. HAIGHT

University of Minnesota, Twin Cities

LAUREL N. BIDWELL

St. Catherine University and the University of St. Thomas

LYCEUM
BOOKS, INC.

5758 South Blackstone Avenue
Chicago, Illinois 60637

© 2016 by Lyceum Books, Inc.

Published by
LYCEUM BOOKS, INC.
5758 S. Blackstone Avenue
Chicago, Illinois 60637
773-643-1903 fax
773-643-1902 phone
lyceum@lyceumbooks.com
www.lyceumbooks.com

6   5   4   3   2   16   17   18   19   20

ISBN 978-1-933478-38-8

Printed in the United States of America.

Library of Congress Cataloging-in-Publication Data

Haight, Wendy L., 1958- author.
    Mixed methods research for social work : integrating methodologies to strengthen practice and policy / Wendy L. Haight, Laurel N. Bidwell.
        pages cm
    Includes bibliographical references and index.
    ISBN 978-1-933478-38-8 (pbk. : alk. paper)
    1. Social service—Research—Methodology.   2. Social service—Practice.   3. Social work education.   I. Bidwell, Laurel N., author.   II. Title.
HV11.H3115   2016
361.3072′1—dc23
                                                                              2015026577

We dedicate this book to our students past, present, and future, and to the social workers who use mixed methods research to improve the lives of people nationally and internationally.

Contents

Figures and Tables

Guidelines for Use with 2015 EPAS

Preface

Chapter 1: Introduction

Part 1: Recovering the Contributions of Social Work Pioneers to Early Mixed Methods Research

Chapter 2: Pragmatism in Social Work and Mixed Methodology: The Legacy of Jane Addams (1860–1935) and John Dewey (1859–1952)

In this chapter, readers will consider the roots of pragmatism, as it plays an instrumental role in shaping our action-oriented approach to knowledge acquisition and theory building. Connections are made between our rich history as practitioner-scholars and the impact that this has on questions that we seek to answer in order to advance human rights and social, economic and environmental justice for marginalized populations. As a profession, we have made a commitment to engaging in ethical research methodologies that are as dynamic as the needs of the populations that we strive to serve.

Competency 1: Demonstrate Ethical and Professional Behavior

- Make ethical decisions by applying the standards of the NASW Code of Ethics, relevant laws and regulations, models for ethical decision-making, ethical conduct of research, and additional codes of ethics as appropriate to context.

Competency 3: Advance Human Rights and Social, Economic, and Environmental Justice

- Apply understanding of social, economic, and environmental justice to advocate for human rights at the individual and system levels.
- Engage in practices that advance social, economic, and environmental justice.

Competency 4: Engage in Practice-informed Research and Research-informed Practice

- Use practice experience and theory to inform scientific inquiry and research.
- Apply critical thinking to engage in analysis of quantitative and qualitative research methods and research findings.

• Use and translate research evidence to inform and improve practice, policy, and service delivery.

Competency 9: Evaluate Practice with Individuals, Families, Groups, Organizations, and Communities

• Select and use appropriate methods for evaluation of outcomes.
• Apply knowledge of human behavior and the social environment, person-in-environment, and other multidisciplinary theoretical frameworks in the evaluation of outcomes.
• Apply evaluation findings to improve practice effectiveness at the micro, mezzo, and macro levels.

Chapter 3: The History of Mixed Methods Social Work Research: The Pittsburgh Survey (1907–08)

For decades, social work scholars have been engaged in multiple research methodologies inspired by a commitment to social, economic and environmental justice. Over the course of time, social work values and ethics have largely remained at the center of our methodological decisions. As a result, social workers have engaged in research practices that shed light on oppression, encourage structural power balances and inform policy. In this chapter, readers will explore the historical foundation of contemporary mixed methods. Readers will also consider ways in which dominant methodological trends have influenced research decisions across time. The legitimacy and quality of social work research is contextualized and explored within this framework.

Competency 1: Demonstrate Ethical and Professional Behavior

• Make ethical decisions by applying the standards of the NASW Code of Ethics, relevant laws and regulations, models for ethical decision-making, ethical conduct of research, and additional codes of ethics as appropriate to context.

Competency 2: Engage Diversity and Difference in Practice

• Apply and communicate understanding of the importance of diversity and difference in shaping life experiences in practice at the micro, mezzo, and macro levels.

Competency 3: Advance Human Rights and Social, Economic, and Environmental Justice

• Apply understanding of social, economic, and environmental justice to advocate for human rights at the individual and system levels.
• Engage in practices that advance social, economic, and environmental justice.

Competency 4: Engage in Practice-informed Research and Research-informed Practice

- Use practice experience and theory to inform scientific inquiry and research.
- Apply critical thinking to engage in analysis of quantitative and qualitative research methods and research findings.
- Use and translate research evidence to inform and improve practice, policy, and service delivery.

Competency 5: Engage in Policy Practice

- Apply critical thinking to analyze, formulate, and advocate for policies that advance human rights and social, economic, and environmental justice.

Competency 9: Evaluate Practice with Individuals, Families, Groups, Organizations, and Communities

- Select and use appropriate methods for evaluation of outcomes.
- Apply knowledge of human behavior and the social environment, person-in-environment, and other multidisciplinary theoretical frameworks in the evaluation of outcomes.
- Apply evaluation findings to improve practice effectiveness at the micro, mezzo, and macro levels.

Part 2: Doing Mixed Methods Research: The Ongoing Contributions of Contemporary Social Workers

Chapter 4: Integrating Research Questions and Contemplating Reasons for Mixing: Men Incarcerated for Violent Crimes

Research questions posed by social workers most often stem from timely topics impacting marginalized and vulnerable individuals, groups and communities. When embarking upon a new research study or program of research, social workers are encouraged to consider, first and foremost, the type of research design that will best fit the central question or problem. This focus is in line with social work ideologies; client systems don't typically benefit from a one-size-fits-all approach. Mixed methods may offer the researcher a more comprehensive picture of a topic or provide a diverse viewpoint rarely explored. Mixed methods may also enhance the rigor of a study to ensure that the findings are ethical and fair and accurately represent the population being studied. In this chapter, a research exemplar focused on perpetrators of sexual abuse and their families, illustrates how mixed methods were used to enhance understanding of a complex phenomenon. Findings from this program of research facilitated the development of a theoretical model explaining the drivers of violent behavior as well as an assessment tool intended to aid clinicians in child sexual abuse prevention and intervention efforts.

Competency 2: Engage Diversity and Difference in Practice

- Apply and communicate understanding of the importance of diversity and difference in shaping life experiences in practice at the micro, mezzo, and macro levels.

Competency 3: Advance Human Rights and Social, Economic, and Environmental Justice

- Apply understanding of social, economic, and environmental justice to advocate for human rights at the individual and system levels.
- Engage in practices that advance social, economic, and environmental justice.

Competency 4: Engage in Practice-informed Research and Research-informed Practice

- Use practice experience and theory to inform scientific inquiry and research.
- Apply critical thinking to engage in analysis of quantitative and qualitative research methods and research findings.
- Use and translate research evidence to inform and improve practice, policy, and service delivery.

Competency 7: Assess Individuals, Families, Groups, Organizations, and Communities

- Apply knowledge of human behavior and the social environment, person-in-environment, and other multidisciplinary theoretical frameworks in the analysis of assessment data from clients and constituencies.
- Select appropriate intervention strategies based on the assessment, research knowledge, and values and preferences of clients and constituencies.

Competency 8: Intervene with Individuals, Families, Groups, Organizations, and Communities

- Critically choose and implement interventions to achieve practice goals and enhance capacities of clients and constituencies.
- Apply knowledge of human behavior and the social environment, person-in-environment, and other multidisciplinary theoretical frameworks in interventions with clients and constituencies.
- Use inter-professional collaboration as appropriate to achieve beneficial practice outcomes.

Competency 9: Evaluate Practice with Individuals, Families, Groups, Organizations, and Communities

- Select and use appropriate methods for evaluation of outcomes.
- Apply knowledge of human behavior and the social environment, person-in-environment, and other multidisciplinary theoretical frameworks in the evaluation of outcomes.
- Apply evaluation findings to improve practice effectiveness at the micro, mezzo, and macro levels.

Chapter 5: Integrating Observational and Cause-Probing Designs: Refugees Experiencing War Trauma

Research designs serve as blueprints for a study or program of research. Social work research might aim to describe the needs of underserved individuals, groups, or communities or it might intend to uncover the cause of a particular phenomenon. In this chapter, readers will consider designs commonly employed in social work research. An exemplar illustrates how a phased research design allowed a group of interdisciplinary researchers and key stakeholders to map out a program of research that captured local, regional, and national data about refugee mental health related to interpersonal trauma. A social justice focus remained at the center of their design decisions. One of the primary goals was to develop culturally grounded screening tools and to integrate them into public health screenings for newly resettled refugee groups. Findings from this program of research resulted in significant changes in practice and policy.

Competency 1: Demonstrate Ethical and Professional Behavior

- Make ethical decisions by applying the standards of the NASW Code of Ethics, relevant laws and regulations, models for ethical decision-making, ethical conduct of research, and additional codes of ethics as appropriate to context.

Competency 2: Engage Diversity and Difference in Practice

- Apply and communicate understanding of the importance of diversity and difference in shaping life experiences in practice at the micro, mezzo, and macro levels.

Competency 3: Advance Human Rights and Social, Economic, and Environmental Justice

- Apply understanding of social, economic, and environmental justice to advocate for human rights at the individual and system levels.
- Engage in practices that advance social, economic, and environmental justice.

Competency 4: Engage in Practice-informed Research and Research-informed Practice

- Use practice experience and theory to inform scientific inquiry and research.
- Apply critical thinking to engage in analysis of quantitative and qualitative research methods and research findings.
- Use and translate research evidence to inform and improve practice, policy, and service delivery.

Competency 5: Engage in Policy Practice

- Apply critical thinking to analyze, formulate, and advocate for policies that advance human rights and social, economic, and environmental justice.

Competency 6: Engage with Individuals, Families, Groups, Organizations, and Communities

- Apply knowledge of human behavior and the social environment, person-in-environment, and other multidisciplinary theoretical frameworks to engage with clients and constituencies.

Competency 7: Assess Individuals, Families, Groups, Organizations, and Communities

- Apply knowledge of human behavior and the social environment, person-in-environment, and other multidisciplinary theoretical frameworks in the analysis of assessment data from clients and constituencies.
- Select appropriate intervention strategies based on the assessment, research knowledge, and values and preferences of clients and constituencies.

Competency 8: Intervene with Individuals, Families, Groups, Organizations, and Communities

- Critically choose and implement interventions to achieve practice goals and enhance capacities of clients and constituencies.
- Apply knowledge of human behavior and the social environment, person-in-environment, and other multidisciplinary theoretical frameworks in interventions with clients and constituencies.
- Use inter-professional collaboration as appropriate to achieve beneficial practice outcomes.

Competency 9: Evaluate Practice with Individuals, Families, Groups, Organizations, and Communities

- Select and use appropriate methods for evaluation of outcomes.

- Apply knowledge of human behavior and the social environment, person-in-environment, and other multidisciplinary theoretical frameworks in the evaluation of outcomes.
- Apply evaluation findings to improve practice effectiveness at the micro, mezzo, and macro levels.

Chapter 6: Integrating Methods and Contemplating Ethical Issues: Parents with Low Incomes Accused of Child Maltreatment

The selection of methods to be used in any research study involves a complex set of decisions that balance research standards with the needs of the participants involved. Sample selection, measures used and procedures for collecting data require careful planning and execution. In this chapter, an exemplar is used to illustrate the complexities of carrying out a mixed methods study with highly vulnerable participants. The ultimate goal of this study was to evaluate a model of legal representation for parents involved with child protection services. For this highly vulnerable group of clients, social work ethics directs us not only to follow IRB guidelines but to take additional steps to ensure protection and support in conjunction with clients' research involvement.

Competency 1: Demonstrate Ethical and Professional Behavior

- Make ethical decisions by applying the standards of the NASW Code of Ethics, relevant laws and regulations, models for ethical decision-making, ethical conduct of research, and additional codes of ethics as appropriate to context.

Competency 2: Engage Diversity and Difference in Practice

- Apply and communicate understanding of the importance of diversity and difference in shaping life experiences in practice at the micro, mezzo, and macro levels.

Competency 3: Advance Human Rights and Social, Economic, and Environmental Justice

- Apply understanding of social, economic, and environmental justice to advocate for human rights at the individual and system levels.
- Engage in practices that advance social, economic, and environmental justice.

Competency 4: Engage in Practice-informed Research and Research-informed Practice

- Use practice experience and theory to inform scientific inquiry and research.
- Apply critical thinking to engage in analysis of quantitative and qualitative research methods and research findings.

- Use and translate research evidence to inform and improve practice, policy, and service delivery.

Competency 6: Engage with Individuals, Families, Groups, Organizations, and Communities

- Apply knowledge of human behavior and the social environment, person-in-environment, and other multidisciplinary theoretical frameworks to engage with clients and constituencies.

Competency 7: Assess Individuals, Families, Groups, Organizations, and Communities

- Apply knowledge of human behavior and the social environment, person-in-environment, and other multidisciplinary theoretical frameworks in the analysis of assessment data from clients and constituencies.
- Select appropriate intervention strategies based on the assessment, research knowledge, and values and preferences of clients and constituencies.

Competency 8: Intervene with Individuals, Families, Groups, Organizations, and Communities

- Critically choose and implement interventions to achieve practice goals and enhance capacities of clients and constituencies.
- Apply knowledge of human behavior and the social environment, person-in-environment, and other multidisciplinary theoretical frameworks in interventions with clients and constituencies.
- Use inter-professional collaboration as appropriate to achieve beneficial practice outcomes.

Competency 9: Evaluate Practice with Individuals, Families, Groups, Organizations, and Communities

- Select and use appropriate methods for evaluation of outcomes.
- Apply knowledge of human behavior and the social environment, person-in-environment, and other multidisciplinary theoretical frameworks in the evaluation of outcomes.
- Apply evaluation findings to improve practice effectiveness at the micro, mezzo, and macro levels.

Chapter 7: Integrating Analyses and Enhancing Rigor: Spirituality and Recovery from Addiction

Realizing the potential of mixed methods social work research does not stop at the integration of concepts, questions and methods. One of the areas in which some mixed methods researchers struggle is in the integration of data analyses. This chapter explores models of integrated data analysis used within a mixed methods study or program of research. An exemplar is used to illustrate the benefits gained by shifting from mono to mixed methods. In order to strengthen previous quantitative findings, the researcher used qualitative techniques influenced by insights that she had gained while providing clinical services to individuals in recovery. Her shift from mono to mixed methods research was intended to both engage participants differently and to enhance the relevance of her quantitative findings by contextualizing the data collected.

Competency 1: Demonstrate Ethical and Professional Behavior

- Make ethical decisions by applying the standards of the NASW Code of Ethics, relevant laws and regulations, models for ethical decision-making, ethical conduct of research, and additional codes of ethics as appropriate to context.

Competency 2: Engage Diversity and Difference in Practice

- Apply and communicate understanding of the importance of diversity and difference in shaping life experiences in practice at the micro, mezzo, and macro levels.

Competency 3: Advance Human Rights and Social, Economic, and Environmental Justice

- Apply understanding of social, economic, and environmental justice to advocate for human rights at the individual and system levels.
- Engage in practices that advance social, economic, and environmental justice.

Competency 4: Engage in Practice-informed Research and Research-informed Practice

- Use practice experience and theory to inform scientific inquiry and research.
- Apply critical thinking to engage in analysis of quantitative and qualitative research methods and research findings.
- Use and translate research evidence to inform and improve practice, policy, and service delivery.

Competency 5: Engage in Policy Practice

- Apply critical thinking to analyze, formulate, and advocate for policies that advance human rights and social, economic, and environmental justice.

Competency 6: Engage with Individuals, Families, Groups, Organizations, and Communities

- Apply knowledge of human behavior and the social environment, person-in-environment, and other multidisciplinary theoretical frameworks to engage with clients and constituencies.

Competency 7: Assess Individuals, Families, Groups, Organizations, and Communities

• Apply knowledge of human behavior and the social environment, person-in-environment, and other multidisciplinary theoretical frameworks in the analysis of assessment data from clients and constituencies.
• Select appropriate intervention strategies based on the assessment, research knowledge, and values and preferences of clients and constituencies.

Competency 8: Intervene with Individuals, Families, Groups, Organizations, and Communities

• Critically choose and implement interventions to achieve practice goals and enhance capacities of clients and constituencies.
• Apply knowledge of human behavior and the social environment, person-in-environment, and other multidisciplinary theoretical frameworks in interventions with clients and constituencies.
• Use inter-professional collaboration as appropriate to achieve beneficial practice outcomes.

Competency 9: Evaluate Practice with Individuals, Families, Groups, Organizations, and Communities

• Select and use appropriate methods for evaluation of outcomes
• Apply knowledge of human behavior and the social environment, person-in-environment, and other multidisciplinary theoretical frameworks in the evaluation of outcomes.
• Apply evaluation findings to improve practice effectiveness at the micro, mezzo, and macro levels.

Chapter 8: Mixed Methods Designs: Children from Rural Methamphetamine-Involved Families

In this chapter, we focus on components of research designs specific to mixed methods research. Readers will explore design dimensions and associated typologies. Typologies provide a starting point for researchers to consider when planning and implementing a study, as they can be useful models for thinking about the potential scope, diversity, and flexibility of complex mixed methods designs. An exemplar will illustrate the evolution of a multi-phased, collaborative mixed methods project concerning methamphetamine-involved families. The impetus for this project was to assist practitioners to better understand the complex needs of these families in order to build more effective interventions. The resulting Life Story Intervention was then implemented and evaluated for effectiveness.

Competency 1: Demonstrate Ethical and Professional Behavior

• Make ethical decisions by applying the standards of the NASW Code of Ethics, relevant laws and regulations, models for ethical decision-making, ethical conduct of research, and additional codes of ethics as appropriate to context.

Competency 2: Engage Diversity and Difference in Practice

• Apply and communicate understanding of the importance of diversity and difference in shaping life experiences in practice at the micro, mezzo, and macro levels.

Competency 3: Advance Human Rights and Social, Economic, and Environmental Justice

• Apply understanding of social, economic, and environmental justice to advocate for human rights at the individual and system levels.
• Engage in practices that advance social, economic, and environmental justice.

Competency 4: Engage in Practice-informed Research and Research-informed Practice

• Use practice experience and theory to inform scientific inquiry and research.
• Apply critical thinking to engage in analysis of quantitative and qualitative research methods and research findings.
• Use and translate research evidence to inform and improve practice, policy, and service delivery.

Competency 5: Engage in Policy Practice

• Apply critical thinking to analyze, formulate, and advocate for policies that advance human rights and social, economic, and environmental justice.

Competency 6: Engage with Individuals, Families, Groups, Organizations, and Communities

• Apply knowledge of human behavior and the social environment, person-in-environment, and other multidisciplinary theoretical frameworks to engage with clients and constituencies.

Competency 7: Assess Individuals, Families, Groups, Organizations, and Communities

• Apply knowledge of human behavior and the social environment, person-in-environment, and other multidisciplinary theoretical frameworks in the analysis of assessment data from clients and constituencies.

• Select appropriate intervention strategies based on the assessment, research knowledge, and values and preferences of clients and constituencies.

Competency 8: Intervene with Individuals, Families, Groups, Organizations, and Communities

• Critically choose and implement interventions to achieve practice goals and enhance capacities of clients and constituencies.
• Apply knowledge of human behavior and the social environment, person-in-environment, and other multidisciplinary theoretical frameworks in interventions with clients and constituencies.
• Use inter-professional collaboration as appropriate to achieve beneficial practice outcomes.

Competency 9: Evaluate Practice with Individuals, Families, Groups, Organizations, and Communities

• Select and use appropriate methods for evaluation of outcomes.
• Apply knowledge of human behavior and the social environment, person-in-environment, and other multidisciplinary theoretical frameworks in the evaluation of outcomes.
• Apply evaluation findings to improve practice effectiveness at the micro, mezzo, and macro levels.

Part 3: Building a Twenty-first Century Mixed Methods Social Work Research Career

Chapter 9: Finding Mentors, Working in Teams, Writing, and Publishing

In this chapter, we discuss issues new social work researchers may confront as they begin to build their mixed methods research careers. Currently, in schools of social work, there exist fewer mixed methods courses and resources than in other related disciplines. Previous chapters emphasize the importance of mixed methods in understanding the complexities of our client systems. We rely upon flexible methodologies in order to conduct ethical research that may be used to generate theory, produce assessment tools, guide intervention, and influence policy. Readers consider the benefits of creating educational opportunities and mentorship in mixed methods, as reflections from early-career social work researchers are presented.

Competency 1: Demonstrate Ethical and Professional Behavior

• Make ethical decisions by applying the standards of the NASW Code of Ethics, relevant laws and regulations, models for ethical decision-making, ethical conduct of research, and additional codes of ethics as appropriate to context.

Competency 4: Engage in Practice-informed Research and Research-informed Practice

- Use practice experience and theory to inform scientific inquiry and research.
- Apply critical thinking to engage in analysis of quantitative and qualitative research methods and research findings.
- Use and translate research evidence to inform and improve practice, policy, and service delivery.

Competency 9: Evaluate Practice with Individuals, Families, Groups, Organizations, and Communities

- Select and use appropriate methods for evaluation of outcomes.
- Apply knowledge of human behavior and the social environment, person-in-environment, and other multidisciplinary theoretical frameworks in the evaluation of outcomes.
- Apply evaluation findings to improve practice effectiveness at the micro, mezzo, and macro levels.

Chapter 10: Opportunities and challenges

Mixed methods research is congruent with social work's commitment to study complex social issues holistically and in context, and with an emphasis on diversity. Mixed methods research draws upon our rich social work history by intentionally and strategically integrating quantitative and qualitative traditions to address particular questions and problems that arise in practice and policy. Not only does mixed methods research add to our commitment to evidence-based practice, but it also strengthens our presence within a multidisciplinary research context. Social work researchers have much to gain from and much to contribute to this emergent field.

Competency 1: Demonstrate Ethical and Professional Behavior

- Make ethical decisions by applying the standards of the NASW Code of Ethics, relevant laws and regulations, models for ethical decision-making, ethical conduct of research, and additional codes of ethics as appropriate to context.

Competency 2: Engage Diversity and Difference in Practice

- Apply and communicate understanding of the importance of diversity and difference in shaping life experiences in practice at the micro, mezzo, and macro levels.

Competency 3: Advance Human Rights and Social, Economic, and Environmental Justice

- Apply understanding of social, economic, and environmental justice to advocate for human rights at the individual and system levels.

• Engage in practices that advance social, economic, and environmental justice.

Competency 4: Engage in Practice-informed Research and Research-informed Practice

• Use practice experience and theory to inform scientific inquiry and research.
• Apply critical thinking to engage in analysis of quantitative and qualitative research methods and research findings.
• Use and translate research evidence to inform and improve practice, policy, and service delivery.

Competency 5: Engage in Policy Practice

• Apply critical thinking to analyze, formulate, and advocate for policies that advance human rights and social, economic, and environmental justice.

Competency 6: Engage with Individuals, Families, Groups, Organizations, and Communities

• Apply knowledge of human behavior and the social environment, person-in-environment, and other multidisciplinary theoretical frameworks to engage with clients and constituencies.

Competency 7: Assess Individuals, Families, Groups, Organizations, and Communities

• Apply knowledge of human behavior and the social environment, person-in-environment, and other multidisciplinary theoretical frameworks in the analysis of assessment data from clients and constituencies.
• Select appropriate intervention strategies based on the assessment, research knowledge, and values and preferences of clients and constituencies.

Competency 8: Intervene with Individuals, Families, Groups, Organizations, and Communities

• Critically choose and implement interventions to achieve practice goals and enhance capacities of clients and constituencies.
• Apply knowledge of human behavior and the social environment, person-in-environment, and other multidisciplinary theoretical frameworks in interventions with clients and constituencies.
• Use inter-professional collaboration as appropriate to achieve beneficial practice outcomes.

Competency 9: Evaluate Practice with Individuals, Families, Groups, Organizations, and Communities

- Select and use appropriate methods for evaluation of outcomes.
- Apply knowledge of human behavior and the social environment, person-in-environment, and other multidisciplinary theoretical frameworks in the evaluation of outcomes.
- Apply evaluation findings to improve practice effectiveness at the micro, mezzo, and macro levels.

Preface

Mixed methods thinking is an integral part of our heritage from nineteenth-century social work pioneers as well as our legacy to twenty-first-century social workers. The foundations of mixed methods social work inquiry are reflected in the work of Jane Addams (1860–1935), who played a pivotal role in the emergence of American Pragmatism, a shared philosophic base of contemporary social work and mixed methods research. Addams philosophized and lived a pragmatic action-oriented approach to knowledge in the pursuit of social justice. This pragmatic approach also is apparent in one of the earliest publicly identified social work research projects, the Pittsburgh Survey conducted in 1907–08.

Contemporary mixed methods research offers modern social workers an approach to addressing complex issues of human struggle with poverty, illness, disability, and oppression. True to our pragmatist roots, we focus on the person-in-environment and emphasize holistic views of human challenges. Our thinking typically is a back and forth conversation between micro and macro levels of analysis. The issues that concern us often involve specific individuals, groups, or communities embedded within macro level sociopolitical, economic, and cultural contexts. These problems addressed by social work researchers are excellent candidates for mixed methods approaches that combine the depth of qualitative with the breadth of quantitative approaches.

Consistent with our shared roots in pragmatism and its progressive ethics, contemporary social work values of social justice, diversity, and empowerment align closely with the values of mixed methods research in which respectful engagement with differences, including bringing to the fore voices that have been silenced, is fundamental. Indeed, pragmatism focuses on gaining knowledge through and in the pursuit of desired ends. This shared pragmatic perspective also is apparent in the work of contemporary mixed methods researchers and social workers who recognize that our values and our politics are always a part of who we are and how we act.

Despite the fit of mixed methods research with social work history, philosophy, and values, social workers have played a very small part in contemporary interdisciplinary discussions of mixed methodology. Leaders in the development of mixed methods research largely have been scholars within applied disciplines such as education, evaluation, and nursing. Similar to social work researchers, researchers from these allied professions address enormously complex, urgent, multilayered issues requiring the full tool chest of social inquiry approaches.

Yet there is increased interest among social workers in engaging in contemporary discussions of methodological issues involved in integrating quantitative and qualitative traditions. Chaumba has called for mixed methods research to be taught to social work students. A recent edition of a popular social work text by Rubin and Babbie includes some coverage of mixed methods inquiry. In the second edition of her qualitative methods text, Padgett notes that the interest in mixed methods approaches to social work research appears greater than ever. Also, the *SAGE Handbook of Social Work Research* includes a chapter on mixed methods research by Greene, Sommerfeld, and Haight. In addition, at the request of members of the Society for Social Work Research, a preconference workshop on mixed methods research was presented by Wendy Haight at the 2013 meeting. Conversations surrounding that preconference workshop served as the impetus for this book, *Mixed Methods Research for Social Work: Integrating Methodologies to Strengthen Practice and Policy*.

Through engagement with methodological theory, social work researchers can strengthen the design of their mixed methods inquiries by combining traditions in a more intentional, strategic, and fully integrated manner. Although social work researchers have been integrating concepts and methods from qualitative and quantitative traditions for decades, relatively few studies are intentionally and fully integrated, especially with respect to design typologies and analyses. Mixed methodologists have moved beyond integration of qualitative and quantitative methods to the development of signature mixed methods designs and analyses that more fully engage the potential of mixed methodology. By engaging with contemporary methodological developments, social work researchers can remain on the crest of rigorous socially relevant research with, and on behalf of, vulnerable clients and communities.

PURPOSE

The purpose of this book is threefold. First, we seek to recover and communicate the historical and ongoing contributions of social workers to the field of mixed methods research. Second, we intend to provide a resource for social workers continuing our mixed methods tradition into the twenty-first century. Finally, we hope to encourage more social workers to join ongoing interdisciplinary efforts to develop and strengthen mixed methods research.

AUDIENCE AND USE OF THIS TEXT

This text is written by and for social workers. Many of the concepts that we present will not be new to social workers. As in other areas of social work practice, mixed methods research is holistic and flexible and it does not prescribe a one-size-fits-all approach. It offers a conceptual framework and set of tools to guide social work researchers.

We intend this text to be used by social work professionals and students who have some grounding in qualitative and quantitative research and who are considering the use of mixed methods in their own research or practice. We also intend it for use in social work research courses. It is appropriate for use in advanced MSW research courses and PhD courses. We encourage instructors to use this text in conjunction with primary source research and methodology articles and book chapters of their choosing. We include some suggestions for additional readings at the end of each chapter with brief annotations describing their appropriateness for assignments in MSW or PhD research courses. It also can be used as a supplementary text in primarily qualitative or quantitative research courses.

ORGANIZATION OF THIS TEXT

This text is divided into several parts. Part 1 focuses on recovering the legacy of early social workers to mixed methods inquiry. In a series of two essays, we first discuss the common roots in American Pragmatism of social work and mixed methodology and then the historical forbearers of modern mixed methods social work research. The second major section focuses on practical issues of how to conduct mixed methods social work research including developing research questions, designs, methods, and analyses. These chapters walk the readers through the development of their own mixed methods inquiry. They also include exemplars of the ongoing contributions of contemporary mixed methods social work researchers. The third section provides some practical guidance for building a mixed methods social work research career in the twenty-first century, including some opportunities and challenges as we move into the future.

A unique feature of this text is the way that we organize discussions of mixed methods around real examples of research by social workers. In a recent study by Bryman, mixed methods researchers in various disciplines identified a relative absence of well-known exemplars as a barrier to the development of mixed methods research. In part 1, we provide a detailed discussion of the Pittsburgh Study conducted from 1907 to 1908. This influential study integrated methods from a wide variety of social science traditions to examine rapid industrialization, urbanization, poverty, and immigration in order to promote reforms. In each of the chapters in part 2, we provide in-depth discussions of mixed methods studies by contemporary social workers investigating a variety of social work issues in a variety of settings. These exemplars were constructed not only from reviews of written literature, but from interviews with the authors, mixed methods social work researchers. Interview excerpts highlight (in the researchers' own words) the nuances of the study that might not be available in the original research publications. Part 3 focuses on opportunities and challenges as we move into the future. It discusses a variety of practical issues involved in building a mixed methods research career including finding mentors; working in mixed methods research teams; and writing, publishing and funding mixed methods research. It also includes interviews with two early career social work researchers and a Taiwanese social work professor as one example of the international interest in mixed methods social work research. All of the examples provide rich details that will highlight the topic under study along with some of the strengths and challenges inherent in mixed methods research.

Several additional pedagogical features will facilitate the learning of social workers new to mixed methods research. First, text boxes precede the in-depth presentations of mixed methods social work research in chapters 3 through 8. These boxes contain questions to guide readers in applying concepts introduced in the chapter to published mixed methods social work research. Second, boxes at the ends of chapters 4 through 8 guide readers in the design of generic mixed methods grant proposals or capstone, thesis, or dissertation projects. These text boxes help readers to apply concepts introduced in the chapter to developing their own research projects. In addition, instructors may use questions contained in both types of boxes to stimulate class discussions or as written assignments. Terms that may be unfamiliar to readers are bolded and italicized throughout the text and defined in the glossary. Finally, Appendixes A and B reproduce sections of a successful mixed methods social work research dissertation proposal and a successful NIH-funded mixed methods social work research grant, respectively, as helpful guides to students and early career professionals.

ACKNOWLEDGMENTS

Many people have had a hand in bringing this book to fruition, and it is a pleasure to acknowledge their generosity here. Our conversations with Tom Meenaghan, advisory editor, and John Creswell were pivotal in the development of this book. Tom Meenaghan provided especially insightful feedback on the importance of embedding mixed methods research in the context of social work. Jennifer Greene shared with us her most recent thinking about integrated analyses. John Creswell, Jane Gilgun, Patricia Shannon, Amy Krentzman, Johanna Creswell Baez, Daphne Watkins, Linda Kingery, and Mary Ku allowed us to interview them about their experiences doing mixed methods research. We also thank our editors and anonymous reviewers. We appreciate their careful reading and incisive criticism.

1

Introduction

I just think mixed methods research is so important to our understanding, especially in the field of social work. It's important to our understanding of the people that we are going to work with. And it doesn't matter whether it's child welfare, human services, hospital social work, wherever we're at—a social worker to me is a person who looks at the whole picture. We would be remiss, I think, to not have mixed methods. (Linda Kingery, MSW, LICSW child protection worker, personal communication, April 2014)

In this interview excerpt, Linda Kingery, a practicing social worker, reflected on her experiences over a six-year period as a coinvestigator in a mixed methods research program. Her interest in mixed methods research reflects the rapid development of this methodology over the past two decades in multiple applied fields. Like Kingery, other practitioners and researchers have become impatient with the *paradigm wars* of the late twentieth century, skeptical of the need to choose sides in an artificial qualitative-quantitative divide, and dissatisfied with the partial picture of complex social phenomena captured by solely quantitative or solely qualitative research programs. Mixed methods research, which has become known as the "third methodological movement" (Tashakkori & Teddlie, 2010), offers exciting possibilities of an integrated social research methodology.

Social workers are keenly aware of the complexity of social issues. We recognize the need for breadth and depth of understanding, for numbers and words, for quantification and interpretation. In the study of rural substance abuse, Kingery wanted to learn not only about the prevalence of methamphetamine abuse in the families she served (a quantitative issue), but she also wanted to learn about the experiences and perspectives of those affected and their family members (qualitative issues). Both types of understanding are critical to designing and implementing effective policies and programs. Kingery viewed the qualitative and quantitative dimensions of this research project not as separate, but as complementary and mutually informative. As will be described in chapter 8, a mixed methods approach led to a more complete and deeper understanding of the issues affecting methamphetamine-involved families and hence to a more effective intervention.

CONCEPTUALIZING MIXED METHODS RESEARCH

It is important to recognize that mixed methods research is not only about research methods, but it is also about methodology. *Methods* are the specific ways we implement our research. They include strategies for sampling, data collection, and analysis. Mixed methods research largely draws on existing quantitative and qualitative research methods. *Methodology*, on the other hand, broadly refers to the underlying logic, worldview, and values that guide the selection of specific methods and their integration (*see* Creswell, 2010; Greene, 2007; Teddlie & Tashakkori, 2010). As we will discuss throughout this book, mixed methodology is reflected in distinct designs, data analysis strategies, and quality criteria.

Defining Mixed Methods Research

Mixed methods research can be broadly defined as the *intentional integration* of qualitative and quantitative approaches to research in order to enhance understanding of complex social phenomena (*see* Creswell & Garrett, 2008; Greene, 2007; Tashakkori & Creswell, 2007). The mixing of qualitative and quantitative research components is *planned* to address the research question(s) of interest, and *flexible* to respond to new information and understanding that emerges as the study unfolds. Furthermore, quantitative and qualitative components are not treated separately, but are *integrated* to provide better understanding of the phenomenon under study. Some research projects described as mixed methods research consist of qualitative and quantitative components minimally connected in their conceptualization or execution (Bergman, 2008). Teddlie and Tashakkori (2010) label such projects quasi-mixed studies to distinguish them from mixed methods research (our concern in this book), which intentionally integrates quantitative and quantitative components.

Mixed methods is a relatively new term expanding and formalizing similar approaches labeled multiple method, multi-method or multi-strategy research (Padgett, 2008). These forerunners of mixed methods research typically mixed for the purpose of method *triangulation*. In other words, they used different methods to offset the limitations of any single method and hence increase confidence in the research results. The mixing, however, often occurred within a particular tradition. For example, a multi-method study may have utilized multiple quantitative measures in order to study a particular phenomenon.

Unlike these forerunners, early mixed methods researchers defined mixed methods research as studies that mixed at least one quantitative method and one qualitative method (Greene, Caracelli & Graham, 1989). Furthermore, as we will discuss in chapter 4, such mixing was conducted not only to enhance rigor through method triangulation, but also to broaden and deepen our understanding of the research problem and to provide new insights.

Contemporary definitions of mixed methods research are broad. They include the mixing not just of research methods, but of all phases of the research process from underlying philosophical positions to final interpretations of results (Johnson, Onwuegbuzie, & Turner, 2007; Tashakkori & Teddlie, 1998). Creswell and Plano Clark (2007) defined mixed methods research as a blending of both methods and methodological orientations with a central assumption that for some research problems such integration provides a better understanding than any single method approach alone. In her definition, Greene (2007) stressed mixed methods research as an orientation to the social world through "multiple ways of seeing." She argued that mixed methods inquiry is about much more than combining quantitative and qualitative research methods. It is about combining mental models: the understandings, assumptions, predispositions, values, and beliefs that frame and guide our work.

Mixed methods research also can be understood within the larger context of social research by considering its relationship to mono method qualitative and quantitative studies (Tashakkori and Teddlie, 2006). Quantitative and qualitative research traditions differ in important ways. Anthropologist Richard Shweder (1996) described quantitative research as focusing on objectivity and eliminating that which is subjective. The emphasis is on sampling, measuring, calculating, and abstracting (generalizing). The metaphor is of the social inquirer as scientist. In qualitative research, the focus is on the subjective, that is, particular points of view. Objective accounts of human behavior are viewed as incomplete. The emphasis is on interpretation, thematization, contextualization, and exemplification. The metaphor is of the social inquirer as interpreter. Shweder argued that the basic difference between quantitative and qualitative social science research traditions is primarily the *object* for study. In quantitative traditions, research questions and hypotheses focus on *quanta*, that is, things that exist and produce their effects independently of our experience of them, such as mathematical truths. Qualitative research questions, on the other hand, focus on *qualia*, that is, all things that are what they are from a particular perspective or experience, for example, child rearing or other cultural practices. People are seen as qualitative beings who have feelings, beliefs, goals, desires, and values. Their subjective mental life is viewed as a proper object of study in the human sciences (Shweder, 1996).

Although qualitative and quantitative research traditions are sometimes presented as dichotomous, it is important to recognize the limitations of this type of categorization (e.g., *see* Bergman, 2008). Both qualitative and quantitative designs and methods encompass broad, heterogeneous social science traditions originating in a variety of disciplines including sociology, psychology, education, economics, political science, public health, and anthropology. In some instances there may be just as much diversity within each tradition as there is across qualitative and quantitative traditions.

What is important to the conduct of mixed methods research, however, is that quantitative and qualitative traditions share many core features. Researchers in both traditions use empirical observations to construct logical arguments addressing their research questions about quanta or qualia. In addition, all social researchers incorporate safeguards into their research to minimize biases inherent in any research project and to strengthen the inferences they draw from their empirical data (e.g., Johnson & Onwuegbuzie, 2004). Further, all social researchers are concerned with interpretation. Interpretation of experience is the focus of qualitative research, but quantitative researchers also rely on interpretation, for example, to determine which questions and hypotheses are important to pursue and the implications of analyses. In addition, social researchers across traditions are concerned with the broader implications of specific research findings. Quantitative research typically seeks to generalize findings from smaller to larger groups of people and settings using the logic of probability theory. Qualitative researchers are concerned with the extent to which findings and concepts transfer across different people and settings through in-depth description of lives lived in various local contexts. Finally, quantitative and qualitative researchers view the knowledge and theory derived from their research as provisional; that is, as potentially incomplete and flawed. Table 1.1 summarizes some of the similarities and differences between quantitative and qualitative inquiry traditions.

Given the important similarities between quantitative and qualitative traditions, Johnson and colleagues (2007), among others, have conceptualized social inquiry not as dichotomous, but as a continuum from mono method qualitative to mono method quantitative studies. Figure 1.1 shows a horizontal color bar that we have designed to symbolize this continuum of social research. On the far left (yellow) end of the bar are mono method qualitative studies. At the far right (blue) end of the bar are mono method quantitative studies. This example allows us to picture the continuum of social science methods from mono method studies at either end of the continuum (yellow or blue), to mixed methods studies in which qualitative (yellow green) or quantitative (blue green) approaches are dominant, and to the center of the continuum (green) where quantitative and qualitative approaches are of equal status.

Assumptions of Mixed Methodology

A core assumption of the methodology underlying mixed methods research is that there are multiple legitimate approaches to understanding the social world through research. Jennifer Greene (2008) explained that a mixed methods way of thinking is an orientation toward social inquiry that actively

TABLE 1.1
Some Similarities and Differences of Quantitative and Qualitative Research Traditions

Quantitative traditions	*Qualitative traditions*	*Both traditions*
Research questions address quanta	Research questions address qualia	Employ logical arguments
Emphasize the objective	Emphasize the subjective	Are empirical: based on deliberate, careful observations
Methodological emphasis on sampling, measuring, calculating, abstracting	Methodological emphasis on interpretation, thematization, contextualization, and exemplification	Incorporate safeguards to minimize biases and strengthen inferences
Social inquirer = scientist	Social inquirer = interpreter	Employ interpretation
		Are concerned with broader implications of empirical findings
		View knowledge and theory as provisional

invites dialogue with diverse ways of making sense of the social world and multiple viewpoints on what is central and valuable. This mixed methods way of thinking offers opportunities to include and even to foreground important but suppressed social science approaches (especially qualitative research) and perspectives (especially client voices). Thus, a mixed methods

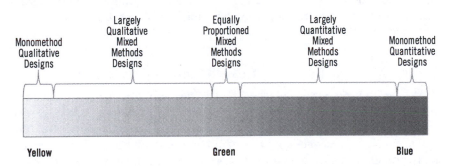

Figure 1.1
Continuum of Social Research Color Bar

way of thinking actively engages us with diversity for greater equity of voice among scholars within diverse social inquiry traditions (Greene, 2007) and social work clients from diverse and vulnerable communities.

A related assumption of the methodology underlying mixed methods research is that the integration of multiple approaches and ways of knowing can result in a better understanding of multifaceted social phenomena than any single inquiry approach (Creswell & Garrett, 2008; Greene, 2007). In other words, the end product of the mixed methods inquiry is more than the sum of its individual qualitative and quantitative parts (Bryman, 2007). By considering qualitative aspects of client experience and quantitative aspects of intervention outcomes, for instance, the mixed methods social work researcher may attain a different understanding of program strengths and limitations than would be attained by a mono method qualitative or quantitative evaluation. The color bar in Figure 1.1 illustrates this idea: blue (quantitative) and yellow (qualitative) are combined to produce a new color, green (mixed methods).

There are a variety of ways in which the mixing of quantitative and qualitative approaches adds to our understanding. In an early mixed methods paper, Rossman and Wilson (1985) described how the combination of "numbers and words" can lead to better understanding in evaluation studies. First, combinations of quantitative and qualitative results can be used to corroborate each other. When sources of data from methods with different limitations converge (triangulate), then the resulting inference is strengthened. Second, quantitative and qualitative methods can elaborate each other. Their integration can provide breadth, richness, and detail. Third, combinations of qualitative and quantitative perspectives can uncover paradoxes and contradictions, leading to an alteration in overall perspective and ways of understanding the phenomenon as a whole. Indeed, when findings are divergent, they may lead to doubt and rethinking often associated with creative intellectual insights (*see also* Greene, 2007). As we will discuss in this book, mixed methods research promises to improve social work practice and policy not only through more rigorous and complete understanding of complex phenomena, but also through suggesting new and creative approaches to persistent social problems.

Common Characteristics of Mixed Methods Research

Mixed methods research is diverse and flexible, and it has a number of common interrelated characteristics and guiding principles (*see* Teddlie & Tashakkori, 2010, 2012) that will be illustrated throughout this book. First, *mixed methods researchers prioritize the research question*. There are many possible starting points for research, such as those suggested by the researcher's facility with particular methods. For mixed methods researchers, however, the research question commonly determines the best tools to use: quantitative, qualitative, or mixed. Researchers construct the design and choose the methods for the specific research question, recognizing that there is no one approach that will fit all research questions (for example, *see* Hesse-Biber & Johnson, 2013). In mixed methods research, methods are the servants of substance, not vice versa.

Second, *mixed methods researchers emphasize continua rather than dichotomies* (*see*, for example, Ridenour & Newman, 2008), as represented in the color bar in Figure 1.1. Mixed methods researchers reject the false dichotomy between qualitative and quantitative research. Instead, they recognize that methods chosen for a particular study may fall anywhere along the methodological continuum. They balance between the extreme positions taken by mono methods scholars at either end of the continuum.

Further, *mixed methods researchers embrace diversity of perspective at all levels.* There are a variety of world views that are compatible with mixed methods research that may inform the underlying philosophy for use in any particular mixed methods study. More generally, mixed methods researchers emphasize diversity throughout the research enterprise from the broader conceptual dimensions to the narrower empirical ones (for example, *see* Teddlie & Tashakkori, 2010, 2012). They value respectful dialog and cooperation across multiple world views (e.g., Greene, 2007), each with its own truths and inherent limitations.

Next, *mixed method researchers are eclectic.* Mixed methods researchers select and intentionally integrate the most appropriate techniques from the entire tool kit of social inquiry research strategies to thoroughly investigate the phenomenon of interest. (e.g., Teddlie & Tashakkori, 2010, 2012). Although this idea may seem daunting to a new mixed methods researcher, we will provide a framework for constructing a mixed methods social work research project in chapters 4 through 8.

Finally, *mixed method research includes inductive and deductive reasoning.* Morgan (2007) viewed mixed methods research as characterized by the **abductive reasoning** described by John Dewey and elaborated in chapter 2. Such reasoning moves back and forth between induction and deduction—first converting observations into theories and then assessing those theories through action. For example, inductive results from a qualitative approach can serve as inputs to the deductive goals of a quantitative approach, or the deductive results of quantitative inquiry can lead to new inductive qualitative explorations.

MIXED METHODS AND SOCIAL WORK

When exploring mixed methods for the first time, many social workers discover that they are already mixed methods thinkers. The complex issues of human struggle addressed by social workers are multilayered and dynamic.

Social workers consider information from multiple sources in a multidimensional assessment of human functioning. In order to gain a comprehensive understanding of an individual, family, group, or community, for example, we ask questions; observe behavior; engage in conversations; and utilize physiological, psychological, and social measures. When information is obtained in various ways and from different sources, there is richness in understanding that would not be available from one type of inquiry alone. When the information that social workers obtain through an assessment, for example, comes together to tell a consistent story, we feel as though we are on the right track. When information does not match or is contradictory, it forces us to reexamine assumptions and dig deeper into the issues at hand in order to form a more comprehensive understanding.

Just like mixed methods ways of thinking in other areas of social work, mixed methods thinking in social work research provides unique possibilities for understanding that mono method approaches cannot match. Indeed, mixed methods research offers an approach to addressing complex issues in a way that is consistent with social work's holistic ecological perspective. Gioia (2012) characterized mixed methods approaches as particularly well suited to social work's focus on the person-in-environment perspective, on understanding individual clients and the micro through macro level social structures in which they are embedded.

Mixed methods research also is consistent with social work ethics. Social work focuses on issues of diversity and social justice and on empowering those whose voices have been silenced as a result of oppression. A cornerstone of mixed methods research is respectful engagement with differences in perspectives, understandings, and inquiry methods. In discussing sociopolitical issues surrounding the place of social inquiry in society, Greene (2008) observed that:

> a mixed methods approach to social inquiry *distinctly* offers deep and potentially inspirational and catalytic opportunities to meaningfully engage with the differences that matter in today's troubled world, seeking not so much convergence and consensus as opportunities for respectful listening and understanding. (p. 20)

Mixed methods research also is in line with a commitment that our research be shaped by our values and politics. As we will discuss in chapter 2, *pragmatism* underlies much of mixed methods research. Pragmatists such as William James, John Dewey, George Herbert Mead, and Jane Addams played key roles in the original American Progressive Movement (Mills, 1969). They focused on gaining knowledge through and in the pursuit of desired ends. These scholars were aware of how their own ethics and values shaped their research goals, and they used their writings to further their social agenda. These pragmatists remind us that our values and our politics are always a part of who we are and how we act. They direct us to investigate how our worldview affects what we choose to study and how we choose to study it (Morgan, 2007).

Mixed methods research clearly offers many advantages to the field of social work. As will be discussed in chapters 9 and 10, however, it is not absent of challenges. Any mixed method research project is vulnerable to the same threats to validity and interpretive adequacy as mono method qualitative and quantitative research projects, as well as additional challenges that emerge from the integration of methods. Furthermore, mixed methods research is in its adolescence, awaiting further development, especially around issues of integrative data analyses (Bergman, 2008).

In this book, we hope not only to encourage social workers to pursue mixed methods research, but also to provide leadership in its continued development into the twenty-first century. Although social workers have been engaged in methodologically integrated inquiry for decades, to date researchers in other applied fields such as nursing, education, and evaluation have played a dominant role in the interdisciplinary dialog about the development of mixed methods research. Yet if we think of mixed methods research as a way to better understand complex human experiences and social structures, social workers are well equipped to take their place alongside their peers from allied disciplines as leaders in this field.

A Social Worker's First Experience with Mixed Methods Research

In Box 1.1, below, a master's level social worker describes her first experiences with mixed methods research. It contains an excerpt from a conversation in which Wendy Haight asked Linda Kingery to reflect back on her involvement in a mixed methods research project described in detail in chapter 8. As you read this excerpt, you might want to consider the following questions:

- What was Linda's initial reaction to participating in this mixed methods research project?
- From Linda's perspective, what is the value of mixed methods research, and how does Linda describe that perspective as changing over time?
- What were some of the challenges of engaging in this research for Linda?
- How did Linda balance her roles as researcher and social worker/ advocate?
- What value may a mixed methods approach have for your own areas of research?
- What challenges might you experience?

••

BOX 1.1
Conversational Excerpt

L (Linda): At the time we were doing it [research], I was just so dang green, Wendy (*both laugh*). I look back on it and I think, "what an opportunity that was just dropped in my lap!" It was like "Wow! I can't believe I was actually involved in something like that." Because this is just pretty heavy stuff. I felt like a wide-eyed innocent (*both laugh*). As a child protection investigator, to me it was about the issue at hand, which was methamphetamine impacting the child welfare process. I mean that was the whole reason we got started on it. "It's hot and heavy right now and it's impacting the way we're doing business." So my interest was totally professional. Even having my master's [MSW] then, I knew so little about research. And the part that appealed to me was the qualitative piece. That we're going to actually talk to these people and get their [perspectives]. It still fascinates me that we got to talk to people who not only had been involved with methamphetamine, an illegal drug, but people who were still in the child welfare system. I still will recall those interviews with people who had been in the throes of addiction and some of them still coping by using other things, like pain killers or smoking pot. So I know when we think of qualitative research we always think of that depth of description and *that* was the part that intrigued me—that we were sitting there with people who had lived the experience and we were getting their take on it. So that's what appealed to me, as a worker. As we moved along though, I saw that we *did* have some quantitative knowledge about how mentally healthy the children we interviewed were. And having that kind of general information that you could look at and say a certain percentage of these kids exhibited significant mental health symptoms added to the description [but] it was that thick, rich, lived experience that intrigued me the most.

When we started out what we did was interview mostly—all the community [professionals], all those folks—and got their perception of the meth problem. Which was interesting, I think to compare the perception of the community [professionals] versus the perception of the people actually living it. And I always think of Bill's story, how much fun it was [for him] to have cereal three meals a day (*laughs*) and to go around the little town and be an adventurous Tom Sawyer type. And he had no idea that he was in the midst of any kind of danger or turmoil and I don't think you can get that from quantitative research. You're just not going to get that kind of a picture, that total view of what it's like to live in that. And that, I'm not saying that was every child's experience, but it certainly was Bill's.

W (Wendy): That was really surprising to me because we do this ethnography and we talk to these community people and we see some of the homes, and think, "these kids have to be traumatized." And many were, but then there was this other experience that you were describing of Bill and Dan—tell the story of Bill and Dan! For the recording (*laughs*)!

L: Yeah! These two boys were actually taken into protective custody within hours of the time that their mom and dad were both arrested for methamphetamine possession in their *home*. And they, I'll never, I mean I just wish there were words to describe that—them standing by that tree and Dan would have been 8, and Bill was 11, and they just had no clue that they were in danger, that there was some kind of a crisis going on, 'cuz their mom and dad had been in jail before, if you remember. And so they were used to Mom and Dad going to jail and Grandma would just come and get them and that was the end of that and they [parents] would be out [of jail] a few days later. So, that was not uncommon for them. But [not] this time. They just presented as such well-behaved, polite little gentlemen. Remember Bill wanted to make sure his book got back to the school library. And they were so convinced because of their strong [extended] family support that someone was gonna be there. Someone would come get them! There was no way they would end up in the system! Someone was going to get them! And it was during the intervention that the resiliency of Bill really stood out. But during the intervention, when Bill would tell the stories, when we were trying to get at what was it like to grow up, to live, for him for 11 years in this home with drug abuse from the get-go, but methamphetamine in the most recent years, what was it like there? And he describes this idyllic small-town, Midwestern childhood where, you know, his mom and dad slept a lot. That was his take on what happened. Now, he said he never saw them do drugs. And the school, if you'll remember, the principal, first perceived them, those two boys, as resilient, but as living a *traumatic* life. And she's the one who saw them the most.

W: Well that was something interesting about the qualitative component. You really got a sense of variation in experiences.

L: That's what I was gonna say. My assumption is that you would not have picked them out of a group, quantitatively, yet when we took the time to get that story and it wasn't just their story, like you said, there was diversity in the stories. There were other kids that were randomly selected for the intervention, that we saw, we got to take a deeper look at their lives. And we got to see all that variety that for me, you just don't capture that quantitatively. You don't need to quote me on this (chuckling), but for me there should never be a quantitative study without some qualitative piece that says *and the rest of the story is this* . . .

W: And that's very much mixed methods—that we have both of those pieces.

L: And I agree with that. That's what gives us at least a *more* complete picture. The quantitative piece does add to the picture because it tells us, *"Yes, Bill presented this way, this is his in-depth story."* But what do we know generally speaking about 11-year-old kids living in methamphetamine affected households? What do we know when we look at many 8- to 12-year-old kids, what do we see? What are the patterns? What are the trends with them? And that is helpful, it really is.

W: Well, . . . if we think of the last part of our meth research where we did the intervention, what were the challenges of engaging in such a relationship for a 6-month period or *more*, 8-month period, with children who were in very difficult situations and living in your community?

L: That was definitely a challenge. When I got ready to leave Joe—more so than Bill—it was traumatic for him and I both. 'Cuz you do build [a relationship]. Who was it that called it "going native?" I do think that is what I did! You know it was hard for me to remain in a role of researcher and not take on an advocate role. And in fact if you remember Bill's case I did utilize the role of advocate and I'm very proud of that because by me bringing that [first foster mother's abuse of Bill] to the [research] group we were able to intervene in that child's life and I think very much for a positive outcome. [Bill and Dan were moved to another foster home where the parents became their legal guardians and where they remained until adulthood.] So, but there was that whole issue of kids like that are so vulnerable and they, *they* attach to anyone who shows a concern. So there was that challenge of the relationship aspect of it. If you [are] going to interview them a few times and gather some information that would have been different but we really engaged in a relationship in that we ate together, we had fun activities together, we rode around in the car together, chatted about many things. It wasn't just a qualitative interview, it was—I wouldn't even call it a counseling relationship—I wanted to know more about them, but they were also gathering information about *me*. They wanted to know this person who was picking them up and taking them out to eat. My favorite story about Joe is the whole thing about him wanting us to go to the same place or have the same meal and for me to eat certain things that *he* found, uh, pleasing to the palate. He wanted me to enjoy the same things he enjoyed and if you remember right at the very end he stopped that; he let go of that. And I've always found that interesting that in the beginning that was one of the most important things and then at the end he didn't care so much. And I remember he told me [about] the gal [at the drive-through window], he said, "I'll bet she thinks you're my grandma." And boy, when you're in that role of gathering information you get connected. . . .

W: I know you didn't completely disconnect, that you were, have been very humane about it. I know you've been to Bill's [high school] graduation and now Dan's. . . .

L: But not so much with Joe. I send him a birthday card, but he sort of moved out of my purview because he didn't live *exactly* in the same town and didn't hang out with my grandson. Although every time I see his [Joe's] foster mom [and permanent guardian] I ask about him and he's doing good. He's getting ready to go to college!

••

CONCLUSION

Over the past two decades, exciting developments in mixed methods research have opened up many new and exciting possibilities for social work researchers. Many of these developments have been led by applied researchers outside of the social work profession who also are addressing complex real-world social problems. This text is intended to introduce social workers to their history and to ongoing contributions to mixed methods research; it is also intended to encourage their contributions to an ongoing legacy.

SUGGESTIONS FOR ADDITIONAL READING

Cowger, C., & Menon, G. (2001). Integrating qualitative and quantitative research methods. In B. Thyer (Ed.) *The handbook of social work research methods.* Thousand Oaks, CA: SAGE.

These authors provide an introduction to the rationale for mixed methods social work research. This chapter would be appropriate to assign to both MSW and PhD students.

Mizrahi, T., & Davis, L. E. (2008). Research. *Encyclopedia of social work.* New York: Oxford University Press.

These authors provide an overview of social work research including the use of mixed methods accessible to MSW students.

Shweder, R. A. (1996). Quanta and qualia: What is the 'object' of ethnographic method? In R. Jessor, A. Colby, & R. A. Shweder (Eds.), *Ethnography and human development: Context and meaning in social inquiry* (pp. 175–182). Chicago: University of Chicago Press.

An older reference, this chapter, which presents Shweder's characterization of the essential difference between quantiative and qualitative traditions not as method but object of study, remains thought-provoking today. It can be viewed as a justification for mixed methodology from the perspective of a qualitative researcher. It is most appropriate to assign to PhD students.

Part 1

Recovering the Contributions of Social Work Pioneers to Early Mixed Methods Research

---

For a time American philosophy, sociology and social work existed in a symbiotic harmony—each not clearly differentiated from the other but benefiting from the interchange. Unfortunately, since the early twentieth century when Mead, Dewey, and Addams were together in Chicago, the intellectual genealogy of American philosophy, sociology, and social work has more drastically diverged to a point where crossover is less likely and perhaps less welcome. Lost in the compartmentalization of these disciplines is how Jane Addams played a role in each (Hamington, 2010, p. 8).

Part 1 presents two essays describing the shared philosophical and historical foundations of mixed methods research and social work:

- Chapter 2: Pragmatism in Social Work and Mixed Methodology: The Legacy of Jane Addams (1860–1935) and John Dewey (1859–1952)
- Chapter 3: The History of Mixed Methods Social Work Research: The Pittsburgh Survey (1907–08)

It establishes the congruence of mixed methodology with the goals, worldviews, and ethics of social work.

2

Pragmatism in Social Work and Mixed Methodology

The Legacy of Jane Addams (1860–1935) and John Dewey (1859–1952)

Mixed methods inquiry and social work share philosophical roots in American Pragmatism. **Classical American Pragmatism** is a grouping of philosophies that were developed from the late nineteenth century through the early twentieth century and were especially influential in the Progressive Era (1890-1915) and up until the Second World War (Whipps, 2010). Influential classical pragmatists included Charles Sanders Peirce (1839-1914), William James (1842-1910), John Dewey (1859-1952), and Jane Addams (1860-1935). Jane Addams, although best known as a Hull House activist and forbearer of American social work, was a founder of pragmatism (Hookway, 2013). American Pragmatism also is a primary philosophical underpinning of contemporary mixed methodology (e.g., Greene, 2008; Johnson and Onwuegbuzie, 2004; Teddlie & Tashakkori, 2009). Over the years, pragmatism, social work, and mixed methodologies have continued to evolve. Yet pragmatism remains a common and significant philosophical framework for many scholars both in social work and in mixed methods inquiry. In this chapter we will first underscore the contributions of Jane Addams to American Pragmatism, and then outline several of the concepts of pragmatism we consider to be key to the practice of mixed methods social work research.

RECOVERING JANE ADDAMS' CONTRIBUTIONS TO AMERICAN PRAGMATISM

Jane Addams was a central figure in the development of American Pragmatism. Although her philosophical work was largely ignored until the 1990s, feminist philosophers and historians have been working to recover her contributions. Jane Addams's role in the development of pragmatist thought, as well as those of her female contemporaries, including Mary Parker Follet, Charlotte Perkins Gilman, and Lucy Sprague Mitchell, were largely mapped onto traditional nineteenth century gender role stereotypes. Male philosophers including Dewey, Williams, James, and Mead were seen as providing original thought, whereas Addams was seen as brilliantly administering their theories. As contemporaries they represent classic archetypes of gender: male as mind—thinking and leading; and female as body—experiencing, caring, and doing. (Hamington, 2010)

Despite nineteenth century gender roles, Addams had close intellectual ties with male philosophers considered to be the founders of American Pragmatism, including George Herbert Mead, William James, and especially John Dewey. Dewey was a dominant philosophical figure into the 1920s. He detailed the most influential strand of pragmatism in the twentieth century philosophy of science and is considered one of the greatest American philosophers. Dewey and Addams were close colleagues and lifelong friends. Hamington (2010) describes them as "intellectual soul mates" from the moment they met in 1892. Dewey visited Hull House shortly after it opened and before he moved to Chicago to teach at the University of Chicago. He became a frequent visitor to Hull House, contributing to the cross-fertilization between Hull House and the University of Chicago. Over the course of a decade, Addams taught a number of courses through the Extension Division at the University of Chicago. Dewey lectured to the Hull House philosophy group, assigned Addams's books in his University of Chicago classes, and became a board member when Hull House was incorporated. Dewey also dedicated his book *Liberalism and Social Action* to Addams and named his daughter, Jane, in her honor. Addams wrote the eulogy for Dewey's son, Gordon. Both Dewey and his daughter, Jane, credited Addams with developing many of his important ideas, including his views on education, democracy, and philosophy (Hamington, 2010; Whipps, 2010).

Clearly, Addams was far more than a competent technician following the lead of male intellectuals. Although characterized as "social housekeeping," Addams's pioneering work in the social settlement movement actually was the radical arm of the Progressive Movement. Addams and colleagues so embraced the ideals of progressivism that they chose to live as neighbors in oppressed communities to learn from as well as help marginalized people. It was through her experiences working in the poverty stricken immigrant neighborhoods surrounding Hull House that Addams developed her pragmatist philosophies. As Hamington (2010) wrote:

> The near half-century that she [Addams] lived and worked as the leader of the Chicago social settlement, Hull House, gave her an opportunity to bring her commitment to social improvement, feminism, diversity, and peace to direct action. These experiences provided the foundation for an engaging philosophical perspective. Addams viewed her settlement work as a grand epistemological endeavor but in the process she also never forgot the humanity of her neighbors. Addams was indeed a public philosopher—one who was not afraid to get her hands dirty. (p. 1)

Addams published a dozen books and more than 500 articles: essays on ethics, social philosophy, pacifism, and social issues concerning women, industrialization, immigration, urban youth, and international mediation. This body of work exemplifies the hallmarks of American Pragmatism: an interplay of experience, reflection, and action. Addams was a founding figure in the National Association of the Advancement of Colored People, the American Civil Liberties Union, and the Women's International League for Peace and Freedom. In 1931, she received the Nobel Peace Prize in recognition of her pacifism, for which she had been harshly criticized during the entry of the United States into World War I (see Hamington, 2010; Whipps, 2010).

THE PRAGMATISM OF ADDAMS AND DEWEY

There are a variety of types of pragmatism relevant to mixed methodology and social work. In this chapter, we will focus on the pragmatism of Jane Addams and John Dewey.

Action and Knowledge

American Pragmatism, social work, and mixed methods inquiry generally share an action-oriented approach to knowledge acquisition and theory building. From a pragmatic perspective, we come to know the world through our experiences and actions in the world. Overt action in combination with reflection is necessary to acquiring knowledge. In short, we can test our ideas, concepts, and theories only by carrying out rational actions that follow from them and observing whether these actions result in expected outcomes. In discussing theory and experience in science, Dewey (1958) observed that

> ventures of a theoretical sort start from and terminate in directly experienced subject-matter. Theory may intervene in a long course of reasoning, many portions of which are remote from what is directly experienced. But the vine of pendant theory is attached at both ends to the pillars of observed subject matter. (p. 2a)

Dewey elaborated the way in which we refine and acquire knowledge as through our *transactions* in nature. Nature is not seen as a fixed world *out there* to be discovered, but as an ever moving whole of interacting parts of which we are a part. Thus, our experience of nature is not extraneous or superimposed on nature, nor does it form a screen that cuts us off from nature unless somehow transcended, for instance, through our scientific research methods. Rather, our experiences are both part of nature and essential to understanding nature (*see* Biesta, 2010). Dewey (1958) observed that human experience is no infinitesimally thin layer or foreground of nature, but . . . penetrates into it, reaching down into its depths, and in such a way that its grasp is capable of expansion; it tunnels in all direction and in so doing brings to the surface things at first hidden—as miners pile high on the surface of the earth treasures brought from below. (p. 3a)

Like other living organisms, we can establish and maintain a dynamic coordination with our environments. Through our transactions in nature, our predispositions or habits become more focused, specific, and attuned to ever changing environmental conditions. In other words, we learn through coordinated transactions with our environment. We acquire a flexible set of predispositions for action. Action that is intelligent and not simple trial and error involves the rehearsal in imagination of various competing possible *lines of action*. However, thinking alone cannot guarantee that our actions will result in coordinated transactions. Whether the chosen line of action will lead to a coordinated transaction will become clear only when we act (*see* Biesta, 2010).

Thus, for Dewey, *knowledge* is concerned with the relations between our actions and their consequences. These relations can be discovered only when experience is modified so that relations become clear. We purposefully introduce changes into the environment that will alter the course of events. This conceptualization of knowledge shifts concern from the world *as is* to knowledge as concerned with conditions and consequences. Dewey's transactional view is that the objects of knowledge are not things out there that exist for us to discover, but the outcomes of processes of inquiry (*see* Biesta, 2010).

An implication of an action-oriented approach to knowledge is that the results of our scholarship, our concepts and theories, reflect works in progress, tools we are continuously refining, rather than finished products. For example, as mixed methods social work researchers we might test our ideas about stress, gained from practice experience and the social science literature, by providing emotional support to individuals experiencing it, observing the outcomes, and reflecting on the implications of those outcomes for refining or revising our ideas.

Social Work's Action-Oriented Approach to Knowledge

Social work has a long history of an action-oriented approach to knowledge. Jane Addams's pragmatism is an applied philosophy embedded in social action. For Addams, local experience, theory, and social action are interrelated. As Hamington (2010) wrote,

Addams did not intend to engage in philosophical narratives removed from social improvement, but neither did she intend to pursue social activism without theorizing about the wider implications of her work. In this respect, through her integration of theory and action, Addams carried pragmatism to its logical conclusion developing an applied philosophy immersed in social action. (p. 1)

From the outset, Addams theorized about her Hull House experience, addressing topics not typical of philosophical discussions such as garbage collection, immigrant folk stories, and prostitution. Eventually, she extended her analyses to issues of race, education, and world peace (*see* Hamington, 2010; Whipps, 2010). In describing Hull House, Hamington (2010) observed:

> From the onset of its operation, Addams theorized about the nature and function of Hull House. The language she used reflected her philosophical insight. For example, in one published essay, Addams describes the application and reorganization of knowledge as the fundamental problem of modern life and then claims that settlements are like applied universities: 'The ideal and developed settlement would attempt to test the value of human knowledge by action, and realization, quite as the complete and ideal university would concern itself with the discovery of knowledge in all branches' (Addams, 1899). This kind of reflective analysis and wider thematization of her work and the work of the social settlement was a hallmark of Addams' writing. (p. 3)

The influence of an action-oriented approach to knowledge remains strong in contemporary social work. One need only peruse the faculty job notices to discern that the vast majority of job openings require not only a PhD and an MSW (a practice degree), but also two years of post-MSW practice experience. There are some very good reasons for this commitment to developing social work faculty consisting of practitioner-scholars following in the footsteps of the Hull House pragmatists. First, when scholars are grounded in social work practice, their work is likely to generate knowledge relevant to social work practice. Such research will target the contemporary questions and ongoing problems faced by practicing social workers. For example, the study of families involved with methamphetamine described in chapter 8 was initiated by practitioner-scholars to address an urgent ongoing problem in child welfare.

Second, research grounded in practice also creates, expands, or corrects existing concepts and theory. As Whipps (2010) wrote,

> Pragmatists, such as John Dewey, William James and Jane Addams, were interested in the intersection of theory and practice, bringing philosophic thinking into relationship with the social and political environment. For these thinkers, philosophizing was an active process, both as a way to change social realities and to use experience to modify the philosophies themselves. (p. 1)

By trying out our concepts and theories in practice contexts, we strengthen our understanding. For example, Sachiko Bamba engaged in participatory action research with professionals staffing a Japanese child care institution for children who could no longer live with their parents primarily because of child maltreatment (Bamba & Haight, 2011). In discussing the children's struggles, participants repeatedly referred to the importance of *Ibasho*, a place where one feels a sense of belonging, freedom, safety, and acceptance. According to Japanese folk psychology, Ibasho is necessary for psychological well-being throughout the lifespan. When Bamba asked professionals to participate in an intervention in which they would directly support children's Ibasho, they resisted. Exploration of the source of this resistance, in turn, clarified the concept of Ibasho. Ibasho is not something that adults can do or give to children. Individuals must create their own Ibasho. Participants understood their role as indirect, as providing a context in which over time children have the opportunity to discover their own Ibasho. Bamba's practice experience in child care institutions allowed her to identify a relevant practice issue. She then tested her understanding by acting on the environment (intervention), which in turn clarified her understanding of Ibasho. This expanded understanding of Ibasho, in turn, has implications for intervention, one far less direct than originally planned.

Mixed Methods' Action-Oriented Approach to Knowledge

Dewey's transactional theory of knowledge provides a rationale for combining **deductive reasoning**, most characteristic of quantitative research, with **inductive reasoning**, more typical of qualitative traditions. Deductive reasoning goes from the general to the specific, for example, by deriving hypotheses from theory and then testing them empirically. Inductive reasoning moves from the specific to the general, for example, by observing individuals' actions and words and then inferring their worldviews. In considering the act of reasoning, Dewey rejected the induction-deduction dualism. In **abductive reasoning** we move back and forth between induction and deduction. Abductive reasoning provides a basis for sequentially mixing quantitative and qualitative inquiry. For example, in some mixed methods designs we use qualitative methods to induce theories from observations and then use quantitative methods to evaluate those theories (*see* Morgan, 2007).

Dewey's transactional theory of knowledge also provides a basis for the combination of the objective and subjective in mixed methods research. Dewey's pragmatism provides an alternative to the mind (subjective) and matter (objective) dualism that has been with us at least since Hume and Descartes. This dualism sets up what for Dewey is a false distinction between objectivity (what is out there in the material world, typically the focus of quantitative research traditions) and subjectivity (the inner world of the mind, often the focus of qualitative research traditions). It sets up what Dewey considered to be an *impossible problem*: how the mind can distinguish a material world outside of itself. For pragmatists both the external world and the inner world of experience are critical to our transactions in nature.

Attention to mixed method inquiry as a third methodology emerged, in part, from the paradigm debates of the late twentieth century (described in chapter 3), which were largely centered on metaphysical issues including Dewey's impossible problem. In the philosophical paradigm debates of the twentieth century, ***ontology***, ***epistemology***, and ***methodology*** typically were fused. Ontology is a branch of philosophy concerned with the nature of being—for example, the nature of the social world. Epistemology is a branch of philosophy that investigates the origin, nature, methods, and limits of human knowledge—for example, how we come to know our social world. Methodology is the underlying logic of inquiry and worldview that guides our selection of specific methods.

Positivism is a theory that theology and metaphysics are earlier imperfect modes of knowledge and that positive knowledge is based on the empirical study of natural phenomena and their properties by the empirical sciences. It combines ontological realism (that there is a real world that exists independently of our senses), epistemological objectivism (that we can come to know that world through our senses), and experimental and quasi-experimental methodologies.

Constructivism is a philosophy of learning founded on the premise that we construct our understanding of the world through acting in that world and reflecting on those experiences. It combines a relativist ontology (what we know is limited by the nature of our minds), epistemological relativism (we can come to know that world only through our imperfect perceptions of it), and qualitative methodologies.

During the paradigm debates, the philosophical assumptions of paradigms such as positivism associated with quantitative research were viewed as fundamentally incompatible with those such as constructivism associated with qualitative research. Thus, combining the traditions of quantitative and qualitative research in one mixed methods study seemed illogical. Yet there is no logical necessity for merging all assumptions underlying various paradigms. Paradigms such as positivism and constructivism are social constructions, historically and culturally embedded discourse practices. A defensible and useful paradigm offers a coherent and internally consistent set of assumptions relevant to the practice of social inquiry, but as Greene & Hall (2010) point out, no particular groupings of assumptions are sacrosanct. Indeed, Donald Campbell, arguably one of the most brilliant and influential social scientists of the twentieth century, endorsed ontological realism and epistemological relativism. He viewed the ontological world and the worlds of ideology and values all as playing roles in the construction of scientific knowledge (Shadish, Cook and Campbell, 2002).

Pluralism and Knowledge

Pragmatists, social workers, and mixed methods researchers all maintain a high regard for the reality and influence of diverse social and psychological worlds on human experience. For Dewey, our transactions with our environment provide *experience*. The things in the world (objects, actions, people, etc.) are what they are as they are experienced, and all experience is equally real. What is experienced is real, but what is real is not necessarily true. Experience in itself does not provide knowledge. Knowledge is a human construction, always plural, changing, and open. That does not mean, however, that anything is possible. Nature does impose constraints. In contrast to how constructivism is often understood under the mind-world duality (as purely mental and hence subjective), Dewey's *transactional realism* holds that knowledge is at the same time real and constructed (*see* Biesta, 2010).

In Dewey's conceptualization of knowledge, *objectivity* as a depiction of the world completely independent of us is simply impossible. If we want to know the world we must interact within the world, and as a result we can know the world only as it responds to us. No knowledge can claim to provide us with a deeper, more real, or truer account of the world. Different knowledge is simply the result of different ways of acting and engaging the world. When we interact with others, we coordinate our subjective worlds to accomplish common goals. Through interaction, cooperation, communication, and coordination we together construct an *intersubjective* world. An intersubjective world is one in which we live and act together and for which we have shared responsibility (*see* Greene & Hall, 2010).

Social Work's Long-Standing Focus on Pluralism

Social work has a tradition of valuing pluralism that extends back to its very roots. Jane Addams's philosophical pragmatism is grounded not only in experience, but also in the experience of those at the margins of society. For example, she felt not only that working class immigrant women should be given a voice, but also that they had something important to contribute to the community of ideas. Furthermore, in *Democracy and Social Ethics* (1902/2002), Addams observed,

> Much of the insensibility and hardness of the world is due to the lack of imagination which prevents a realization of the experiences of other people. Already there is a conviction that we are under a moral obligation in choosing our experiences, since the result of those experiences must ultimately determine our understanding of life. We know instinctively that if we grow contemptuous of our fellows, and consciously limit our intercourse to certain

kinds of people whom we have previously decided to respect, we not only tremendously circumscribe our range of life, but limit the scope of our ethics. (p. 24)

Today schools of social work offer classes in diversity as well as infusing into the general curriculum the plurality of experiences of various groups such as ethnic minorities, individuals from various income groups, women, and those living with disabilities. Our understanding of complex social issues is greatly enhanced through the multiple perspectives afforded by individuals occupying different social vantage points. Such understanding is prerequisite to successfully addressing complex social issues through practice and policy. For example, nationally, in the United States, black children are three times more likely than white children to be suspended from school (Losen, 2011). Yet black students are no more likely than other students to engage in unsafe or rule breaking behaviors at school (e.g., *see* review by Gregory Skiba, & Noguera, 2010). Rather, they are more harshly punished than other students for the same misbehaviors. Such racial disproportionality is a persistent social justice issue that negatively affects the school achievement of black children (*see* Haight, Gibson, Kayama, Marshall, & Wilson, 2014). From the philosophical position of American Pragmatism, school administrators, school social workers, children who are suspended, and their parents all experience such disciplinary practices. If their accounts of the events surrounding the disciplinary action turn out to be different, there is no reason to assume that the content of only one of them can be real and the experiences of others are necessarily any less real. Differences in their accounts of suspensions reflect different real experiences of disciplinary practices. For example, out-of-school suspensions may be experienced by an educational administrator as imposed by district policy to maintain a safe and orderly learning environment for all students and avoid legal charges of bias. They may be experienced by a school social worker as a barrier to maintaining working relationships with African American families who are disproportionately affected by exclusionary school discipline practices. They may be viewed by parents and children as racially motivated impediments to learning. An adequate understanding of this complex human problem is facilitated by attention to these diverse and real experiences and perspectives. Such an understanding is prerequisite to the design of effective policies and practices that holistically address this complex problem at the micro and macro levels.

Mixed Methods and Pluralism

From a mixed methods perspective, pluralism is the substance of what is being studied and how it is being studied. The overall rationale for mixing methods in social inquiry is for better understanding of the inherent complexities and contingencies of human phenomena. Mixed methods researchers claim that such understanding can be attained only by using a plurality of seeing, interpreting, knowing, and valuing. Any one theoretical or methodological tradition is inevitably partial because human phenomena are extraordinarily complex. Better understanding of this complexity can be attained with the use of more than one perspective and more than one methodology (Greene, 2007).

Mixed methods researchers assuming a dialectical stance actively and respectfully explore difference in the very questions they ask; for example, how do participants who differ in such characteristics as culture, ethnicity, gender, religion, and sexual identity perceive and experience particular social problems and interventions? They also actively engage with difference in thinking about and designing their research. Indeed, they may actively welcome more than one way of thinking and addressing problems throughout the inquiry (Greene & Hall, 2010). A dialectic stance "seeks not so much convergence as insight . . . the generation of important understandings and discernments through the juxtaposition of different lenses, perspectives and stances" (Greene, 2005, p. 208). These mixed methods researchers seek meaningful engagement with difference to generate new insights that are of conceptual and practical consequence.

Knowledge as Warranted Assertions

Pragmatists, social workers, and mixed method inquirers also share a view of knowledge as both generalizable and context bound. Given that knowledge is the relationship between our actions and their consequences, Dewey argued that knowledge can offer us only possibilities, not certainty. What is possible in one situation may be impossible in another. The assertions we make as a consequence of our actions are warranted on the basis of careful observation and control. They are, however, warranted in relation to the particular situation in which they were produced. Thus, Dewey referred to the outcomes of inquiry as *warranted assertions*, not truth. This does not mean that conclusions from one situation cannot be useful in other situations. Knowledge *transfers* from one situation to another by guiding our observations and suggesting possible ways for resolving problems. Whether or not these possibilities will address the new problems in a specific new situation can be discovered only when we act in the new situation. Thus, Dewey rejects the need to choose between extremes in which inquiry results are either completely specific to a particular context or an instance of more generalizable principles.

Social Work and Evidence-Based Practice

In the past decade, *evidence-based practice* has received a great deal of attention in social work. Broadly conceived, evidence-based practice is the

use of current empirical evidence in conjunction with professional knowledge of the sociocultural context (including beliefs, values, and behaviors)
and particular client as a guide to practice and policy decisions (Gambrill,
2006; Sackett, Strauss, Richardson, Rosenberg, & Haynes, 2000). Knowledge
of empirical research is essential for social workers to consider questions
such as:

- Do we understand the origins and factors contributing to this com-
  plex human problem?
- Did this intervention produce the desired results?
- Did this intervention have unintended negative consequences?
- Could scarce resources be better spent elsewhere?

Implicit in evidence-based practice, however, is the recognition that the
product of empirical research is warranted assumptions. In making practice
and policy decisions, social workers must combine warranted assumptions
from empirical research in specific contexts with their practice experience
with particular individuals and in specific communities. The extent to which
warranted assumptions apply to new contexts can be assessed only when
they are actually tried and evaluated in those contexts.

Mixed Method Research as an Iterative Process

In describing mixed methods research from a pragmatist perspective,
Greene and Hall (2010) described an iterative process of applying warranted
assertions to new contexts. Mixed methods researchers who are pragmatists
recognize that knowledge is fallible because we can never be certain that
our current knowledge will be appropriate for future inquiry problems. Similarly, these researchers understand that assertions can be warranted only in
specific inquiry contexts and that their value must be reestablished in new
inquiries. Like Dewey, these pragmatists also reject the need to choose
between extremes where inquiry results are either completely specific to a
particular context or an instance of some more generalized set of principles.
They consider transferability: the ways in which findings are relevant and
useful in other settings.

Progressive Ethics

Pragmatists, social workers, and many mixed methods inquirers also share a
commitment to progressive ethics. Pragmatism is an activist-oriented philosophy. It provides a set of tools to address actual social problems. Pragmatists
such as Dewey, Addams, James, and Mead shared commitments to the values
of democracy, freedom, and equality. In *Democracy and Social Ethics*,
Addams wrote:

We know, at last, that we can only discover truth by a rational and democratic interest in life, and to give truth complete social expression is the endeavor upon which we are entering. Thus the identification with the common lot which is the essential idea of Democracy becomes the source and expression of social ethics. It is as though we thirsted to drink at the great wells of human experience, because we knew that a daintier or less potent draught would not carry us to the end of the journey, going forward we must in the heat and jostle of the crowd. (p. 25)

American pragmatists saw the social environment as malleable, capable of improvement through human action and philosophic thought. Because of this, many of the classical pragmatists were engaged in social action, often participating in experiments in education and working for egalitarian social reforms (Whipps, 2010). Shared inquiry directed at resolving social and political problems was central to Dewey's conception of the good life and the democratic ideal. The classical pragmatists also were aware of how their own values shaped their research goals, and they each used their writings to further their own political agenda. They remind us that our values, ethics, and politics affect what we choose to study and how we choose to study it (*see* Beista, 2010; Morgan, 2007).

Although her philosophy was respected by her male colleagues including Dewey, Jane Addams's pragmatism was arguably more radical than that of other American philosophers of her era. A central tenet of pragmatism is that philosophy should address problems in the current social situation. This tenet supports critiques of gender, race, and class oppression, but it was Jane Addams who consistently and forcefully brought oppression to the fore. Jane Addams and other feminist reformers such as C. P. Gilman were continually involved in fighting oppression, especially of women, children, those living in poverty, and members of minority groups. Addams continually gave voice to the experiences of those who were marginalized, addressed their issues, and saw a vibrant democracy as possible only if there was participation by all (*see* Hampton, 2010).

Furthermore, although pragmatists of her era advocated for social progress, Addams radicalized the extent of that social progress. Rather than defining progress by the achievements of the *best and brightest*, Addams advocated for the betterment of all through ***lateral progress***. Lateral progress meant that social advancement was not the breakthroughs or peak performances of a few, but social gains held in common. For example, Addams believed that unions were important to the extent that they contributed to lateral progress, that is, improving working conditions, raising wages, reducing hours, and eliminating child labor for *all* Americans. Addams argued that the poor are often victims of circumstance and that it is the responsibility of society to first understand those who are marginalized and then develop the means for their participation in lateral progress. Charity, although necessary, is not lateral progress (*see* Hamington, 2010).

The Social Work Code of Ethics

The values of progressivism radicalized by Addams are reflected in social work today. Social work values include service, social justice, respect for the dignity and worth of each person, respect for diversity, and the importance of human relationships. Social work, like other professions such as law and medicine, has developed from its values ethical standards, guides for professional conduct. The most visible compilation of the profession's standards is the Code of Ethics of the National Association of Social Workers (NASW, 2008). It begins by explicitly stating core social work values. According to the preamble, "The primary mission of the social work profession is to enhance human well-being and help meet the basic human needs of all people, with particular attention to the needs and empowerment of people who are vulnerable, oppressed, and living in poverty" (p.1).

Ethics of Mixed Methods Research

Many of the leaders in contemporary discussions of mixed methodology share progressive and humanistic values with social work (e.g., Greene, 2008; Johnson & Onwuegbuzie, 2004). They are in applied fields such as nursing, education, and evaluation. They take an explicitly value-oriented approach, addressing their studies toward desired ends such as reducing discrimination, minimizing human suffering, and educating children.

CONCLUSION

American Pragmatism provided a foundation for contemporary social work and mixed methodologies. It is a multifaceted philosophical tradition with many strands. In this chapter we have focused on the pragmatism of Jane Addams and John Dewey. Their pragmatism shares features with other strands of pragmatism (*see* Whipps, 2010), as well as with social work and mixed methodologies. These features include an action-orientated approach to knowledge, understanding that knowledge is shaped by multiple experiential viewpoints (pluralism), recognition of the importance of both the natural or physical world as well as the emergent social and psychological worlds (including language, culture, human institutions, and subjective responses), a view of knowledge as being both constructed and based on the reality of the world we experience, emphasis on the social context of all knowledge claims, understanding of research as yielding provisional truths and warranted assumptions, and ethical obligation to use the products of research to improve social life.

Of course, not all social workers or mixed methodologists are pragmatists. As is healthy for vibrant areas of scholarship and practice, contemporary mixed methodologists and social workers assume a variety of paradigmatic stances. For example, we described the paradigmatic stance taken by Greene (2007) as dialectical. She emphasizes the importance of deliberately and respectfully engaging different ways of knowing, each of which affords only a partial view as having the best potential for generating new insights. The transformational paradigm also is assumed by both mixed methodologists and social workers who focus, like Jane Addams, on the lives and experiences of marginalized people and asymmetrical power relationships. It prioritizes linking the results of research to action and wider issues of social justice. Both the dialectical and transformative views are certainly consistent with American Pragmatism, but also distinct in their emphases.

SUGGESTIONS FOR ADDITIONAL READING

Biesta, G. (2010). Pragmatism and the philosophical foundations of mixed methods research. In A.Tashakkori & C. Teddlie (Eds.) *SAGE handbook of mixed methods in social and behavioral research* (pp. 95–117). London: SAGE.

This chapter examines the claim that pragmatism can provide a philosophical basis for mixed methods research including an overview of Dewey's philosophy. This chapter would be challenging for MSW students, but appropriate to assign to PhD students.

Greene, J., & Hall, J. N. (2010). Dialectics and pragmatism: Being of consequence. In A. Tashakkori & C. Teddlie (Eds.), *SAGE handbook of mixed methods in social and behavioral research.* (2nd ed., pp.119–144). Thousand Oaks, CA: SAGE.

Greene and Hall describe both dialectic and pragmatic stances as legitimate frameworks for mixed methods research. This is an excellent article appropriate for PhD students.

Hamington, M. (2010). Jane Addams. *Stanford Encyclopedia of Philosophy.* Retrieved from http://plato.stanford.edu/entries/thomaskuhn

Hamington has made important contributions to the recovery of Jane Addams's work as a philosopher. This entry is a fascinating exploration of the life and philosophy of Addams that would be accessible to MSW students.

Maxwell, J. & Mittapalli, K. (2010). Realism as a stance for mixed methods research. In A. Tashakkori & C. Teddlie (Eds.), *SAGE handbook of mixed methods in social and behavioral research* (2nd ed.). Los Angeles, CA: SAGE.

Not all mixed methods researchers are pragmatists. Maxwell and Mittapalli describe realism as a basis for mixed methods research. This is an excellent article appropriate to assign to PhD students.

Mertens, D., Bledsoe, K., Sullivan, M., & Wilson, A. (2010). Utilization of mixed methods for transformative purposes. In A. Tashakkori & C. Teddlie (Eds.), *SAGE handbook of mixed methods in social and behavioral research* (2nd ed.). Los Angeles, CA: SAGE.

Mertens and colleagues use the transformative paradigm as a basis for mixed methods research. This is an excellent article appropriate to assign to PhD students.

3

The History of Mixed Methods Social Work Research: The Pittsburgh Survey (1907–08)

Given the common roots of mixed methods inquiry and social work in pragmatism discussed in chapter 2, it is unsurprising that social work has a long and evolving heritage of integrating quantitative and qualitative methodologies to address complex social issues. In this chapter, we will first identify an early social work study as a precursor to modern mixed methods research. At this time, mixed methods research was not developed as a distinct methodology with specific designs or analytic strategies, for example; rather, integration of methods occurred as a natural approach to addressing complex social issues. Then, we will describe the broader context of social work as a profession in relation to social science research. Indeed, the grounding of social work in social science has been central to the field's professional identity from its nineteenth-century origins in scientific philanthropy through today. Yet gender and ideological divisions between social work and other areas of social science soon appeared, undermining the mutual benefits to be derived from their dialectical relationship. Next, we will describe the broader context of mixed methods social work research within debates surrounding the legitimacy of social science methodologies grounded in traditions other than quantitative. As ideas of *legitimate* social science research were disputed during the great quantitative-qualitative debates of the mid- to late-twentieth century, division appeared within social science including within social work research. As with many other areas of social science, social work research became more narrowly focused on quantitative methodologies. Yet there was tremendous pushback from qualitative researchers including those in social work. Mixed methods research reemerged in the 1980s as one response to these paradigm wars. Then, we will describe mixed methods approaches in relation to concerns about the relevance of social work research to social work practice. Given their fit with the mission of social work, mixed methods approaches were seen as enhancing the relevance of social work research to other areas of practice, long-standing and unresolved issues. Finally, we will present an illustration of early mixed methods social work research: the Pittsburgh Survey.

INTEGRATED APPROACHES WERE IMPLICIT
IN THE NINETEENTH CENTURY ORIGINS
OF SOCIAL WORK RESEARCH

Although they were not so named, integrated approaches to inquiry are apparent even in the work of nineteenth century forbearers of modern social work researchers. Charles Booth (1840–1916), a wealthy Englishman, investigated the *Life and Labour of the People of London* (1903) from 1886–1902. His goal was to understand the conditions of the poor. He created qualitative categories describing people by their employment and their apparent social status. Category rankings included "the lowest class of occasional labourers, loafers, and semi-criminals" through "regular standard earnings—above the line of poverty" and "upper middle class" (*see* Macdonald, 1960). These qualitative categories were then quantified to measure the extent of poverty in London. In 1926, Beatrice Webb remarked on Booth's methodology:

> Charles Booth showed us for the first time how best to combine the qualitative with the quantitative examination of social structure. By the masterly use of the method of wholesale interviewing (i.e., the use of a set of intermediaries who . . . were themselves acquainted with the whole aggregate of individuals to be investigated), amplified and verified by all sorts of independent testimony and personal observation of various parts of the immense field, he succeeded in making a qualitative examination of a magnitude never before attempted. By combining this with the merely mechanical enumeration of all the individuals in successive censuses, and by drawing out the eightfold indices of social condition that he had discovered, he was able to give to his qualitative categories a numerical measurement of an accuracy and over a field far greater than had ever before been attempted. (As cited in Macdonald, 1960, p. 8)

Integrated approaches to inquiry also were apparent in the work of mid–nineteenth century U.S. social work research pioneers. These social reformers systematically studied social problems to reform public policy. Dorothea Dix, for instance, traveled more than 60,000 miles on nineteenth-century tracks, roads, and rails accumulating information on mental illness. She described spending "eight years of sad, patient, and deliberate investigation" (Macdonald, 1960). Although she did not use these modern terms, her "quantitative data," the rough statistics she collected, were contextualized and expanded through vivid "qualitative case studies." She then used this investigation in her influential address to Congress in support of federal aid to the states to improve the terrible conditions of the "indigent insane."

By the early twentieth century, support for social work research became available on a wider scale through the establishment of the Russell Sage Foundation. Its 10-million-dollar endowment was targeted to the improvement of social and living conditions in the United States. One of its earliest funded projects was the Pittsburgh Survey, publically identified as a *social work* study (Austin, 2003).

The Pittsburgh Survey exemplifies early integrated research not only in its deliberate blending of what today we describe as quantitative and qualitative methods, but also in its mixing of diverse perspectives from multiple disciplines. Within a one-year period (1907–08), social reform leaders came together to systematically study, from multiple perspectives, the social conditions related to rapid industrialization, massive immigration, and urban congestion in a major U.S. city. Investigators including social workers, economists, philanthropists, and photographers produced a set of six books, each focusing on various facets of the larger study. This collective group of researchers recognized that the phenomenon under study called for an equally complex set of observations and questions from multiple perspectives in order to truly understand the social issues. Their survey thus included both quantitative studies of the occurrence of social problems and qualitative case studies concerned with causative factors. In 1908, Edward T. Devine, an economist, social worker, and director of the New York School of Philanthropy (later to become the New York School of Social Work), wrote about the Pittsburgh Study in the *American Economic Association Quarterly*. In his writing, he clearly identified multiple perspectives and methods as the greatest strengths of the study:

> The Pittsburgh Survey represents one way of studying family life in an industrial and urban community. The method of personal observation by an individual investigator is obviously inadequate to such an undertaking. Life is too short, prejudices too ineradicable, individual qualifications too specialized, the personal equation too disturbing, to permit any single individual, however gifted, to see for himself the community as a whole, and to measure the influences and forces that shape the family destiny. (1909, p. 207)

The design of the Pittsburgh Survey allowed examination of multiple interrelated phenomena from multiple perspectives utilizing multiple techniques. The primary goal was to provide comprehensive in-depth information to civic leaders for legislative reform initiatives to address social problems. Indeed, the Pittsburgh Study contributed directly to the development of workers' compensation legislation intended to deal with what was identified in the survey as the major cause of household poverty at the time: industrial accidents (Fitch, 1910).

Today, the Pittsburgh Survey is considered the first of its kind in breadth and depth in the United States. Along with its predecessors, including Charles Booth's study of poverty in London, Dorothea Dix's study of the care of the insane, and Jane Addams's study of the conditions of settlement housing, the Pittsburgh Survey marked the beginning of the social survey movement, a significant turning point in U.S. social work research. During the first decades of the twentieth century, hundreds of community surveys were conducted in the United States describing local needs for social services (Maas, 1977; Polansky, 1971). This survey movement was the predecessor of most contemporary forms of needs assessments and various forms of action research (Reid, 1987).

SOCIAL SCIENCE RESEARCH BOLSTERED THE DEVELOPMENT OF SOCIAL WORK AS A PROFESSION

Mixed methods social work research also has its professional roots in the broader context of social science research. In the late nineteenth century, a scientific orientation to social work was made explicit by leaders of the scientific philanthropy movement, whose aim was to make giving relief to the poor a systematic rational professional endeavor. By the early twentieth century, writings by prominent social workers such as Edith and Grace Abbott, Jane Addams, and Florence Hollis emphasized the importance of the scientific study of social work practice. They believed that social science could provide both the necessary understanding of the causes of social problems such as poverty and delinquency and a method for the systematic study and treatment of individual cases (Reid, 1987, 1998). Of particular note is Mary Richmond's (1917) classic, *Social Diagnosis*. In this book, Richmond developed a scientific methodology and techniques for casework. She provided broad instructions on how to gather and use social evidence including methods for interviewing. Her first principle was that care had to focus on the person within his or her situation. Her portrayal of the client within the environment was a precursor to modern systems theory.

During much of the first half of the twentieth century, social workers turned to social science as a means to develop professional identity. In 1915, Abraham Flexner, a reformer from the General Board of Education in New York City, spoke on "Is Social Work a Profession?" at the forty-second annual meeting of the National Conference of Charities and Correction in Baltimore. The conclusion of his talk was that social work was not a profession (Flexner, 1915). According to Kirk and Reid (2002), this conclusion caused a "ringing in the ears of social workers that lasted nearly a century" (p. 1), in part because of Flexner's credibility as the leader of turn-of-the-century U.S. medical education reform. That effort involved closing many commercial non-university-affiliated schools and allowing the American Medical Association to gain greater control over education and practice.

Flexner's conclusion that social work was not a profession was based on consideration of a number of criteria he viewed as characteristic of professions such as law, medicine, engineering, architecture, and university teaching. Flexner described social work as meeting a number of criteria for a profession including that it involved intellectual work based on science and learning, a professional self-consciousness, and the pursuit of the broader social good. However, he viewed social work as primarily serving a "mediating function" of bringing other professions and institutions together rather than being an autonomous profession. He also was troubled by social work's broad, diffuse aims, limited autonomy, and primitive curriculum. Flexner's challenges to social workers included clarification of their autonomous responsibility, refinement of their aims, and development of their education. These charges, however, were overshadowed by his characterization of social work as lacking a specific, separate, scientific body of knowledge. According to Kirk and Reid (2002), "It was this lack that became social work's accepted failing, the budding profession's Achilles heel" (p. 6).

In subsequent decades, social workers were concerned with identifying and developing an autonomous knowledge base. This quest facilitated the emergence of university-based graduate programs in social work (Pumphrey & Pumphrey, 1961). Traditionally, social work research had been located in social agencies, state welfare departments, or national agencies such as the Child Welfare League of America. In 1931, Edith Abbott argued that social work education would be facilitated by university affiliation and furthermore that social research was a critical component of a good professional school. At the time, however, she also observed that: "most schools have neither the funds nor the staff to make any provision for this important method [social research] of instructing professional students and advancing the knowledge of social welfare" (Pumphrey & Pumphrey, 1961, pp.295–296). From about 1947, however, U.S. social work research increasingly was done under university auspices (Maas, 1977).

Beginning in the late 1940s, advanced training for social work researchers became more available through the development of doctoral programs in schools of social work. The development of these doctoral programs brought a new emphasis on research training using tools from the social sciences as part of the social work curriculum. By the mid-1960s, there were nineteen social work doctoral programs in U.S. universities (Kirk & Reid, 2002). As the professional schools gained in academic recognition, the need for faculty with research skills who could contribute to theory and knowledge building in social work increased. By 1976 there were thirty-three doctoral programs in social work in U.S. universities (Bernard, 1977) and by the turn of the twenty-first century there were seventy-one (Watkins & Holmes, 2008).

Engagement in social science research served an important symbolic function by anchoring professional activity in rationality rather than in tradition or legislative politics. This may be why developers of the social work profession focused more on the need to identify a "body of scientific knowledge" than on some of Flexner's other concerns. Flexner understood that, to gain community sanction, a profession needs a body of knowledge not available to laypersons that confers authority, guides service to clients, and forms the content of professional education. He viewed the mastery of a body of knowledge and theory, rather than of practice skills per se, as an important criterion that distinguished professions from other occupations (Kirk & Reid, 2002).

EARLY TWENTIETH CENTURY IDEOLOGICAL AND GENDER DIVISIONS ISOLATED SOCIAL WORK FROM SOCIAL SCIENCE

Despite the centrality of the broader field of social science research to the emergence of social work as a profession, the relationship of social work researchers to social scientists in other fields has been complex. The development of social science and social work in the United States began together in the mid-nineteenth century. The first leaders of social work hoped that the profession might follow the example of medicine and engineering in drawing its knowledge from basic sciences. The logical basic science base for social work seemed to be the social sciences, with ancillary sources in related helping disciplines. In the early years of the twentieth century, empirically based knowledge available to social workers came mostly from the social sciences with additional contributions from medicine and psychiatry (Kirk & Reid, 2002; Reid, 1987). The report of the Milford Conference (American Association of Social Workers, 1929) suggested the following as a base of casework: biology, economics, law, medicine, psychiatry, sociology, and statistics. Anthropology, education, and social psychology were added by Karpf (1931) in one of the first major works concerned with the scientific base of social work.

Social workers were committed to social science research, but problems related to ideology and gender soon emerged. Early social work practitioners were interested in solving immediate problems. They were driven by a reformist ideology. Many social scientists were primarily concerned with developing research methods and theory. Complex gender and other politics also contributed to the split between social work and the social sciences. Jane Gilgun (1999b) described how, in the 1890s, John Dewey, George Herbert Mead, and other pragmatist philosophers were recruited to the University of Chicago where their ideas influenced Chicago's emerging social science departments. In the early years of the twentieth century, there was a great deal of interdisciplinary work including that between anthropology and sociology. Although not so named, the emerging mixed methods approach included social surveys, in-depth interviews, participant observation, document reviews, analysis of demographic data, and social mapping. These early years of Chicago sociology were characterized by links between academic settings and the community. As described in chapter 2, faculty members such as Dewey and Mead were close associates of Jane Addams, who along with her Hull House colleagues including Sophonisba Breckinridge and Edith Abbott contributed to the emergence of American Pragmatism and the Chicago school of sociology. The work of Addams was enriched by her association with the University of Chicago faculty, *and* her ideas influenced subsequent developments in sociological research.

Ideas of social reform proposed by Addams and her activist colleagues were compatible with the reformist ideas of Dewey and other male pragmatists, who also sought to improve social conditions. Reformist ideas, however, were heavily critiqued by male sociologists for what they viewed as moralistic and paternalistic underpinnings. These sociologists disassociated themselves from what they considered *do-gooder* ideologies and the women whom they viewed as embodying them. One such sociologist, showing obvious disrespect for social workers, discouraged his students from taking courses with Abbott and Breckinridge, and he told students in a seminar that women reformers had done great damage to the city of Chicago. Abbott and Breckenridge eventually broke away from the sociology department, forming an independent School of Civics and Philanthropy in 1920, later renamed the School of Social Service Administration. By the close of the second decade of the twentieth century, there was limited contact between the primarily female social work reformers and the primarily male sociology faculty at the University of Chicago (Gilgun, 1999b). By virtue of this early division of the fields at Chicago and elsewhere, social work was largely stripped of scientific skills and cut off from formal connection with the major sources of theoretical social thought (Austin, 2003). Likewise, social scientists were stripped of important opportunities to learn from emerging social issues on the ground and to use that understanding to develop theory and methods.

By the mid-twentieth century, these two fields began to come together again as social workers looked to the social sciences for tools for assessing the effectiveness of their interventions. In the 1980s, a collaboration began between social work and the National Institute of Mental Health (NIMH) that led to the establishment of the Task Force on Social Work Research in 1988, followed by the creation of the Institute for the Advancement of Social Work Research (IASWR), NIMH funding for social work research development centers, and the development of programs of interdisciplinary research to strengthen social work practice (Austin, 2003).

THE MID-TWENTIETH-CENTURY QUANTITATIVE/ QUALITATIVE DEBATE WITHIN SOCIAL SCIENCE AND SOCIAL WORK EXACERBATED THE STRUGGLE FOR THE LEGITIMACY OF SOCIAL WORK RESEARCH

Social work has a long history of drawing on multiple methodologies to understand and address complex social issues. Yet the soaring rise in prominence of quantitative methods in the mid-twentieth-century social sciences resulted in a more restricted set of questions and method choices viewed as yielding legitimate evidence for social work research (*see* Gilgun, 1999b). In particular, the great quantitative/qualitative debate of the mid- to late-twentieth century raged within social science circles *including* social work research, and had real consequences for how and what research got done. Most research funders openly preferred, and to some extent still do prefer, studies using apparently objective quantitative methodologies. Issues of funding, especially external funding from faculty grants, were critical to schools of social work, helping to fund programs. In addition, funders of social service agencies and other settings where social workers practiced typically emphasized evaluations describing seemingly straightforward quantifiable outcomes. Yet there was consistent and strong pushback to this preference given to quantitative perspectives and methods from qualitative researchers, including those who viewed quantitative research as generally lacking in depth and attention to human experience and context necessary for understanding complex social phenomena.

In the mid-twentieth century, social work research methods, largely borrowed from sociology and psychology, emphasized quantitative methodologies. During the 1960s and 1970s, impressive advances were made in quantitative analyses and the use of computers. Beginning in the 1970s, there was an increasing use of multivariate methods of data analysis including factor analysis, multiple regression, and multivariate analysis of variance. Multivariate techniques allowed researchers to analyze their data more rapidly and thoroughly, to ascertain patterns in the interrelationships among numerous variables, and to build causal explanations by controlling statistically for the influence of different variables (Reid, 1995).

In addition, emphasis on quantitative social work research was further fueled by the development of more discriminating measurement techniques in the social sciences and psychiatry that were contributing useful knowledge for assessments. Social workers became increasingly interested in using these techniques for monitoring and assessing policies, programs, and interventions (Reamer, 1998). During this time, research became more oriented toward experimental methodology (Polansky, 1971; Stuart, 1971) with the testing of hypotheses seen by many as the purpose of social science research (Maas, 1977).

The shift among the helping professions to an emphasis on evidence-based practice (EBP; *see* Gambrill, 2003) also propelled the use of quantitative methods in social work research (Guo, 2008). As originally conceived in medicine, EBP was an integration of the best evidence from research with the practitioner's knowledge of the context and the patient's preferences (Sackett, 1997). In medicine and in social work, scholars describing EBP took a capacious view of *evidence* to include results from qualitative as well as quantitative studies. In practice, however, quantitative methods were often preferred as apparently more objective, easier to implement, and more straightforward to interpret. Unease in social work began to stem not only from the sidelining of qualitative approaches, but also from the close association of EBP with managerial agendas and an emphasis on cost effectiveness and performance measurement at the expense of other equally legitimate interests, especially those of service users (Powell, 2002).

The privileged status given to quantitative research was not without vigorous and sustained criticism including by social work researchers. Polansky (1971) predicted that the "current enchantment with statistics" would decline and that insightful, case-based analyses of individuals, groups, and communities would regain respectability. Reid (1995) argued that, although sophisticated statistical techniques had contributed enormously to the methodology of social work research, they also had created problems:

1. Consumers of research didn't understand the statistics and so had to rely on authors' interpretations.
2. Many researchers who used the techniques did not understand their mathematical foundations; therefore, they were often ignorant of their pitfalls and limitations.
3. The measurements that provided the raw material for the analyses, for example, entries in administrative databases, were not necessarily rigorous enough to warrant elaborate statistical manipulation.

Other concerns with the privileged status of quantitative methods, including in social work, were raised. In 1977, Henry Maas argued that the "total commitment to measurement and quantitative analyses seems now to have been premature in a field of inquiry [social work] still lacking a clear description of how things happen" (p. 1190). He argued that one needs an understanding of the totality to know which parts warrant precise observation and pointed to the research of early qualitative social work researchers of the 1920s and 1930s. Unfortunately, none of those qualitative studies had touched the mainstreams of social work research because social agencies remained focused on service statistics, demographic mapping of multi-problem neighborhoods, and "other poorly conceptualized and fragmenting perspectives on social science and social work services," none of which has yielded "new knowledge of enduring value" (Maas, p. 1190). He expressed concerns that social work researchers had become more preoccupied with methods and techniques than with the purpose and substance of their inquiries to social work. In other words, he argued that social work researchers had let the study methods determine the questions rather than the other way around. He predicted that the range of methods used in social research would broaden. In particular, he argued that the ability afforded by qualitative methods to study subjective experience as well as objective events and to examine issues in their natural environments was most consistent with the organismic, dynamic systems view of social work.

By the mid-twentieth century, the prominence of quantitative ways of thinking and conducting research also were being challenged along philosophical lines from many fronts in the social sciences (*see* Greene, 2007; Ladd, 1992) and in social work (e.g., Haworth, 1984). Social sciences in many western societies were originally modeled after the natural sciences. In the mid-nineteenth century, the forbearer of modern sociology, August Comte, warned that progress toward understanding human beings was hampered by unfounded and speculative notions advanced by philosophers. He proposed that an important goal of social science was to account for the regularities in human social behavior and that the methods employed in the physical and natural sciences could be used for this purpose. He also believed that once these regularities were discovered they could be converted to principles or laws and used to create a utopian society. John Stuart Mill, a contemporary of Comte and forbearer of modern experimental methods, also advised using empirical methods of the natural sciences to study the social domain. Mill's approach to science, however, went beyond simple observation and the search for regularities to the relations between events, specifically, the conditions under which one could infer causal relations (*see* Ladd, 1992). In the model of social science evolved from Comte and Mill, theory is induced from observations and then tested under carefully controlled experimental conditions. The desired result is empirically sound and generalizable propositions about the social world, especially causal explanations of universal truths. The goal is to explain and thereby predict and control the social world, just as scientists explain and then endeavor to predict and control the physical world.

Such *positivist* or *post-positivist* social science research assumes that the social world exists independently of our knowledge of it, that we can come to know this social world through objective observations, and that we can set questions of value outside the perimeter of scientific questions of fact. Post-positivists understood that our ability to observe the social world objectively is limited by our own social positions and human biases, and they devised a variety of increasingly sophisticated designs and methodological strategies to minimize human biases including when studying human beings in naturalistic contexts (for example, *see* Shadish et al., 2002).

Positivist and post-positivist approaches have been criticized by philosophers of science since the latter part of the nineteenth century. William Dilthey (1883) contended that there is a fundamental difference in subject matter between the natural and the social sciences. Physical science deals with inanimate objects that exist outside of us whereas the social sciences focus on products of the human mind with all its subjectivity, emotions, and values. Although there are discernible, quantifiable patterns of human behavior, eliminating inner experience and interpretation from those behaviors robs social science of that which is most interestingly human and, at best, yields an incomplete understanding of those patterns (Shweder, 1996).

Furthermore, in social science, it is impossible to fully separate what is being studied from the investigator. It is people (including investigators) who participate in the social world and who interpret it. Thus, the social researcher can attain an understanding of the social world only through a process of interpretation. Furthermore, human experience and behavior are inextricably bound to context. Instead of objective, realist, and generalizable claims of universal truth, critics of positivist and post-positivist approaches generally argue that knowledge is inherently and inevitably subjective, contextual, contingent, and value laden.

In the mid-twentieth century, quantitative social science methods based on positivist and post-positivist approaches also were challenged based on the products of their research. During evaluation of the effectiveness of the War on Poverty, experimental methods were not meeting the challenges of evaluation. Humans did not behave like inanimate objects, crops, chemicals, or magnetic forces, for example. They behaved unpredictably and with intention in contexts over which the researcher had limited control (Greene, 2007). Experimental methods of post-positivist social science did not provide sound empirical data on the quality and effectiveness of the War on Poverty programs. The need for control and standardization did not work well in the real world, and the need for randomization raised questions of ethics. Greene (2007) observed that "defensible experimental research required standardized strategies in tightly controlled contexts, but good practice required constantly adjusting strategies to changing circumstances" (p. 35). Further, confining social inquiry to observable phenomena constrained and biased research on social programs and problems to analysis of inputs and outcomes with little attention to program process or participants' experiences. In social science as a whole, interest increased in qualitative approaches examining people's contextualized experiences gleaned through narrative and thick description (Greene, 2007).

The systematic and self-conscious consideration of broader philosophical issues in discussions of social science methodology also erupted within social work in contentious debate in the 1980s as critics challenged the philosophical and methodological foundations of social work research (*see* Kirk & Reid, 2002; Reid, 1987). Some critics saw a place for post-positivist research in social work, but argued that it had been erroneously equated with *good science*. They proposed other paradigms based on different assumptions about what constitutes valid research (*see* Haworth, 1984). Critics argued that the paradigms commonly taught, used, and accepted by social work researchers were inadequate to understanding and responding to the social issues addressed by social workers. More specifically, post-positivist paradigms placed undue value on quantitative approaches, experimental designs, objective measurement, and statistical analyses. Critics sought to replace post-positivism with paradigms in the tradition of qualitative methodology that had long been part of such disciplines as sociology and anthropology. As within the broader social science community, these criticisms and proposals were vigorously disputed by quantitative researchers (e.g., *see* Hudson, 1982).

Debates over the place of qualitative and quantitative traditions continued throughout the rest of the twentieth century (Austin, 2003) with many researchers becoming increasingly frustrated. Reid and other social work researchers (e.g., Kirk & Reid, 2002) argued that grand epistemological debates are unlikely to yield practical consequences, and for social work practical consequences are what matters. Other scholars in the applied professions and social science more generally argued that epistemological debates do not get research done. Greene (2007) argued that we need to redirect attention away from dualistic attributes of paradigms, including objectivism-subjectivism and realism-idealism, and get on with the work of applied social inquiry by intentionally and thoughtfully employing the full extent of our methodological repertoire.

In addition, frustrated researchers pointed out that social inquiry paradigms are themselves social constructions and so are not inviolate, immoveable, or static. Greene (2007) argued that we need to broaden the abstract notion of philosophical paradigm to reflect the more grounded, intuitive, dialogic notion of a *mental model* as the underlying framework or logic of justification for social research. Mental models are the set of assumptions, understandings, predispositions, values, and beliefs with which we approach our work. They include basic philosophical assumptions (ontology, epistemology, methodology) underlying the quantitative-qualitative debate, but also our values, beliefs, disciplinary understandings, practice wisdom, and life history. Certain philosophical assumptions may be incommensurable with others, but most mental models are inherently dialogic as we seek correction, elaboration, and understanding.

In addition, paradigms are not the sole determinant of the choice of methods in social research. Crotty (1998) described hierarchical levels of perspectives and decisions reflected in any research study including broad epistemological perspectives (e.g., objectivism, subjectivism), but also content-specific theoretical perspectives (e.g., feminism), methodological expertise (e.g., experimental research, ethnography), and methods (e.g., specific decisions regarding sampling and observation). In addition, researchers' actual methodological choices are affected by the demands of the research situation. For example, educational researchers make decisions primarily on the basis of the context, purpose of the study, and concrete problem at hand rather than paradigm issues (Greene, 2007). In other words, qualitative and quantitative dichotomies are not characteristic of actual research practice. It is the concrete research problem and inquiry purpose that importantly determine the design and methods of an applied study. Depending on the problem the design can be quantitative, qualitative, or mixed.

In his opinion expressed in 1988, Epstein perhaps best summed the frustration with the great quantitative-qualitative debate: "to imply that we, as professional social workers, must make a choice between one or the other research method is senseless, idiotic, and simple-minded, to say the least. Both methods make meaningful contributions to our understanding of the social world and, when used *together*, can obviously augment it" (p. 194). In his discussion of research methodologies in 1980, Fanshel argued that:

> no single methodological approach to the conduct of social work research is adequate; the needs of the profession dictate that a pluralism prevail. Scholars' willingness to live with differences in investigative procedures and styles will create the best yield for social work. Sociologists prefer survey methods; anthropologists are inclined to use naturalistic field methods . . . and psychologists are strongly committed to experimental methods. Social work, however, has no need to develop a special identification with any particular approach. The profession's research experience has been characterized by diversity and multiple communities of investigators. (p. 8)

Although the great qualitative-quantitative debate of the twentieth century was divisive, it did serve some important purposes both in social science research more broadly and in social work research specifically. Reid (1995) argued that this debate stimulated a much needed examination of the methodology rationale of mainstream social work research. It also provided an impetus and favorable climate for qualitative research. Even though qualitative methods had long been accepted in mainstream social work research, they were not widely used during the heyday of quantification because they were viewed by some as second best if not second class. Finally, Reid argued that the great quantitative-qualitative debate of the late twentieth century fostered efforts to develop integrative pluralistic frameworks that accommodate diverse epistemological viewpoints.

Thus, deliberately mixing methods in a thoughtful, reflective manner reemerged in social work and other areas of applied research, legitimizing multiple rationales and multiple ways of practicing social inquiry. Most social researchers maintained an allegiance to one particular methodological tradition but also accepted a plurality of legitimate traditions. The idea of mixing methods had appeal in part because of long-standing acceptance of methodological triangulation in both quantitative and qualitative methodological traditions. All methods have inherent strengths as well as biases and limitations. The intentional use of multiple methods, with offsetting or counteracting strengths and limitations, in investigations of the same phenomenon can strengthen the depth, breadth, and rigor of findings. In other words, one method does not preclude another. One can quantify beliefs, behaviors, and actions AND interpret their meaning from diverse perspectives in various contexts. Qualitative methods are good for gathering certain types of information and quantitative methods are good for others. The two traditions can operate in complementary fashion, each contributing uniquely to our understanding of complex social phenomena.

MIXED METHODS SOCIAL WORK RESEARCH ENHANCED THE SEARCH FOR RELEVANCE

The recognition that qualitative and quantitative methods can be compatible may have resulted in a truce in the paradigm wars, but tensions remained between social work research and other areas of social work practice; specifically, the relevance of social work research to social work practice. As Mary Macdonald so aptly observed in 1960:

> The great problem in social work research is to bring together knowledge of the field and knowledge of [research] method. . . . In general, those who have known the most about a given social work subject have not been methodologists. Those who have acquired expertise in research method have seldom been experts in some branch of social work. . . . Hence, there have been many disasters . . . the abortive study that fails for lack of competence in application of appropriate research method, the irrelevant study that fails to contribute to social work knowledge because the research design does not utilize concepts and variables that are meaningful to social work theory. (p. 19)

As the research leadership in social work shifted to the academy, the concern about a gap between research and professional practice increased (Austin, 2003; Reid, 1987, 1995). Practitioners were especially concerned that academic researchers were not in sufficient touch with the realities of practice to provide the best kind of leadership (Kirk & Reid, 2002).

At the same time that these concerns about relevance were being articulated, a number of social work researchers began to argue that integration of methods could mend the increasing estrangement between researchers and practitioners. In 1994, Harrison explained that, with the mid-twentieth century rise of quantitative methods, a hierarchy of research methods had been established in the research community, preferring hypothesis testing and statistical methods. The methodological status hierarchy was related largely to the social science research community's allegiance to social science technologies that assumed objectivity and the independent existence of a social world. According to Harrison (1994), this alliance of social work researchers with mainstream social science led to an estrangement between social work practice and research because the methods hierarchy was not related to the nature of social work practice (e.g., in which practice interventions might be altered during the course of treatment) or to the ways that practitioners use information (e.g., as guides rather than preset protocols). This application of conventional social science to social work was a good effort, but it was an effort that needed redirection, expansion, and integration. Harrison argued that social work researchers needed to develop their own research methodologies that integrated both qualitative and quantitative methodologies. This integration, he argued, was not only inevitable, but would make more likely the integration of research and practice.

In 2001, Cowger and Menon similarly argued that an integration of quantitative and qualitative methods would help to mend the divide between social work research and practice. They argued that the integration of methods "allows congruence with the principles of social work to study things holistically, in context, and from more than one frame of reference." They described the problem situation of the typical client as presenting the social worker with multiple stakeholders, multiple contexts, and multiple perspectives on the nature and meaning of the problem. Social work practice simply does not lend itself to a single narrow research method to understand what is going on, to evaluate a service, to examine one's own practice, or develop new practice knowledge. Furthermore, they argued that useful knowledge relevant to the multiple contexts of social planning and administration is unlikely to be acquired by singular and narrow notions of research methods. Cowger and Menon then moved the mixed methods discussion forward in social work by articulating purposes for integrating qualitative and quantitative methods including (a) qualitative research as a beginning step to quantitative research, (b) quantitative research as a beginning step to qualitative research, and (c) simultaneous triangulation of methods. (The purposes of mixed methods research are discussed further in chapter 4.)

By the twenty-first century, social work scholars were discussing the integration of research methods internationally. For example, Powell (2002) argued in the *British Journal of Social Work* that for social work research to be relevant to practice it must be both generalizable and widely relevant on the one hand and particularized and context-specific on the other. To address this challenge, he recommended an "eclectic methodology" considering a multiplicity of views. Furthermore, he argued that "the continuing development of mixed methods approaches is also important in addressing the complexity of interests within the policy and practice arena, ranging from funders to service users, and the differing conceptions of what constitutes relevant research in this context" (p. 23).

In 2013, Chaumba identified forty-seven social work research articles published between 1995 and 2010 that involved the integration of quantitative and qualitative techniques. She argued that mixed methods research integrates the voices of the participants with a comprehensive analysis of the phenomena and enhances the validity of findings.

ILLUSTRATIVE EXAMPLE OF AN EARLY PRECURSOR TO MIXED METHODS SOCIAL WORK RESEARCH: THE PITTSBURGH SURVEY

As you read about the Pittsburgh Survey consider the questions listed in Box 3.1.

●●

BOX 3.1
Guide to the Pittsburgh Survey

1. In what ways does this early study include characteristics of mixed methods social work described in chapters 1 and 2? Consider definitions, assumptions, common characteristics, and pragmatism.
2. From the perspective of contemporary mixed methods research, how might the Pittsburgh Survey have been strengthened?
3. In what ways might the Pittsburgh Survey have contributed to the emergence of social work research methods?
4. To what extent are methodological insights from the Pittsburgh Survey reflected in contemporary social work research?

●●

The Pittsburgh Survey was a precursor to modern mixed methods social work research. It marked the beginning of the U.S. social survey movement, a significant turning point in social work research. The Pittsburgh Survey resulted in six volumes, each reporting on a different social issue in turn-of-the-century Pittsburgh. Here, we will focus on *Women and the Trades*, authored by Elizabeth Beardsley Butler (1911). This work discusses the social and economic climate experienced by women in the trades and provides vivid examples of what working conditions were like in Pittsburgh in 1908–09.

Butler generated a rich understanding of the working and social conditions of women in the trades through an integration of qualitative and quantitative methods (although such dichotomization of methods was not articulated). In the first chapter, Butler began with an ethnographic description of a city booming with industry:

> Look down from Mount Washington at the merging of the two dull brown rivers, at the irregular succession of bridges, at scows and small river craft slowly finding way from wharf to wharf; and on either shore, at the black enclosures, gleaming now with leaping flames, now with the steady white-hot glow of Bessemer converters, but everywhere swarthy from the rising columns of black smoke. (p. 17)

Throughout the book Butler used participant observation and historical documents review to generate thick descriptions. It is clear that she spent a great deal of time on the *inside*, forming an **emic** understanding of the community and the people who lived and worked within. For example, she embedded an insider perspective into her broad description of immigration patterns in the city:

When the industries of the district first drew on Europe for laborers, it was the men of Ireland and Germany, of Italy, Austria and Poland who came. Later in smaller numbers the women followed. They came because their husbands and brothers were here, but not often for the purpose of forging out a life of their own. Similarly the women of the later immigrant races, the Slavs and the Southern Europeans, are lagging behind. Giuseppina keeps a little Italian cottage, sure that Pietro will return or will make his way before he sends for her. Life in America for her is not a settled destiny. It is a growing probability, to be sure, for all those populations whose demands exceed the productive power of the soil; but even to the strong it remains something of an experiment, something for which peasant women must await the issue before they follow in numbers equal to the men. (pp. 20-21)

Throughout the book, Butler's description includes a variety of types of qualitative data including maps and photographs in order to illustrate what she described in words. She also integrated quotes from insiders working within the trades under study. For instance, in her racial analysis of women working in different types of trades, she highlighted a quote from a factory foreman working with Slavic workers: "They would work all night . . . if I would give them the chance. We never have any trouble with them. We can't give them enough work to do" (p. 24). Butler used this quote to illustrate her finding that the historical suffering and lack of training, in addition to a "stolid physical poise," placed Slavic women at a particular advantage to cope with some of the poorest working conditions. Furthermore, she asserted that the Slavic women, perhaps because of their new immigrant status, or perhaps because of other physical or psychological traits, were taking inferior positions and competing for physically demanding positions typically occupied only by men.

Such rich descriptions continue throughout the volume. They present a detailed account of the physical working conditions in Pittsburgh at the time. For example, Butler vividly described a visit to a sweatshop:

I went into one cellar opposite a Hill factory where two women and one man, all Negroes, were stripping [tobacco] in a room less than seven feet in height. The only source of air was a narrow door leading by a flight of steps up to the street. A tiny slit of a window at the far end was close barred, and two-thirds of the cubic space in the room was occupied by bales of tobacco and cases of stripped stock. Pools of muddy water stood on the earth floor, and the air was foul beyond endurance. (p. 83)

Consistent with the traditions of ethnographic research, Butler integrated quantitative data into her primarily qualitative descriptions and analyses. For example, she reviewed U.S. Census information to describe the number of women in various trades. To extend her understanding of the work environment, she also documented, quantitatively, information about work hours as well as wages earned within different trades. She included these data in the body of the text, as well as in illustrative tables and figures. She included comparisons, not only among different races but also among men and women. She also included historical artifacts, for example, a reproduction of pay regulations that were posted on a workroom door, as well as documents that were generated to publicize, for other workers, the amount of work accomplished by the most productive workers in a given week.

Butler's use of qualitative and quantitative data is well integrated throughout the book. For instance, in her discussion of wages within the canning industries she presented a range of pay rates for different types of jobs and she elaborated the reasoning behind the discrepancies in pay. For instance, she wrote, "Bottling is enough of a trade to warrant a higher level of wages. High dexterity, like skill, can only be acquired by time. Whereas some of the older hands exceed the standard pay, many others are not able to earn more than $.90 to $1.00 per day" (p. 38).

She also used summative techniques to quantify qualitative data. For instance, in her description of the physical environment of garment workrooms, Butler examined four broad domains: the arrangement of the windows, the use of artificial light, the cleanliness of the workroom, and the quality of protection (or guards) on machinery. She provided a frequency table showing the results of her inquiry, using a four-point scale within each domain. For example, her findings indicated that there were six garment workrooms included in her study that did not have a need for artificial light due to sufficient daylight, eight workrooms where there was a shaded light above the machine, two where there were only electric bulbs shining directly on the needles of the machines, and five workrooms that were dark and without provision for artificial light. Following this quantification, she provided a detailed (qualitative) description of each category. For instance, returning to the example of artificial lighting, she wrote:

> Eleven factories have no artificial light. This does not mean that in these eleven factories the workrooms are flooded with daylight; on the contrary, in five cases the reverse is true. Manufacturers of stock or custom goods for discriminating customers must provide sufficient light for their employees so that the work will be turned out well, but when the articles manufactured are of cheap quality the standard of finish is low, light in the workroom becomes of less importance. In the former case daylight or well-planned artificial lighting has a commercial value; in the latter case its value is considerably lowered. That this kind of economy results in eyestrain among the employees does not go down on the ledger of the business. (pp. 106–107)

In this early study, it is clear that there was a great deal of attention to the rigor and to the alignment of methods and analysis with the goals of the study. Butler outlined her sampling criteria and methods of inclusion and exclusion of participants from the study. She also discussed her use of triangulation (although it wasn't called that at the time). For instance, managers were asked to provide information about the number and type of employees as well as the hours and wages paid. She also engaged in both document reviews and qualitative interviews in order to collect comprehensive information about hours and wages. Butler discussed the use of such triangulation in detail:

> Each statement made by the management was tested by interviews with employees and by interviews with people familiar with the trade, who stood on neutral ground. Conversely, statements made by employees were tested by interviews with employers. In consequence, the discussion of each trade may justly be regarded not as a reflection of either the employer's or the employee's point of view, but as a description resulting from consideration of the several viewpoints and neutral truths concerned. (p. 381)

Not only did she focus her attention on interviewing workers and managers inside each trade, but she also spent time talking with people within the union as well as social workers and other leaders whose work was, as she indicates "on the fringe of that undertaken here" (p. 381). This use of triangulation contributed to the strength of the qualitative analysis in each section of the book.

Butler clearly articulated how the methods employed in this study were used to achieve a broader understanding of this particular time period in Pittsburgh:

> Little prominence has been given to individual cases of exploitation and injustice, unless these cases were characteristic of a trade group rather than of individual method. Meanness is a personal trait. Night work may be the result of meanness in a single firm, or it may be the result of a commercial maladjustment. In the former case it deserves passing mention, but in the latter case it must be commented upon as, temporarily at least, characteristic of the industry. My effort has been to study the conditions growing out of the trade itself, not out of the foibles or the unkindness of any individual, and to present a sketch of the trade process in terms of the life of the workers and of its place in present day industrial methods. (p. 381)

Conclusion

Learning lessons from the past can better prepare us to understand implications for the role of mixed methods approaches in contemporary social work. A solid sense of mission and history of social work research is important for us to maintain focus, to avoid getting pulled off course by pendulum swings toward particular methods and perspectives, and to set the course of social work research in the twenty-first century. In this chapter, we described how an integrated style of research emerged and evolved as embedded within the broader contexts of social work, other applied professions, and social science research more broadly. Precursors of modern mixed methods approaches were present in the first instances of social work research in the late nineteenth and early twentieth centuries. Their development, however, has been complexly interwoven with the development of social work as a profession by trends and debates occurring within the social sciences across the twentieth century and by political and administrative imperatives. Issues involved in the blending of theoretical perspectives and methodologies across disciplines discussed in this text, however, were not explicitly addressed until the latter part of the twentieth century.

SUGGESTIONS FOR ADDITIONAL READING

Kirk, S. A., & Reid, W. J. (2002). *Science and social work: A critical appraisal*. New York: Columbia University Press.

> Kirk and Reid provide a critical appraisal of past and present efforts to make social work practice more scientific. This book is accessible to MSW as well as PhD students.

Ladd, G. (1992) Perspectives on the aims, assumptions, and activities of human science: An historical overview. In R. D. Parke and G. W. Ladd (Eds.), *Family-peer relations: Modes of linkage* (pp. 1–36.). Mahwah, NJ: Erlbaum.

> Ladd discusses the considerable debate over the last several centuries about what the purpose of science should be and how it should be conducted. He describes various responses to these debates as often depending on assumptions about the nature of science, and the type of knowledge it can yield. An excellent reading for PhD students.

Part 2

Doing Mixed Methods Research
The Ongoing Contributions of Contemporary Social Workers

"It is unlikely that understanding in a professional field can be enriched by research whose methods are alien to other practices in that field. What we know and how we come to know it are of one piece" (Maas, 1977, p. 1193).

In part 2, we will discuss the step-by-step process of planning a mixed methods research project such as a grant proposal, capstone project, thesis, or dissertation. The focus in chapters 4 through 8 is on how to actually do mixed methods research, drawing on examples from contemporary mixed methods social work researchers:

- Chapter 4. Integrating Research Questions and Contemplating Reasons for Mixing: Men Incarcerated for Violent Crimes
- Chapter 5. Integrating Observational and Cause-Probing Designs: Refugees Experiencing War Trauma
- Chapter 6. Integrating Methods and Contemplating Ethical Issues: Parents with Low Incomes Accused of Child Maltreatment
- Chapter 7. Integrating Analyses and Enhancing Rigor: Spirituality and Recovery from Addiction
- Chapter 8. Mixed Method Designs: Children from Rural Methamphetamine-Involved Families

4

Integrating Research Questions and Contemplating Reasons for Mixing
Men Incarcerated for Violent Crimes

I got interested in perpetrators [of violence] because like everybody else, every other feminist anyway, I was interested in survivors of violence. My dissertation research was on girls between the ages of 10 and 15 who had been sexually abused. I did life history interviews of these little kids. I interviewed them five times each and I also interviewed them and their parents once. So I had six interviews with each of these kids. And I was just enraptured by them, by the stories they told, how they told the stories, and how committed they were: how much they wanted to tell their stories so other girls wouldn't go through what they went through. I mean to see an 11-year-old saying that, it's like how can that not totally change you and influence what you wanna do for the rest of your life? So I was just totally taken with these kids. There were a couple who found it very hard to talk and I understand that [but] the kids by and large talked their heads off. So anyway one of things that several of the kids said—not all of them but several of them—[was] "I really loved him." And they were all men who abused these girls. "I loved him and I'm so sorry he's in prison and I wish he would just get help." And then they'd describe all the fun things they did. They didn't want the abuse; they hated that part. But they still loved them. And I thought, "This is a little bit more complicated." So I got very interested in perpetrators. I did work closely [as a social worker] with one man who had sexually abused all three of his children and he opened my eyes. He wasn't a psychopathic type. He was just a terribly abused child growing up. That's just one type of perpetrator, the abused child growing up who never got any help. So from there I thought, "I really am curious about perpetrators now." (J. Gilgun, personal communication, April 30, 2014)

Thus, Jane Gilgun launched a decades-long program of mixed methods social work research focused on perpetrators of violence. Throughout her mixed methods program of research, Gilgun's research questions have been closely linked to her social work practice experience. For example, her clinical social work experience with boys who had experienced abuse sensitized her to the possible connections between early life experiences of abuse and later perpetration of abuse. Gilgun's mixed methods research program also illustrates reasons for mixing methods in social work research. Driven by a strong desire to understand violence, she used that understanding gained from qualitative approaches to develop clinical assessment tools for practitioners using quantitative approaches. Finally, Gilgun's research underscores the importance of the ethical treatment of all people who participate in social work research. She explained her stance towards the highly stigmatized individuals who participated in her research including perpetrators of sexual assault and murder:

> I was very honest with them, but in a way that fully accepted them as human beings. I wanted them to feel like they were human beings and important despite what they'd done, which is not a very popular perspective on perpetrators. A lot of people want you to just hate them. And, you know, they are human beings. They did terrible things, but they are human beings. (J. Gilgun, personal communication, April 30, 2014)

In this chapter, we will consider the initial stages in the development of a mixed methods study: how to identify a research question or hypothesis and choose a mixed methods or a mono method approach. We also will return to Gilgun's research program to illustrate two classic reasons for choosing mixed methods approaches: addressing research questions focused on understanding and development.

IDENTIFYING THE RESEARCH QUESTION

Asking an important question is at the heart of any successful research project, whether mono method or mixed method. How one identifies the *right* questions is a critical but under- discussed component of the research process. In mixed methods inquiries, quantitative and qualitative research questions are closely linked or integrated. In Gilgun's research, for example, research questions included qualitative questions of how perpetrators experienced violence, as well as quantitative questions of how reliably and validly an instrument developed from this understanding assessed them. In addition, new questions may emerge or be adjusted as the mixed methods inquiry progresses and new issues emerge. For example, qualitative components of the mixed method study may raise new questions about potential risk or protective factors for violence that have implications for the quantitative components or vice versa.

To identify important research questions social work researchers often look to urgent issues in practice and policy. These research questions are framed within specific content theories and existing empirical research. Many of the issues of concern to social workers such as violence, substance abuse, poverty, and oppression are interdisciplinary. Thus, developing important research questions often involves delving into literature in multiple disciplines such as psychology, sociology, anthropology, and political science; allied professions such as education, nursing, and public health; and social work practice and policy literatures. All of the research exemplars presented in this book focus on important social issues: violence, war trauma, addiction, child maltreatment, racism, poverty, and mental health; they develop concepts that may be applicable to diverse social work and policy contexts. Furthermore, the questions addressed in the research exemplars are framed within a variety of theories in particular content areas (e.g., attachment theory or critical race theory).

Some of the most significant social work research questions have implications not only for direct practice and policy, but also for theory development. Gilgun's research questions, for instance, address indisputably important practice and policy issues: the prevention of violence. They are framed within existing theories of violence, but also contribute to these theories by putting concepts to the test through action. True to the pragmatic roots of social work and mixed methodology, some of the best mixed methods social work research questions not only provide direct opportunities to further the social good, but they also provide important opportunities to test, refine and elaborate theories.

At a more practical level, research questions address empirical issues that are appropriate in their scope given the state of the knowledge. If very little is known about a given program or policy, for example, addressing specific questions about causality (e.g., if the program resulted in the desired change) may be premature. Empirical questions directed at program description and implementation may be more appropriate. Likewise, asking specific descriptive questions about particular community practices may be premature if very little is known about the cultural context in which the practices are embedded.

In addition, it is important to consider resources available for any given project. If resources are modest, as they often are for dissertation research, it may be wiser to address a research question that is relatively limited in scope than to attempt to answer a more ambitious question, for example, to address a question about a particular community rather than a national group. The question that is more limited in scope may result in a stronger study that can then be built upon in subsequent research, whereas attempting to address the more ambitious question with inadequate resources may result in a weaker study that yields inconclusive or uninterpretable findings.

Finally, if enough existing research is available to make a prediction, then the researcher may specify a hypothesis or hypotheses. For example, after designing an innovative intervention the mixed methods social work researcher hypothesizes that it will be experienced positively by clients and will result in observable changes in behavior.

CHOOSING A MIXED OR MONO METHOD DESIGN

Greene and Hall (2010) recommend that when planning a mixed methods study the researcher begin with careful consideration of the reasons for mixing quantitative and qualitative approaches for that particular study. Such consideration is important for first determining whether or not a mono or mixed methods design is most appropriate for any given study. Although mixed methods approaches are becoming increasingly popular, not all research projects are strengthened by a mixed methods design. Some questions are better addressed through focused qualitative or quantitative approaches. In addition, resources from funding to researcher energy to participant patience are not unlimited. Attempts at integration can dilute as well as strengthen a study. Furthermore, when a mixed methods design is appropriate for any given study, careful consideration of the purpose for mixing can maximize the benefits of mixing so that the study becomes more than the sum of its quantitative and qualitative parts. In this chapter we will present an integration of several general methodological frameworks describing the purposes of mixing quantitative and qualitative approaches (e.g., Creswell & Plano Clark, 2011; Teddlie & Tashakkori, 2003). Then we will discuss reasons for mixing qualitative and quantitative approaches more specific to social work.

REASONS FOR MIXING METHODS

In 1989, Jennifer Greene and colleagues (Greene, Caracelli, & Graham, 1989) conducted a classic study of the purposes for mixing methods. They began by reviewing the existing theoretical literature in social inquiry methodology. One important area of methodological theory is that of triangulation (e.g., *see* Campbell & Fiske, 1959, Denzin, 1978). *Triangulation* refers to the use of multiple methods to offset or counteract biases and limitations inherent in any single method. For example, a face-to-face interview may be combined with a standardized test to assess mental health functioning. Interviews and standardized tests have different strengths and limitations. Interviews offer an opportunity to engage participants, clarify items for them, and probe their responses, activities more difficult with a standardized test. On the other hand, standardized tests offer consistency in their administration across participants and may be less vulnerable than interviews to social response bias, in which participants answer in a way that seems socially acceptable to the researcher. When different research methods with offsetting strengths and limitations converge or corroborate one another, then our confidence in the findings is enhanced. In other words, multiple measures of the same phenomenon may be employed to strengthen the validity of the inquiry results.

Another important area of theory considered by Greene and colleagues was that of *multiplism*. Thomas Cook (1985) extended the theory of triangulation to all aspects of the research process. He considered the use of multiple methods in a single study, but also multiple theoretical orientations and political and value perspectives. Furthermore, Cook considered not only convergence of findings, but also complementarity. In other words, Cook's *critical multiplism* uses different methods, theories, or perspectives, for example, to consider their convergence on the *same* component of the study, but also their analysis of *different* components of a study. For example, a social work researcher might choose particular methods to assess children's educational achievement and other methods to assess their enjoyment of school in a study examining the multifaceted phenomenon of children's school engagement.

Greene and colleagues (1989) developed a conceptual framework of the primary purposes for integrating quantitative and qualitative research from these and other methodological sources. They then refined this framework through a review of fifty-seven empirical mixed methods evaluation studies, primarily of education programs, published between 1980 and 1988. Their goal was to develop methodological theory to guide the increasing use of mixed methods designs in education evaluation research. Their conceptual framework remains relevant to this day, not only for evaluation research, but also for mixed methods research in a variety of applied fields. Indeed, Alan Bryman, professor of Organisational and Social Research at the University of Leicester in the United Kingdom, began with Greene and colleagues' conceptual scheme for coding evaluation studies. He reviewed more (232 articles) and more recent studies (published between 1994 and 2003) from a wider range of social science fields (e.g., sociology, geography, management and organizational behavior, media, and cultural studies) than Greene and colleagues (Bryman, 2008). Based on his content analysis of these journal articles, Bryman provided a more detailed scheme of rationales than did Greene and colleagues, but the most frequently cited rationales overlap considerably with Greene and colleagues' categories. Below we describe four of the primary reasons for mixing identified by Greene and colleagues and other prominent mixed methodologists including Bryman (2008), Teddlie and Tashakkori (2010), and Creswell and Plano Clark (2011): enhanced understanding, enhanced rigor, development, and new insights.

Enhanced Understanding

A commonly discussed reason for mixing methods is to enhance understanding through a more comprehensive or expanded examination of complex psychosocial phenomena. In Bryman's (2008) study, ***enhanced under-standing***, identified in 32 percent of articles, was the most frequently cited rationale for mixing qualitative and quantitative approaches. Bryman charac-terized enhancement as augmenting either quantitative or qualitative find-ings by gathering data using the other approach. In addition, he found that authors of 13 percent of articles listed ***completeness*** as a rationale for mix-ing methods. Completeness refers to the researcher's ability to bring together a more comprehensive account of the area of inquiry by employing both quantitative and qualitative approaches. Finally, 11 percent of studies cited ***diversity of views*** as a rationale for mixing methods; that is, enhanced understanding of complex phenomena occurs when multiple per-spectives, each with inherent insights and limitations, are considered.

Greene and colleagues (1989) first described how a more comprehen-sive understanding of complex psychosocial phenomena may be achieved through the use of qualitative and quantitative methods: ***complementarity*** and ***expansion.*** Complementarity refers to the use of data from different methods to generate a deeper, broader, and more comprehensive portrait of a complex phenomenon. Different methods are used to tap into different dimensions of the (same) phenomenon under study. In one program of social work research, Haight and colleagues examined the visits of parents with their young children who were in foster care. They conducted struc-tured quantitative observations of parent-child interactions during weekly scheduled visits (Haight, Black, Workman, & Tata, 2001; Schoppe-Sullivan et al., 2007) and qualitative interviews with parents about their experiences of such visits including factors that facilitated and impeded their interactions with their children during visits (Haight et al., 2002). In subsequent phases of their mixed methods research program, these social work researchers designed and evaluated an intervention to improve visiting using a mix of quantitative outcome measures and qualitative interviews to help interpret quantitative findings (Haight, Mangelsdorf, et al., 2005). Thus, quantitative and qualitative approaches tapped somewhat different dimensions of the complex process of visiting and the intervention.

As discussed by Greene and colleagues (1989), expansion refers to the use of different methods to assess *different* phenomena as a way of broaden-ing the scope and reach of the study. For example, Rose Korang-Okrah (2012) combined ethnographic examination of the experiences and living conditions of Ghanaian widows within particular Akan communities with an analysis of national policy related to property rights violations. She examined different phenomena (local experiences, living conditions, and national pol-icy) to expand the scope of her study of women who were widowed in Ghana.

Teddlie and Tashakkori (2003) also emphasized the use of mixed meth-ods approaches to enhance understanding through a more comprehensive examination of complex phenomena. Similar to Greene and colleagues' purposes of complementarity and expansion, they emphasized that mixed methods approaches allow researchers to simultaneously address a range of confirmatory and exploratory questions. For example, a study mixing for the purposes of *complementarity* might test a hypothesis confirming the effectiveness of an intervention on specific outcomes and also explore participants' perceptions of effectiveness. Another study might confirm hypotheses about quantified outcomes (e.g., educational achievement scores) and also explore meaning and experience (e.g., children's educational histories and goals) for the purpose of *expanding* understanding of school achievement. Similar to Byran's *diversity of views*, Teddlie and Tashakkori also described the use of mixed methods research to incorporate a greater assortment of views, for example, of researchers working within different disciplinary traditions and paradigms, of cultural insiders and outsiders, and of dominant and marginalized groups.

Similar to Greene and colleagues' discussion of mixing for the purposes of *complementarity* or *expansion,* Creswell and Plano Clark (2011) argued that the combination of quantitative and qualitative approaches can result in a more comprehensive understanding of the research problem than either approach by itself. For example, they observed that initial results of any single study or study component may need explanation. A second study or study component may be needed to explain the first. For example, a quantitative component may reveal relationships between variables, and a subsequent qualitative component may help to explain or understand those relationships.

Enhanced Rigor

A number of scholars cited ***enhanced rigor*** through triangulation as a rationale for mixing methods (e.g., Creswell and Plano Clark , 2011; Greene et al., 1989; Teddlie and Tashakkori, 2003). Indeed, 13 percent of studies reviewed by Bryman identified triangulation as a rationale for mixing, especially using quantitative and qualitative approaches to corroborate each other. They used the term triangulation primarily to describe the use of mixed methods to enhance the validity or accuracy of the conclusions drawn from the data. Greene and colleagues (1989), however, underscored that deeper understanding and fresh insights may occur when data from different methods do *not* triangulate. For example, in a study of children who had experienced trauma (Black, Haight, & Ostler, 2006), qualitative interviews with a supportive adult yielded different information about children's experiences than did a standardized paper-and-pencil test. Many children whose test scores were invalid due to frequent denial of common experiences (e.g., occasional bad dreams or angry feelings) opened up to a supportive adult during qualitative interviews. This resulting lack of triangulation not only raised questions about the validity of the standardized test for this group of children, but also led to a deeper understanding of children's experiences, especially harsh discipline by parents for revealing family business and feelings to outsiders.

Note also that triangulation can occur throughout the research process, not just in the choice of measures or instruments. For example, in a study of children's socialization within an African American community, Haight (2002) triangulated interviewers' characteristics, specifically their European American or African American ethnicity. The basic idea was that study participants would respond in various ways to researchers with different characteristics; that is, the stories they tell and the thoughts they share would be related to relevant characteristics of their audience (e.g., interviewers' ethnicities). With cultural insiders, for instance, they might more readily develop trust and openly discuss sensitive topics, but they also might assume a level of shared knowledge, thus leaving some critical perspectives unspoken, for example, on race relations. With cultural outsiders, participants might be more hesitant, but also might assume the role of cultural interpreter, voicing perspectives left unspoken with cultural insiders. The ways in which participant interviews with cultural insiders and outsiders both converge and *diverge* can be important to a broad understanding of participants' perspectives and experiences.

Development

Greene and colleagues also identified ***development*** as a purpose for mixing qualitative and quantitative approaches. Development is broadly construed to include instrument design, sample selection, and data collection. In such studies, data from one method are used to inform the development of another method. For example, qualitative interviews might be used to develop a quantitative survey instrument. Bryman described 13 percent of studies he reviewed as identifying one type of development, sampling, as a rationale for mixing. In these cases, one approach is used to facilitate the sampling for the other approach. For example, a survey instrument may be used to identify typical and atypical cases for in-depth qualitative case study.

New Insights (Initiation)

Greene (2007) identified an important but less frequently used purpose for mixing methods. She emphasized the deliberate engagement with differences as a critical characteristic of mixed methods research throughout the research process, from asking questions derived from different philosophical or theoretical stances to being willing to consider alternative interpretations of the data. When researchers mix methods for the purpose of ***initiation***, they use data from different methods to evoke paradox, contradiction, or dissonance to gain new insights. They design the divergence of data from different methods in order to initiate original understandings of a complex phenomenon.

Such initiation can involve the further investigation of what Thomas Cook (1985) referred to as ***empirical puzzles***. Empirical puzzles arise when data do not converge. If the empirical puzzle can be interpreted, however, then understanding may be enhanced. For example, in her dissertation research with Japanese child welfare workers, Sachiko Bamba (2008) explored the lack of convergence between her individual interview data and focus group data. Less experienced child welfare workers' interview responses varied from their focus group responses when the focus group contained senior workers whose views differed from those the younger workers had previously expressed during individual interviews. Interpreting the absence of convergence illuminated important issues concerning the status and role of less experienced workers, as well as the interaction of cultural context with research methods.

REASONS FOR MIXING METHODS IN SOCIAL WORK RESEARCH

A number of social work scholars also have reflected on the reasons for integrating quantitative and qualitative approaches. As would be expected, many of these reasons overlap with those described by mixed methodologists outlined above. Similar to these mixed methodologists, Padgett (2008) described mixed methods social work research as motivated by researchers' desire to enhance their understanding of a particular problem. She also underscores the use of mixed methods to improve study rigor through triangulation.

Chaumba (2013) likewise pointed to enhanced understanding and rigor as reasons for mixing methods in social work. Mixing methods allows a more comprehensive analysis of a phenomenon, and enhanced validity of the findings. Chaumba also noted that a researcher may have multiple purposes for mixing methods in a single study, such that there can be primary and secondary reasons for mixed methods. Additionally she underscored the importance of researchers explicating the rationale for mixing so that readers have an opportunity to assess the value of combining quantitative and qualitative methods.

In their social work research text, Rubin & Babbie (2016) described three broad reasons for combining quantitative and qualitative approaches. Similar to Greene and colleagues' description of *complementarity*, the first reason Rubin and Babbie described for mixing methods is to extend the main (quantitative or qualitative) findings, that is, to use one set of methods to illustrate cases or provide numbers for the other set. Qualitative findings may be used to illustrate how quantitative findings apply in particular cases, or quantitative findings may be used to indicate the number of cases in qualitative categories. Similar to Greene and colleagues' description of development, Rubin and Babbie's second reason for mixing was the use of one type of method (quantitative or qualitative) to initiate ideas or techniques that subsequently can be pursued by the other methods. For example, qualitative methods may be used to identify research questions to assess using quantitative methods or to facilitate the development of quantitative measurement instruments. Finally, they stated that mixing may occur through triangulation for the purposes of corroboration. Note that these social work researchers did not specify the generation of new insights (initiation) as a purpose for mixing methods, a possible lost opportunity that we will return to in chapter 9.

In addition to these general reasons for mixing methods, there may be reasons for mixing methods that are more specific in emphasis to social work research.

Congruence with Social Work Practice and Theory

Cowger and Menon (2001) argued that "useful knowledge that is relevant to the multiple contexts of social planning and administration is unlikely to be acquired by singular and narrow notions or research methods. . . ." (p. 10). They described the integration of qualitative and quantitative traditions as allowing "congruence with the principles of social work to study things holistically, in context, and from more than one frame of reference" (p. 7). They remind us that social work has always been grounded in ecological theory with the central premise of understanding the person-in-situation and the need for a variety of approaches to comprehend the person within micro- through macro-level contexts. Consistent with social work's holistic emphasis on the person in the environment, mixed methods social work research provides both contextualized understanding of human experience and broad trends and outcomes.

Strengthening Evidence-Based Social Work Practice

In social work research, mixed methods approaches strengthen contemporary *evidence-based practice*. Evidence-based social work practice integrates empirical evidence (qualitative, quantitative, or mixed) with the practitioner's professional understanding of the particular sociocultural context including clients' beliefs, values, and behaviors to guide intervention (Gambrill, 2006). Thus, in applying evidence-based practice, social work practitioners typically mix qualitative and quantitative perspectives. They apply general knowledge from qualitative or quantitative research to their qualitative understanding of specific clients in particular contexts. In addition, quantitative and qualitative approaches within evidence-based practice counteract weakness inherent in either mono method approach. The qualitative components of mixed methods social work research can aid us in avoiding the pitfalls of decontextualization and reductionism, that is, seeking to understand a complex phenomenon out of context and by reducing it to its parts that can be a problem in some narrowly quantitative social work research. On the other hand, the quantitative components of mixed methods social work research can aid us in avoiding the pitfalls of some narrowly qualitative research that focuses on issues relatively idiosyncratic to particular contexts and does not provide generalizable concepts or understandings.

Congruence with the Requirements of Social Work Research to Address Multiple Audiences

On a related and more practical note, social work research often addresses multiple audiences or stakeholders with somewhat different emphases and priorities best approached through different methods. Administrators and funders may require quantitative outcome data on the functioning of particular programs. Social work practitioners in those programs may be more interested in using qualitative process evaluations of client perspectives and experiences to improve their practice. In addition, many social work researchers, like social workers more generally, work in interdisciplinary settings including professionals with different intellectual preferences and styles best addressed by different methods. For example, in a recent evaluation study of a law school clinic providing legal counsel to indigent parents (described in chapter 6), lawyers on the advisory board were most interested in in-depth qualitative case analyses consistent with the reasoning they used in representing clients, whereas funders wanted quantitative outcome data comparing the family outcomes of parents who did and did not receive services from the clinic.

RESEARCH EXAMPLE: APPLYING CONCEPTS—A LONG-TERM PROGRAM OF RESEARCH WITH MEN INCARCERATED FOR VIOLENT CRIMES

Jane Gilgun's decades-long program of research with men convicted of violent crimes illustrates the integration of qualitative and quantitative methods for the general purposes of enhanced understanding and development, as well as research deeply connected to social work practice and values. Gilgun was motivated by her desire to support social workers and other clinicians in stopping violence. Qualitative methods allowed in-depth understanding of the meanings of violence to perpetrators necessary to the development of effective assessment tools that Gilgun evaluated using quantitative methods. She has written many articles on this research (key pieces include Gilgun 1999a, 1999b, 1999c, 2004, 2008). Note that Gilgun's research program is a sequence of qualitative and quantitative studies in which results from the qualitative studies inform the design of the quantitative studies.

This section also draws heavily on Bidwell and Haight's 2014 interview with Gilgun. Before you read abut Gilgun's research, consider the questions posed in Box 4.1.

••

BOX 4.1
Guide to Gilgun's Research

We use Gilgun's research program with violent men to highlight the concepts presented in this chapter. As you read about this work, consider the following:

1. How are Gilgun's research questions tied to social work theory and practice?
2. To what extent and how do her questions also address issues of theory development?
3. In what ways does Gilgun's research exemplify the general purposes of mixed methods inquiry (i.e., enhanced understanding, enhanced rigor, development, and new insights)?
4. In what ways does Gilgun's research exemplify purposes of mixed methods research more specific to social work research (congruence with social work practice and theory, strengthening evidence-based social work practice, addressing multiple audiences)?

••

Enhanced Understanding

Approximately thirty-seven years ago, Jane Gilgun began her research career as a doctoral student studying girls who had survived sexual abuse. What emerged from intensive qualitative study was a surprising story about the relationship between the perpetrator and the victim of sexual abuse. Many of the girls who were abused by a family member expressed love for the perpetrator. This highlighted a complex phenomenon of sexual abuse that Gilgun sought to understand from multiple perspectives, especially that of the perpetrator, in order to develop strategies to stop the violence:

> I chose to interview the girls and then the perpetrators and do a long series of comparisons because I wanted to stop violence. It is such a terrible thing to do. Just because you are more powerful than somebody else doesn't give

you the right to do whatever the hell you want. And so I wanted to understand what goes on in the minds of these people that they think they can do this to little cute girls, to their wives, to little cute boys. (J. Gilgun, personal communication, April 30, 2014)

In 1986, Gilgun began to explore the experiences of perpetrators of sexual abuse. She started by conducting qualitative interviews with couples: perpetrators of sexual abuse and their spouses. She expected that, for a couple to endure the effects of disclosure of sexual abuse and stay married, they must have something very important in common: "I figured that if they stayed married after disclosure of sexual abuse and incest, they must be joined at the hip. Otherwise, she would have been out of there in a New York second." More specifically, Gilgun hypothesized that both members of the couple must share similar risks. Indeed, she found that all of the twenty participants (ten couples) had experienced complex trauma in childhood, that is, multiple traumatic events often of an invasive interpersonal nature such as physical or sexual abuse. She observed that women and men responded somewhat differently to these traumatic events in adulthood, in ways that might account for why fewer women than men perpetrate sexual abuse. The men, she found, were engaging in sexual abuse specifically and violence more generally as a coping mechanism, a way to make themselves feel better:

> He'd have a fight with his wife and feel really terrible, or another man would have a setback at work and feel really bad. And so they'd think, "well what can I do to feel better?" And so having sex with their children made them feel better, so that was good for them. That was "good." Another man, and this was a guy who was an athlete here at the university, a star here on a scholarship and then he was injured, and so he got kicked off the team and he left the university. And he got addicted to drugs and so even though he had a really good job in town, he hung out with a lot of drug addicts at night. And so the four of them decided to kill this guy because the one woman who was with them said that this guy had molested her or something when she was a kid. So the four of them went over there to this man's house and started beating the hell out of him. And the guy whom I interviewed knew that they were gonna kill him. He said that he wanted to leave, but he was all muddled because he was so high on drugs, so he said to them, "Would you please just kill the bastard so we can get it over with? I can't stand this one more minute." So, he was trying to get himself to feel better. He couldn't stand the tension of this prolonged beating that this guy was getting in the bath tub. They put him in the bath tub because they didn't want to be splattered with blood. So then this guy left them after the murder and he described what it was like to walk home. And I'm telling you, it was [like] a Bergman movie when he described how he felt. I felt what he must have felt when he knew his life was over. He knew the enormity of what he had done

and that there was no going back. (J. Gilgun, personal communication, April 30, 2014)

As her research progressed, Gilgun launched a program of qualitative research with perpetrators of violence incarcerated at the state prison. She engaged in repeated individual interviews with each man over the course of one year. This extended engagement allowed her to develop trust with her participants. It also allowed a more complete story of developmental processes underlying risk and resilience to emerge as she filled in missing details or asked clarifying questions to understand information gathered from previous interviews. She also wrote field notes and summaries of her reflections. Gilgun describes her first visit to the prison where she subsequently collected data for fifteen years:

> It was like descending into hell. You go up to this big door and it clangs open and you walk through and then it clangs shut, go down a flight of stairs, you get to another door, clangs open, you walk through, clangs shut, walk down another flight—five flights of stairs I walked down. Each time this huge door slid open and clanged shut. And I got down to the treatment unit and I felt like there was no air there. It had windows but they were about six inches wide so nobody could break them to get out. And the air circulation just felt weird. I thought, how could I possibly, how could anybody live here? How could anybody work here? Little did I know that I would spend 15 years there myself. They did get used to it. I did get used to it, but it was a shock. (J. Gilgun, personal communication, April 30, 2014)

Based on her interviews and observations and using a strengths-based perspective, Gilgun began to build a theoretical model that accounted for different patterns of development for perpetrators. Although her overarching purpose for engaging in this work was concern for the survivors, she was deeply interested in explaining, theoretically, the nature of violence. Her interest in theory was both academic and pragmatic. If she better understood what was driving violent behavior, especially what violence meant to perpetrators, she could inform theory, social policy, prevention, and intervention.

Development

Gilgun's interest in violence prevention fueled her desire to use her understanding to create a clinical assessment instrument. The purpose of this instrument is to aid clinicians in child sexual abuse prevention and intervention efforts. It is completed by clinicians to aid practice in a variety of settings such as child mental health and child welfare including foster care, in-home services, and residential treatment.

The resulting tool, CASPARS (Clinical Assessment Package for Assessing Client Risks and Strengths), assesses resiliency through five scales, each of which yields a risk and an asset score:

- Family Relationships is a twenty-item scale that helps to identify patterns in families that support or undermine children's development (e.g., "parental figures sympathize with child's problems").
- Emotional Expressiveness is a fourteen-item scale that identifies how children understand their own emotions and those of others and how they manage and express their emotions (e.g., "child does not show a range of feelings . . .").
- Family's Embeddedness in the Community is a thirteen-item scale that identifies the connections or lack thereof that family members have with their extended families, neighbors, and other community members (e.g., "family members are involved in positive community activities, such as PTA or help at church").
- Peer Relationships is a sixteen-item scale that helps practitioners identify patterns of peer relationships (e.g., "child has maintained a relationship over time with another child who is about the same age").
- Sexuality is a thirteen-item scale that aids in the identification of patterns of healthy and unhealthy sexual development and expression (e.g., "child stops sexually inappropriate behaviors when parents set limits").

The CASPARS was originally tested on 146 boys and girls aged five through thirteen years (mean = 9 years) and their families from a variety of ethnic communities (including 51% European Americans and 12% African Americans). Sixty-three percent of children had experienced out-of-home placements in foster or residential care. They had a variety of behavioral, mental health, and neurological issues, and most had several challenges. Seventy-one percent of children had sexually inappropriate behavior. They had experienced a variety of types of maltreatment including sexual abuse (58%) and witnessing physical and/or sexual abuse (47%). Experienced service providers completed the CASPARS and a variety of scales from established measures of similar and dissimilar constructs. They included social workers, clinical psychologists, child care workers, and therapeutic foster care providers.

Gilgun examined the psychometric properties of the CASPARS including its reliability and validity using quantitative methods. **Reliability** refers to the stability of a measurement including its ability to yield the same data upon repeated assessments of the phenomenon. The internal consistency of CASPAR scales was high (i.e., items within each scale were highly correlated). **Validity** refers to the approximate truth value of an inference, for example, that the CASPAR scales are measuring the constructs they were intended to measure. Indeed, when clinicians completed the CASPARS and other established scales measuring similar constructs, their ratings were significantly correlated. In addition, scales of the CASPARS were not significantly correlated with those of a somatic complaints factor of an established scale, indicating that the CASPARS discriminated the constructs of interest from other constructs.

Purposes More Specific to Social Work

Gilgun's research clearly is congruent with social work practice and theory including the study of complex phenomena holistically and in context. Furthermore, her mixed methods approach engages multiple audiences from clinicians to theoreticians. Indeed, throughout her career, Gilgun has been deeply interested in model building and committed to learning with and from social work practitioners. As she moves toward retirement, she has begun writing about her theoretical model of violence based on her decades-long research program. Her plans are to test her model on a new sample and then to develop an intervention based on that model.

CONCLUSION

In this chapter we have focused on the initial steps in planning mixed methods research: identifying an important research question and choosing a mixed methods or a mono method design to address that particular question. Identifying mixed methods social work research questions involves knowledge of current practice and policy, as well as an interdisciplinary review of research and theory. It also is necessary to consider whether a mono method or mixed methods design is most appropriate. Methodologists have identified enhanced understanding, enhanced rigor, development, and initiation as purposes for choosing a mixed methods approach for addressing any given set of research questions. In addition, mixed methods social work research is congruent with ecologically based social work theory, strengthens evidence-based practice, and facilitates communication with diverse audiences with diverse goals. Although methodologists have articulated a variety of rationales for mixing qualitative and quantitative approaches, there is room for improvement. Interestingly, the second largest category Bryman coded under rationale for mixing was not stated (27%). As we shall see in chapters 5 and 6, explicating those purposes also has important implications for choice of research design and method.

As we move through the chapters in part 2 of our text, we will provide some general guidance to students and researchers new to mixed methods approaches for developing a project such as a grant proposal, capstone project, or a dissertation in their own areas of interest. Box 4.2 provides some general guidelines for identifying an area of research, choosing a mono or mixed methods design, and identifying a specific research question or hypothesis.

••

BOX 4.2

Building a Mixed Methods Social Work Research Project: Identifying Your Research Questions/Hypotheses and Reasons for a Mixed Method Approach

1. A first step in developing the research proposal is to identify the general area of research. Similar to Jane Gilgun, who first identified violence as her area of focus, you may wish to begin by identifying an important social issue in your area of specialization. Particularly fruitful areas of study contribute *both* to practice/policy and to theory. Gilgun's research contributed not only to the CASPARS assessment tool, but to theory on the origins of violence. In the tradition of American Pragmatism presented in chapter 2, consider approaches to your identified social issue suggested by particular content theories and then consider how addressing your particular concrete social issue can advance theoretical understanding.

2. Once you've identified the social issue on which you will focus, it is time to conduct a thorough review of the relevant theoretical, scientific, policy, and practice literature. It is likely that this review will be multidisciplinary, encompassing not only social work journals, but journals in allied disciplines such as psychology, sociology, anthropology, and allied professions such as education, medicine, public health, and nursing. What are the gaps in knowledge, the underresearched or poorly researched questions, for example?

3. Next consider whether your topic might be advanced through a mono or mixed methods approach. As discussed in this chapter, not all studies are enhanced by a mixed methods approach. Do the benefits of mixing methods in your area of research outweigh the costs, for example, in terms of resources and focus?

4. Now identify your specific research questions or hypotheses. You may choose a mixed methods research question/hypothesis, or a sequence of qualitative and/or quantitative questions/hypotheses that build on or otherwise relate to one another. Identifying an important research question/hypothesis involves consideration of the literature review you conducted, as well as your own practice/ policy experience. Consider the integration of your qualitative and

quantitative research questions or hypotheses. Will answers to these questions and hypotheses mutually inform one another in a manner that justifies an integrated approach? What particular *purposes* would mixing methods serve for your particular research question(s)?

••

SUGGESTIONS FOR ADDITIONAL READING

Cook, T. D. (1985). Postpositivist critical multiplism. In R.L. Shotland and M. M. Mark (Eds.) *Social science and social policy* (pp. 21–62). London: SAGE.

This classic article provides one of the methodological bases for mixed methods research. It is most appropriate for PhD students.

Cowger, C., & Menon, G. (2001). Integrating qualitative and quantitative research methods. In B. Thyer (Ed.) *The handbook of social work research methods.* Thousand Oaks, CA: SAGE.

This chapter would be appropriate to assign at the end of chapter 1 or 4. Authors Cowger and Menon provide an introduction to the rationale for mixed methods social work research. This chapter would be appropriate for both MSW and PhD students.

Greene, J. C., Caracelli, V. J., & Graham, W. F. (1989). Toward a conceptual framework for mixed-method evaluation designs. *Educational Evaluation and Policy Analysis, 11*(3), 255–274.

This classic study of the purposes for mixing methods remains relevant today. The article is clearly written and is accessible to many advanced MSW students as well as PhD students.

5

Integrating Observational and Cause-Probing Designs
Refugees Experiencing War Trauma

Mary is a sixty-year-old grandmother and refugee from the civil war in Sierra Leone. She joined her three adult children in the U.S. last year. They are living together in a Midwestern city where the adult children and grandchildren are successfully assimilating. Mary's children are living in their own homes, raising families, and working at middle income jobs. Initially, Mary appeared to have adjusted very well. She was delighted to be with her family and embraced the role of homemaker for her daughter's family. Her daughter soon noticed, however, that her mother was struggling with the toll taken by the torture she had endured in Sierra Leone. Mary was tormented by nightmares and suffered from terrible insomnia. She had little appetite and was losing weight. Her body hurt all over from the physical effects of the torture. She no longer enjoyed her familiar tasks of cleaning, cooking and caring for her grandchildren. She no longer left the house, but spent most of the day on the couch. She refused to talk with her family about her experiences in Sierra Leone. In addition, her primary care physician had neither explored the impact of torture on her general health, nor screened for trauma.

Mary's daughter brought her to be evaluated at their local Center for Victims of Torture, part of a worldwide organization to provide support to survivors of torture. Initially, the psychiatrist there chose not to focus directly on trauma, but instead established trust by talking with Mary about her family, and routine activities such as cooking. Addressing somatic symptoms of trauma, especially the insomnia and pain, then served as a bridge to understanding Mary's underlying trauma and formulating a treatment plan. Mary eventually was diagnosed with post-traumatic stress disorder (PTSD) and major depression, along with chronic pain related to torture. Her treatment included medication and trauma-informed culturally sensitive psychotherapy. (Based on Wendy Haight's notes from an interview with Mary's psychiatrist)

In recent years, the United States has seen an influx of refugees from war-torn countries around the world. Refugee resettlement programs focus on the basics of health, housing, second language learning, and employment, with much less attention to critical areas of mental health. Yet many refugees like Mary suffer from the traumas of war: torture, the death of family and friends, and loss of homeland. Mixed methods social work researchers carefully consider *how* to learn about and understand the experiences of others, especially clients like Mary, who have culturally distinct experiences that may affect how their challenges are expressed, the assets available to address these challenges, and which remedies are acceptable to them. How to integrate qualitative and quantitative traditions to accomplish this greater understanding and then use that understanding to strengthen social work practice and policy is the subject of this chapter. Mixed methods design—that is, the nuts-and-bolts of planning mixed methods research—is then illustrated using Patricia Shannon's program of primarily observational research with refugees to the United States experiencing war trauma.

DESIGN

Research designs, quite simply, are the plans we make for integrating different components of a study to address broad study aims and specific research questions. At the most general level, social work research designs aim to describe, for example, the needs of a community for particular services using observational designs, or to probe causality, for example, the extent to which particular interventions or policies had the intended effect using experimental or quasi-experimental designs.

Observational Designs

Observational designs aim to describe, not to manipulate, phenomena. They can employ quantitative, qualitative, or mixed methods. For instance, *ethnography*, the systematic study of culture from the point of view of people living within the culture, is associated with qualitative methods in anthropology. Yet ethnographers have long included quantitative analyses of demographic as well as linguistic and behavioral data in their inquiries. Observational designs are appropriate for addressing a number of general aims of social work research. For example, observational designs can describe the functioning of particular groups of social work clients, how clients experience social work interventions, the living conditions of particular families or communities, the extent and severity of particular problems, and the acceptability of specific policies to citizens in diverse local communities.

Observational research also can play a critical role in theory development. For example, Haight and Miller (1993) used an observational mixed methods design as an *existence proof* to address a theoretical issue in human development. Their quantitative analyses revealed that mothers from a middle-class community routinely exposed very young children to pretend play before those children produced their first spontaneous gestures of pretending. These analyses challenged the prevailing Piagetian theory (1962) that such child behavior (e.g., gesturing as if eating or treating a stuffed animal as if it were a baby) necessarily is a solitary accomplishment emerging spontaneously from the child's developing ability to use symbols (i.e., that the development of symbolic thought is not influenced by social contexts). Their qualitative description of how mothers used pretend play when interacting with toddlers and young children instead raised the possibility that the development of children's early use of the symbols for pretend play is scaffolded by more experienced individuals. This possibility is consistent with Vygotsky's theory (1962) that higher order cognitive processes such as symbolic thought first emerge in a social context and only then are internalized. In other words, the development of aspects of complex human thought moves from the interpersonal to the intrapersonal.

Observational designs also can play important roles in defining important problems to be addressed in social justice efforts. In his doctoral dissertation, for instance, Douglas Sperry (2014) used an observational mixed methods design to address a problem critical to school social work: why do many children from low-income and working-class communities struggle in school? Many researchers, educators, and policy makers have turned to a 1995 study by Hart and Risley for an explanation. Hart and Risley reported significant differences in the amount of vocabulary addressed by a small sample of primarily white caregivers from professional families to their children and that addressed by a few black caregivers from low-income families to their young children in Kansas. They reported that, on average, the children in their study from six black families on public aid heard 616 words per hour whereas the children from the thirteen professional families (8% black) heard 2,153 words. Hart and Risley extrapolated these averages across the first four years of children's lives and then generalized to suggest that there is a 30-million-word gap between the number of words heard by the economically poorest and the most advantaged children in the United States (Hart & Risley, 1995, 2003). Attention to this *word gap* has steadily increased since Hart and Risley released their monograph as an explanation for the subsequent school struggles of many children around the country from families with low- and working-class incomes. Indeed, on October 16, 2014, the White House Word Gap Event (Too Small to Fail) presented a number of new initiatives to "bridge the word gap."

Yet Sperry was critical of Hart and Risley's study. He was skeptical that the problem lay in differences in the amount of speech heard by young children and hence that interventions aimed at increasing parent speech to children would achieve the desired effect. Not only were Hart and Risley's data based on a small sample from Kansas, but their methods departed in significant ways from the rigorous methodological underpinnings of the study of everyday language. For example, although the study by Hart and Risley was observational in method, it did not employ the culturally sensitive ethnographic methods in which observers spend significant amounts of time within the communities and with the families under study, not only to gain trust but also to better understand the meaning of the practices observed. In the Hart and Risley study, the black families living in poverty and depending on social welfare may have had a very different response from (mostly white) professional families to middle-class strangers from the university videotaping in their homes. Those different responses may well have affected the amount of spontaneous speech directed to young children. Indeed, studies in the language socialization tradition that combined extensive ethnographic methods with quantification of language have not found deficiencies in the language addressed to young children in low-income and working-class families, or in white and black families (e.g., Heath, 1983; Miller, 1994; Ochs & Schieffelin, 1984).

In the tradition of language socialization, Sperry's mixed methods approach combined qualitative ethnographic methods of sustained involvement with families and communities with quantitative analyses of the amount of vocabulary addressed to young children. Furthermore, he used observational data from a sample of five geographically, ethnically, and economically diverse communities: white families in south Baltimore with low incomes, black families with low and working-class incomes in the Black Belt of Alabama, white families with working-class incomes in rural Indiana, white families with working-class incomes in Chicago, and white families with middle-class incomes in Chicago. In short, he found no evidence of a word gap for children in low-income families. Instead, like other studies within the language socialization tradition, Sperry found that children in various communities are exposed to a rich verbal tradition.

Clearly, other more complex explanations than the debunked language deprivation hypothesis must be sought in our efforts to close the achievement gap between white and ethnic minority students, and between children from privileged and impoverished families. In other words, efforts to reduce achievement gaps that target parents are addressing a problem that may not exist. Rather than engaging in the harmful practice of pathologizing families, for instance, efforts to promote the achievement of children from low-income and ethnic minority communities might begin by examining racism and classism in schools as well as inequities in school funding in low-income areas as problems underlying the achievement gap.

Cause-Probing Designs

Social work research aiming to evaluate interventions and policies make use of any number of *cause-probing designs*. These designs mirror the classic analysis of causality formulated by the nineteenth century philosopher John Stuart Mill. He argued that a causal relationship exists if (1) the cause precedes the effect in time, (2) the cause is related to the effect, and (3) there are no other plausible alternative explanations for the effect other than the cause (*see* Shadish et al., 2002).

Experimental Designs

In ***experiments***, we first manipulate the presumed cause and then observe the presumed effect as per Mill's first criterion. As per Mill's second criterion, we next observe whether or not variation in the presumed cause is related to (correlated with) the presumed effect. Finally, various structural features of the experiment reduce the plausibility of explanations for the observed effect other than the presumed cause as per Mill's third criterion.

An important structural feature of experimental designs is the ***random assignment*** of participants (people, families, communities) to experimental and control groups using a random numbers table or other tool. Random assignment equates groups prior to exposure to the presumed cause (e.g., social work intervention). With random assignment of participants to groups, other factors that may affect the outcome are equally likely to affect the experimental and the control group and thus cannot explain any observed differences between groups after exposure to the presumed cause. Random assignment thus allows us to use the control group to test the counterfactual: what would have happened to the experimental group participants in the absence of the cause. For example, a social work researcher evaluating the effects of an intervention (the cause) to reduce aggressive behavior in children (the effect) would need to distinguish any observed changes in children's aggression over time due to maturation, developmental history, or other changes in the environment. By randomly assigning children to experimental and control groups, the social work researcher would eliminate these alternative explanations for greater improvement in the experimental group over the control group because children in both groups would be equally likely to experience these impacts on their aggressive behavior. Thus, any remaining differences between groups in aggressive behavior must be due to the intervention.

Some social work researchers struggle with ethical issues around the random assignment of participants to groups. How, for example, can we justify withholding a promising intervention from people in need who stand to benefit? Our response is that we do not know that an intervention is beneficial until we test it. Furthermore, interventions that appear promising may, in fact, have unintended negative consequences. Scared Straight, for example, is a popular intervention with youth who have committed or are at risk to commit delinquent acts that has been implemented across the United States and internationally in at least six nations. Youths meet in prisons with convicts who "scare them straight," in part by vividly describing to them the harsh realities of prison life. This intervention has much appeal: it is inexpensive, brief, gives convicts an opportunity to make a positive contribution, and powerfully exposes youth to the consequences of continuing along the delinquent pathway. Unfortunately, experimental evidence indicates that youth who participate in the program are *more* likely than youth who do not participate to commit further delinquent acts (e.g., *see* Petrosino, Turpin-Petrosino, & Buehler, 2003). This unintended negative consequence may result because some youth are traumatized by their experience in the program or come to admire and identify with the convicts.

One response to ethical issues surrounding the use of experiments with social work clients is to use *wait-list control groups*. Participants are randomly assigned to groups. The experimental group receives the intervention and the control group is assigned to a wait list or receives the usual intervention. If the new intervention is effective and does not cause unintended harm, then those clients on the wait list or other control group are offered it.

Quasi-experimental Designs

What if the cause-probing social work researcher is unable to randomly assign participants to groups? Perhaps the school or agency has already determined group assignment due to logistical or other factors, balks at randomization, or solicits volunteers for the new intervention? In this case, the treatment (experimental) and comparison (control) groups are not equivalent at the beginning of the experiment. If treatment and comparison groups are not the same at the outset of the intervention, how can we determine whether subsequent differences in the outcomes of interest are due to these initial differences or to our intervention?

To deal with this challenge, social work researchers may choose any number of *quasi-experimental designs*. These designs share the aim of experiments to determine causal relationships. They also share many of the important structural features: the presumed cause is made to precede the effect, any covariation is noted, and plausible alternative explanations are eliminated. By definition, however, participants in quasi experiments are not randomly assigned to groups. This creates a challenge: in quasi experiments plausible alternative explanations for the observed outcome other than the presumed cause must be eliminated one by one using logic, design features, and measurement rather than random assignment to groups. For example, children volunteering to participate in an intervention designed to improve their social skills are found to be more socially skilled at the end of the intervention than those children choosing not to participate. One might conclude that the intervention was effective. A plausible alternative explanation, however, is that the children who volunteered to participate were more socially skilled at the outset than those children who chose not to participate. By adding pretests of social skills, this plausible alternative explanation for the superior post-test performance of participants assigned nonrandomly to the treatment group relative to the comparison group can be assessed. Adding design features such as pretests, multiple comparison groups, and multiple pretests and posttests makes it possible to systematically eliminate plausible alternative explanations of the cause (*see* Shadish et al., 2002). Thus, quasi-experimental designs can rival experiments in their ability to determine causality. Yet they will never match experiments because there may be alternative explanations for the presumed effect that we do not anticipate.

Experiments and quasi experiments are designs typically associated with quantitative methods. Yet in their classic text on experimental and quasi experimental designs, Shadish and colleagues (2002) essentially advocated for a mixed methods approach to experimentation:

> One of the most important developments in recent social research is the expanded use of qualitative methods. . . . These methods have unrivaled strengths for the elucidation of meanings . . . the discovery of new hypotheses, and the description of how treatment interventions are implemented or of possible causal explanations. . . . Field experiments will benefit from including qualitative methods both for the primary benefits they are capable of generating and also for the assistance they provide in the descriptive causal task itself. For example, they can uncover important site-specific threats to validity and also contribute to explaining experimental results in general and perplexing outcome patterns in particular. (p. 478)

Correlational Designs

Correlational designs are widely used in social work research, especially quantitative survey research and research using large-scale administrative databases. These designs sit at the intersection of descriptive and cause-probing designs. Like descriptive studies, they typically involve observation rather than manipulation. Yet they do provide one of the three components of Mill's causal argument: correlation between variables.

Further, correlational designs can be strengthened through advanced statistical techniques. ***Structural equation modeling*** (SEM), which refers to a family of statistical methods used to test conceptual or theoretical models, can strengthen causal interpretations in correlational designs (*see* Kline, 2011). Although researchers do not directly manipulate cause and effect relations in a correlational design, structural equation modeling allows them to examine the fit of complex theoretical models of causality to their actual data. Unlike correlation coefficients or multiple regression models, SEM allows researchers to explore various pathways through which multiple factors may affect causal relationships by identifying ***mediating variables*** or ***moderating variables***. Mediating variables are the causal mechanisms through which an independent variable affects the dependent variable. For example, an independent variable (the social work intervention for children's problematic peer relationships) has its impact on the dependent variable (children's peer relationships) through children's increased self-confidence (mediating variable). Moderating variables affect the strength or direction of a relationship between independent and dependent variables. For example, the quality of the child's relationship to the clinical social worker presenting the program to improve children's peer relationships (moderating variable) affects the strength or direction of a causal relationship. The exploration of various potential causal pathways entails the use of large data sets and advanced statistical techniques such as path analysis, and confirmatory factor analysis.

We offer a note of caution. A common social work research strategy involves the use of large administrative databases or other secondary sources. In this research, many decisions have already been made regarding study method. Furthermore, these decisions may have been made for administrative and not research purposes. For example, child welfare researchers examining complex relationships among multiple variables in the state social services database likely will not have the opportunity to choose the study instruments/measures. The measures chosen for administrative purposes may not have been assessed for reliability and validity or implemented with the rigor required for research. Researchers using administrative and other secondary data sources will devote significant time to planning and describing the statistical analyses. It is easy, especially for students, to inadvertently neglect issues of method. Yet in these studies, no less than in social work research involving the collection of primary data, it is essential to be aware of the quality of data under analysis—to ask critical questions about participant selection, procedures, and instruments, for example—before planning analyses, drawing conclusions, and making recommendations for practice and policy. It makes little sense, for example, to employ complex statistical analyses or draw conclusions from poor-quality data.

Employing mixed methods in correlational designs also can strengthen causal interpretations through triangulation of methods, establishment of temporal precedence, and elimination of plausible alternative explanations for the observed outcome other than the presumed cause. For example, a social work researcher discovers a positive relationship between the implementation of a new program for parents involved with child welfare and rates of family reunification. Qualitative interview data indicate that those parents receiving these services attribute their successful reunification to the new program (triangulation of method) as well as describe how services affected their success (suggesting causal mechanisms). Furthermore, these interviews establish that participant parents received no other services different from those received by parents not participating in the program prior to or during implementation of the program (elimination of a plausible alternative explanation that differences in reunification resulted from other differences between the two groups in services received).

Mixed Method Specific Design Elements

As described, above, there may be a number of mixed-methods-specific design components within observational and cause-probing studies. These mixed-methods-specific design elements include integration of qualitative and quantitative methods (concurrently or sequentially), the relative weight given to qualitative and quantitative components, and the purposes for integration. Mixed-methods-specific descriptive and cause-probing designs and design elements will be described in detail in chapter 8. These designs can be complex and can evolve over the course of the study. Mixed methods researchers have described a number of mixed methods designs, but do not prescribe a one-size-fits-all approach or even provide an exhaustive list of different designs (design typologies). Far more important than enumerating a list of designs is learning to think about how quantitative and qualitative traditions may be integrated. The dynamic and flexible characteristics of mixed methods designs can be both liberating and intimidating for a new researcher: liberating because they offer the potential for much creativity and intimidating because they offer no set pathway to a successful study.

Some common notation has emerged to describe some of the design characteristics of mixed methods research (*see* Creswell & Plano Clark, 2011). This notation provides a convenient shared shorthand for describing designs, as well as introducing mixed methods design components. A plus sign ($+$) indicates a simultaneous or concurrent form of data collection with both quantitative and qualitative data collected at the same time. A right-pointing arrow ($\rightarrow$) indicates a sequential form of data collection with one form of data building on the other (i.e., quantitative builds on qualitative or vice versa). Capitalization also is used to indicate the weight or priority given to the study's qualitative and quantitative components. In any given mixed methods study, either the qualitative or the quantitative component may be emphasized (notated as QUAL quant, or qual QUANT, respectively) or both components may be equally emphasized (notated as QUAL QUANT). Thus, a mixed methods social work study in which qualitative interviews of social service recipients are used to develop a national survey might be notated as qual$\rightarrow$ QUANT. In other words, this descriptive study employs a sequential design with priority given to the quantitative component.

Some mixed methods studies occur within a larger sequence, for example, over a series of observational and cause-probing studies in a program of research. To distinguish mixed methods studies in a series of studies, brackets [ ] may be used. For example, a primarily qualitative study may be followed by a primarily quantitative study in a larger research program. This series of studies may be notated as [QUAL→qant] → [QUANT→ qual]. Box 5.1 summarizes some basic mixed methods notation.

●●●

BOX 5.1
Some Mixed Methods Notation

+ indicates a simultaneous or concurrent data collection
→ indicates sequential data collection
CAPITALIZATION indicates weight or priority
[ ] can be used to indicate the sequence of studies, for example, over a program of research.

●●●

RESEARCH EXAMPLE: APPLYING CONCEPTS—REFUGEES EXPERIENCING WAR TRAUMA

A [QUAL →quant] →[QUANT] →[QUAL→QUANT] program of research

Patricia Shannon's research with refugee groups illustrates a program of mixed methods research. In the first phase of the research program intended to describe the problems of refugee mental health, qualitative methods were prioritized and sequenced before the quantitative component. Phase 2 was a mono method quantitative study to describe the scope of the problems. Phase 3 emphasized qualitative and quantitative components equally in developing screening tools, but the qualitative component was sequenced first.

Shannon's research also illustrates some intentional decisions that a mixed methods researcher must make in selecting a study design. (Shannon has published widely, but some key articles we draw upon in this chapter include Cook, Shannon, Vinson, Letts, & Dwe (2015); Shannon (2014); Shannon et al. (2012); Shannon et al. (2015); Shannon, O'Dougherty, & Mehta (2012); Shannon, Vinson, Cook, & Lennon (2015); Shannon, Vinson, Wieling, Cook, & Letts, (2014); Shannon, Wieling, Becher, & Simmelink-McCleary (2014); and Shannon, Wieling, Simmelink-McCleary, & Becher (2014). As we've discussed previously, these decisions will be based on the questions that the researcher seeks to answer. In addition, Shannon reflected on the fit between the research methods and participants, that is, how various individuals from various communities may respond to particular research designs and methods: "With mixed methods, [it's] not just about the purpose of the research, but also about the [research] population. I think it's informed by the population you're dealing with and what's the best way to work with that particular group to better understand them" (P. Shannon, personal communication, November 3, 2014). Before reading about Shannon's research consider the questions posed in Box 5.2.

•••

BOX 5.2
Guide to the Example

In reading about Shannon's research, you may wish to consider the following:

1. Would you describe Shannon's research as employing primarily observational, cause-probing, or some combination of designs? Why?
2. How do the qualitative and quantitative design components and studies in this research program build on and elaborate on one another?
3. How do the goals and purposes of this research program fit with social work values, ethics, practice, and policy?

•••

Shannon's questions explored in this example emerged from her clinical mental health practice at the Center for Victims of Torture. The Center for Victims of Torture is part of a worldwide network of organizations whose goal is to support victims of torture in rebuilding their lives. Through her clinical practice, Shannon observed the devastating effects of torture on survivors' mental health. Yet local refugee resettlement programs were not addressing mental health needs. They focused instead on other important issues such as employment, housing and physical health needs. During our interview, Shannon described her overarching research goal:

> For this [research] we were interested in the state's largest groups of new arrivals. Which are the Somalis, the Bhutanese, and the Karen from Burma because the whole goal of this [research] is not to have people arrive with mental health problems and get into the community and never surface again for 15 years or 20 years, which was the Cambodian and the Hmong story. We want to understand [mental health needs] with the newest populations so that we can catch them [earlier] and get them better service and get them better integrated. The whole goal has been to get mental health screening integrated within the public health screen, which happens within the first three months of arrival. (P. Shannon, personal communication, November 3, 2014)

Shannon elaborated on how she began her program of research:

> I completed a dissertation focused on the treatment relationship with sexual abuse survivors followed by a post doc on therapy relationships with trauma survivors. I read extensively including post-modern critiques and they made

a ton of sense to me in terms of power dynamics and the helping relationship, not to mention the research relationship. So I came here [to Minnesota] and interviewed at the Center for Victims of Torture [CVT] and what I liked about them is their philosophy. [They] talked explicitly about power and politics. And I thought, healing is a political act. I always felt like healing trauma survivors, who are vulnerable disempowered populations in the first place (that's why they become victims of interpersonal trauma)—that healing their dignity and restoring their sense of power and leadership was in and of itself a political act. Just like their victimization is a political act. So for that reason, I felt like it was a perfect social justice fit. And then working at CVT opened my eyes not only to gendered violence around the world, but to violence around the world in general: all of the different populations and the very political nature of that kind of trauma. And then through doing my job, which was half clinical practice and half teaching, training and capacity building in the community, I was often going out to new communities to respond to crises: schools, medical clinics, that's how I got to know everybody. [I] developed a network of providers in [Minnesota] to respond to the Liberians and Sierra Leoneans who were coming. And then even the recent Kenyan political crisis. My colleagues and I pulled the Kenyan community together around the political violence. We had a number of support meetings and talked with them about self-care and trauma and did a couple things on campus for the Kenyan students. So I just started to see all the people in the community who were isolated and suffering and how different it was for them to be in a community in the United States as opposed to where they came from and how hard then it would be for them to access care. And how the first points of contact—churches, schools, medical clinics—were not picking up on the mental health needs of these folks at all. They didn't want to ask. When you sit in a room with physicians, they'll say well we don't know how to ask such uncomfortable questions. (P. Shannon, personal communication, November 3, 2014)

Phase 1: A Series of Observational, Qualitative and Quantitative Studies to Understand the Problem

These observations, coupled with Shannon's desire to place culturally informed mental health screening tools and mental health training in the hands of service providers, led her to begin a program of mixed methods research using observational designs. Shannon's program of research involves a sequence of mutually informing qualitative and quantitative studies. She embarked on the first phase of this research in 2009 by talking directly to refugees to understand their experiences (if any) discussing the effects of war trauma on their health with their primary health care providers. She chose qualitative methods for several reasons, including the lack of information about this topic in the literature, her desire to consider whether there was a need for improved mental health screening for refugee groups, and her need to identify facilitators and barriers to such discussions. Her individual face-to-face interviews included questions about any discussions refugees had had with their doctors about mental health concerns and what they felt might improve the process of communicating about these needs with health care providers. Shannon reflected during our interview:

> [At this point in time] I felt like I was [encountering] what I thought were a lot of myths in the professions. So one of the myths that bothered me a lot is people constantly saying that refugees (or people from other cultures) won't talk about mental health because of stigma. First of all, [their concept of] stigma is an American idea. What does it [stigma] mean in these other cultures? We don't know. And in the literature you hear it being said over and over again by professionals and I thought maybe they [professionals] are on to something that makes people uncomfortable. Maybe this really does capture what practitioners experience when they're trying to talk with people about mental health, but it can't be the whole story. This is practice-informed research also. I know as a clinician that, when I talk to people about mental health, they talk to me about their mental health. So what is going on? What is the problem? And so we asked them [refugees]: "Can you talk about this? How do you talk about this? And what's the best way? And when you're not able to talk about it, why aren't you able to talk about it?" (P. Shannon, personal communication, November 3, 2014)

These qualitative interviews indicated, that although most of the refugees would be open to discussing their mental health with health care providers, they wouldn't feel comfortable *initiating* those conversations.

Shannon then turned to service providers in order to determine their knowledge about trauma in refugees. She conducted a quantitative survey with local ethnic, community-based organizations working with newly resettled refugees. In this survey, she found that, although professionals from most agencies (93%) served refugee groups, they had not received any training specific to mental health screening and/or referral.

Shannon reflected on some of the practical and methodological factors that influenced her design and method choices during this initial phase of qualitative and quantitative research:

> The [quantitative] survey that we did of the providers was partly for ease of access for them. But you wouldn't do a survey with the people I work with that aren't literate. And also I think I would tend to do more [qualitative] interviews [with clients]. You get more information from interviews when you don't know anything about the populations, when the whole research area is unknown. (P. Shannon, personal communication, November 3, 2014)

Phase 2: Quantitative Research to Observe the National Scope of the Problem

The next phase of the research program was quantitative and used an observational design. Shannon found that there also was no national information about mental health screening practices for newly resettled refugee groups.

She wanted to get a sense of what was happening at the national level. She developed a quantitative survey that was disseminated to professionals across the United States to explore (and document) screening practices used with refugee groups. She also wanted to learn about the type and frequency of training frontline professionals received, and to better understand their training needs.

During our interview, Shannon described some of the processes involved in creating this national survey. She collaborated with university colleagues who wanted to take a largely quantitative focus due to the nature and scope of their questions. When asked to comment on how some of the decisions were made about the design of this study, she explained:

> The [quantitative] research question was to get the lay of the land concerning what's really going on nationally and to establish the gap [in services]. And so it seemed like survey data was the way to go. There were a lot of check boxes that made it easy [to collect data]. So I would say it's the research question and the practicalities of accessing data in a certain way. And the practicality of who your [research] partner is. The researcher [whom I was collaborating with] said, "Try to make as many close-ended questions as you can [for analysis purposes]." Now I wish we had more open-ended questions, but that's just how it goes. And so we sent that out because I had a good relationship with the refugee health leader and she was the coordinator of the national group of refugee health folks, so we sent it out nationally. And then I had graduate students continually follow up with states that weren't answering it and do phone interviews. They would say, "If you can't do the online one, can I just do it over the phone with you?" We tried to get a really high response rate, which we did. And then the purpose of that survey was just to substantiate: "Do you screen for mental health? If not, why not? Do you screen for trauma? What are some of the barriers? If you had a screening tool, would you be able to do it in your short time frame?" Just trying to establish need and feasibility and training needs. So that was the standard survey [design]. (P. Shannon, personal communication, November 3, 2014)

Her findings showed that only twenty-five states provided any type of mental health screening and fewer than that specifically asked about issues such as exposure to torture or war. Her findings also indicated that, although it would be feasible to implement a screening protocol, frontline professionals lacked the training necessary to do so.

Phase 3: A Series of Qualitative and Quantitative Observational Studies to Develop Screening Tools

In the next phase of research, Shannon and her colleagues used a series of qualitative and quantitative studies to develop screening tools to assess the mental health needs of refugees. She described how they began by conducting focus group interviews with participants from four of the largest refugee groups in Minnesota to better understand "culturally grounded concepts of mental health" from refugees themselves, and then used that information to design a survey to assess the prevalence of mental health issues in refugee groups:

> [For] the focus group interviews, we did those because we were trying to generate knowledge in an unknown area about what is mental health across these refugee groups. Do they have things in common? And are there culturally unique ideas? We were focused on vulnerable, understudied, underserved populations with cross cultural and linguistic challenges. We chose ethnographic methodologies because they really speak to those issues in terms of crossing cultures. Now we're demonstrating prevalence or frequency of torture or trauma and the mental health symptoms in a large population. That study is mixed methods. To document the frequency of torture and war trauma we had to ask them if they experienced torture and war trauma, and if they did, what was it? We had to know what the acts were and to hear some of the stories. Then we had to go back and code it [the narratives] according to U.S. definitions of torture and trauma. So there was qualitative coding of narratives. And then the scaled scores [based on narratives] were analyzed quantitatively. That's the screening tool. It was both open-ended and scaled. (P. Shannon, personal communication, November 3, 2014)

The data from these studies were then used to develop screening tools that would later be piloted at local health clinics. During the pilot phase, the clinics used these screening tools with newly arriving refugees, culturally adapting them and rephrasing questions that were problematic or not understood. While Shannon was engaged in her pilot screening practices, the state of Minnesota took note of the progress that she and her colleagues had been making and involved them in an initiative to engage doctors and other community stakeholders. In the following excerpt, she comments on the various interests of key stakeholders and how that impacted her research design and methods:

> I think, from the health department's point of view, if they were going to start screening they wanted to feel like they had mental health resources to [address] what they're up against. Because there's a lot of liability from the doctor's point of view. You don't [want to] screen for things for which there's no treatment. Ethnic leaders felt like there were no services in the state; that was their interest. I felt like we could improve on service linkages. I knew that clinically. We decided to evaluate the mental health service delivery system in preparation for screening. (P. Shannon, personal communication, November 3, 2014)

Like many social work researchers, Shannon was working with individuals from vulnerable groups. She reflected on the ethics involved in her mixed methods research:

I would just be thinking when you're researching political things about the politics of it. Especially with victim populations. You don't want to disempower them in assuming that they can't defend themselves. Let me give you an example of the ethical complexities. One of the authors on that paper is a cultural leader in the community. We said to him, "You know, if you publish this you are probably not going to be able to go back to [country of origin]. We know you have family in [country of origin]. Do you want to be named as an author? Do you want to pick a different name?" And he said, "No, I've given worse testimony to human rights groups and been in and out of [country of origin] tons of times; they've followed me all the time." You know so there are people who can clearly make an informed decision about whether or not they want to be a political advocate or not. It's a little similar to when you work with clients and trauma survivors, there's some stage in their healing where they want to go give a public speech [at church or to survivor groups]. You want to reign them back in for fear of unanticipated consequences. And so sometimes I feel that way about these kinds of issues. (P. Shannon, personal communication, November 3, 2014)

Shannon's research has resulted in practice and policy change at the local, national, and international level. She was able to accomplish this through her multiple partnerships and collaborative work with community and national stakeholders, as well as refugee communities most affected by the central issues being explored. As a mental health clinician, Shannon took a pragmatic approach to her research. At the root of her research was the desire to inform practice and policy in order to improve the lives of refugee trauma survivors. Mixed methods approaches allowed her to explore multiple questions that, together, led to a comprehensive understanding of trauma experienced by refugees in sociocultural, political contexts, which then led to the development of mental health screening instruments.

CONCLUSION

After identifying the research question(s) and purposes for the mixed methods approach, social work researchers may make a number of decisions about overall research design. They may choose observational or cause-probing designs or an integration of designs. Observational designs such as those used by Patricia Shannon aim to describe, do not involve manipulation of variables, and can employ qualitative and quantitative methods. Researchers also may elect to use cause-probing designs: for example, to evaluate any effect of a social work intervention. In experimental designs the presumed cause is manipulated to precede the presumed effect, the relation of cause and effect is observed, and alternative explanations are eliminated through random assignment of participants to groups. If it is not possible to randomly assign participants to groups, then quasi-experimental designs may be employed. Like experimental designs, these designs also involve manipulation of the presumed cause to precede the presumed effect and observation of any relationship between cause and effect. Alternative explanations are eliminated through logic and design, for example, through the use of multiple comparison groups and pretests and posttests. Mixed methods researchers also may combine observational and cause-probing designs. Any of these designs can employ both quantitative and qualitative methods. In chapter 6, we will begin our description of such methods with a discussion of site selection, sampling and participant selection, identifying instruments/measures, procedures, and human research concerns.

Box 5.2 provides additional guidelines for continued development of the mixed methods grant proposal, capstone project, master's paper, or dissertation proposal: integrating designs.

••

BOX 5.3
Building a Mixed Methods Social Work Research Project: Integrating Designs

1. Consider your general design. Will you employ an observational or cause-probing design or some combination? How does this design relate back to your research questions or hypotheses?
2. What are the mixed methods specific design elements within your observational and/or cause-probing design? How would you notate them?
3. How would you illustrate your design using mixed methods notation?

••

SUGGESTIONS FOR ADDITIONAL READING

Creswell, J., & Plano Clark, V. (2011). *Designing and conducting mixed methods research* (2nd ed., Chapter 4: Examples of Mixed Methods Designs). Los Angeles: SAGE.

Chapter 4 of this influential text includes discussion of design notations and excellent graphics of mixed methods studies. It is appropriate for MSW as well as PhD students.

Shadish, W. R., Cook, T. D., & Campbell, D. T. (2002). *Experimental and quasi-experimental designs for generalized causal inference* (chapters 1–3). Boston: Houghton Mifflin..

In this classic text, Shadish and colleagues discuss the logic of inferring causality in research designs, their typology for validity threats, and how to address these threats through design remedies. These chapters are especially appropriate for PhD students, but advanced MSW students should find chapter 1 accessible.

6

Integrating Methods and Contemplating Ethical Issues
Parents with Low Incomes Accused of Child Maltreatment

Upon fleeing from an abusive husband to another state, Lynne was unemployed, homeless and unable to support her three young children. Accused of child neglect, she described her subsequent experiences with child protection services: "My kids were traumatized for life and there was no flipping reason for any of this to happen. They [child protection workers] could have done wrap-around services, they could have helped so that I could get back on my feet. They caused intense psychological trauma to my children. In court there's no voice [for the parent]. And that's the part that's crazy making for me. That's what made me angry. You want justice for these kids? Then you give me the time and you listen to me" (Haight, Marshall, & Woolman, 2015, p. 12). After the judge assigned her legal counsel through a local law school clinic, Lynne described, "I felt like, ok, thank God. Because I was terrified of a court appointed attorney. I felt like I was in good, capable hands. The services [of the law school clinic] are amazing. I'm just grateful" (p.12). Lynne specifically described a positive working relationship with her student attorney [Joe], "I could share things with him: my frustration, my anger. I could trust him with what was going on. He was always very forthright, said it like it was" (p. 12). She also described how Joe helped her to engage with court mandated services, "What I needed was somebody to be just like Joe was: cool, even-tempered: 'This is what we're doing, this is why we're doing it,' instead of somebody shouting me down" (p. 12). After six months, Lynne was employed, had found stable housing and was reunited with her children.

Providing parents with low incomes who are accused of maltreatment such as Lynne with access to quality legal representation is both a social justice issue and potential resource for improving their children's well-being. Although defendants in criminal proceedings have the right to legal counsel under the Sixth Amendment, there are no such mandates under juvenile law. Furthermore, not all states provide a statutory right to counsel after child protection proceedings have been initiated or in termination of parental rights proceedings. The U.S. legal system is based on the assumption that justice is most likely to result from an equal contest of opposed interests. Yet when parents already stigmatized by child welfare involvement enter into this contest without competent counsel and handicapped by a lack of economic resources and knowledge of the judicial system, the contest can be grossly unfair to them and potentially devastating to their children (see Haight et al., 2015). In this chapter, we will first discuss how to develop the research method and consider the protection of vulnerable individuals like Lynne who participate in our research. Then, we will illustrate the integration of qualitative and quantitative research methods in a cause-probing design to evaluate a law school clinic providing representation to parents like Lynne who have low incomes and are accused of child maltreatment.

PLANNING THE METHOD

The research *method* refers to how the design is implemented, that is, how the study is actually conducted. Planning of method includes making decisions about the selection of sites, participants, instruments or measures, and procedures necessary in mono and mixed methods social work research. One of the primary method challenges in mixed methods research is balancing tensions between the priorities of the qualitative and quantitative study components when making decisions about their integration. The defining feature of mixed methods research is not the particular methods, but the *planned integration* of methods from diverse social inquiry traditions with various goals and corresponding strategies.

In planning their mixed methods, researchers typically begin with the research question. Then they make decisions about site selection, sampling participants, measures, and procedures. Although for the purpose of this discussion, we treat these decisions separately, in practice they are interdependent. To underscore these two important points about planning the methods, we designed a mixed methods research dial, shown in Figure 6.1. The research question (or hypothesis) is at the center of our planning and decision making. The concentric circles surrounding the research question represent moving parts of the dial. These rings are labeled with some basic methods decisions regarding sampling, measurement, procedures for collecting the data, and analyses necessary when designing any research project. In a mixed methods inquiry, however, these rings represent the continuum of qualitative (yellow), mixed (green), and quantitative (blue) strategies. For example, the *samples* ring represents the range of sampling strategies from solely purposive (qualitative) to solely probabilistic (quantitative). For each research design, we will turn each ring so that our decisions are aligned with our particular research question. The example in Figure 6.1 shows a mixed methods design in which qualitative components are

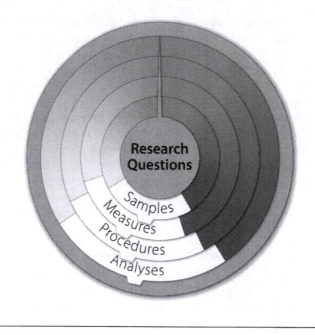

Time

Figure 6.1
Planning the Research Design

emphasized. For example, the research questions are primarily qualitative, but also include embedded quantitative components.

This research dial analogy underscores the holistic character of research designs in which decisions about particular methods for sampling, measurement, procedure, and analysis are made in relation to and constrained by other methods decisions. For example, choosing a primarily quantitative analysis technique would not make sense if primarily qualitative sampling, measures, and procedures also were chosen. What this two-dimensional dial does not represent is the flexible and dynamic nature of mixed methods designs that may evolve throughout the course of any given study. At any point in time, each ring of this design dial may shift slightly in one direction or another based on alterations to the research questions as we gain more information and insight as the study progresses (represented by the arrow labeled *time*).

The research dial analogy also underscores the importance of considering design priorities in planning any mono or mixed methods social science inquiry. When we choose in an evaluation study, for example, to increase the sample size to strengthen our statistical analyses, we reduce resources that could be used to prevent *attrition* (people dropping out of the study) that could threaten *internal validity*. Internal validity refers to whether the relationship between two variables is causal in a given study (e.g., the inferences we make about whether our intervention caused observed changes). Similarly, if we tighten controls to enhance internal validity, then *external validity* may be weakened. External validity refers to whether the causal relationship holds over variation in participants, settings, and measures (e.g., that a social work intervention will yield the same results with European American and Asian American clients, when administered to clients at school and at home, and when outcomes are measured by standardized assessments or semi-structured interview protocols).

Selecting the Site

The research *site* is the place where the research is conducted, for example, the particular school, social service agency, nonprofit organization, community, state, or country. In making decisions about the site, mixed methods researchers face some of the same challenges as mono method researchers. In addition, they may face the challenge of balancing qualitative and quantitative priorities.

In all research, mono method or mixed methods, careful consideration and description of the research site always will be essential. From the perspective of qualitative traditions, human behavior is shaped within particular sociocultural and historical contexts. There is no reason to assume that findings from one site will necessarily generalize to other sites with varying characteristics. Social service agencies in different counties within the same state, for instance, likely have varying historical relationships with other agencies and may serve clients from different cultural communities. The extent to which findings transfer from one site to another is an important and open empirical question. For example, to what extent and under what conditions might a social work intervention experienced as helpful within a particular cultural community be positively received in other cultural communities? The responsibility of the researcher is to describe the site in sufficient detail so that others can anticipate the extent to which particular findings may transfer to their own sites.

Likewise, site selection and description are important in quantitative traditions. Shadish and colleagues (2002) noted, for instance, that "most experiments are highly local but have general aspirations" (p. 18), but that "to different degrees, all causal relationships are context dependent, so the generalization of experimental effects is always at issue" (p. 5). They pointed out that many factors are usually required for an effect to occur, but we rarely know all of them or how they relate to each other. For example, an experimental or quasi-experimental design may indicate that a social work program (independent variable) causes a reduction in client distress (dependent variable). This effect, demonstrated at a social service agency (site) with particular characteristics—workers have relatively light caseloads, receive supportive supervision, and are involved with administrators in selecting programs—may not hold in an agency (site) with different characteristics, any one of which may be necessary, redundant, or irrelevant to the causal relationship of interest.

Shadish and colleagues also noted that a high degree of localization is not unique to the experiment. All research—including survey research widely used in social work—is conducted in a particular place. Yet researchers are rarely concerned with what happened in that particular place. They often want to learn about more general concepts, theoretical constructs, intervention strategies, or policy approaches. At other times, producing more generally applicable findings is not the aim. For example, social work researchers may intend to demonstrate that a particular outcome of an intervention is possible under optimal conditions, or that a particular outcome is common in a particular state, without expecting that the effect necessarily would be produced more generally at other sites.

Of course, practical considerations also affect site selection in mono or mixed methods research. Researchers may need to use their professional connections and community ties to even gain access to the site (for example, an international social work research project in a developing country). For both the quantitative and qualitative study components, mixed methods researchers may need to gain the trust and support of community gatekeepers. In social work research with vulnerable and diverse communities there may be a relatively extended period of time before such trust and support are earned. Gaining access to communities also is affected by historical contexts. For example, Haight spent nearly a year living and working within an African American community in Salt Lake City (2002) before even broaching the topic of a research study, and that proposed study focused on an area of concern among community gatekeepers. These community gatekeepers were well aware of a history of exploitation of African American communities in research (see the discussion of the Tuskegee Study later in this chapter) and generally skeptical of university researchers. Although such an extended period of trust building is more typical in qualitative research, it would have been equally necessary to the collection of any quantitative data from this site.

In addition to the considerations of site selection common to any research project, mixed methods researchers must balance and prioritize the sometimes competing aims of qualitative and quantitative study components. They do so by carefully considering any advantages of integrating qualitative and quantitative traditions of site selection relative to employing a mono method strategy. If the relative emphasis of study aims and questions is either quantitative or qualitative, then those aims will drive decisions regarding site selection. Such decisions become more complex in studies with equal emphasis on qualitative and quantitative components. Consider, for example, a mixed methods social work evaluation study of a model substance abuse prevention program for youth using a concurrent QUAL + QUANT design. The qualitative component may be enhanced through in-depth ethnographic study and description of a single site. This description may aid the researchers in interpreting strengths and challenges in program implementation (for example, the administrators' motivation to recognize and address adolescent substance misuse, problematic relations with local substance misuse treatment programs, and parent and community pressure). A quantitative aim to generalize findings across sites to scale up the intervention across the state may be enhanced by the inclusion of multiple randomly selected sites, some of which will be in suburban and some within urban locales, some in northern and others in southern regions of a state, for example. Of course, both in-depth description of a single site and inclusion of multiple sites, whether within a single study or sequenced across studies, require considerable resources. Is the primary aim interpretation of the processes involved in program implementation or generalization across sites? If resources are sufficient to encompass both goals, then the researchers may choose to select multiple sites studied in-depth. If resources are not sufficient for such an ambitious agenda, then tensions between study components must be balanced in site selection. In planning site selection, researchers would need to consider the impact of a compromise in which more than one site (but fewer than "multiple" sites) is selected to allow some diversity and also some depth of (but not in-depth) study. Mixed methods researchers can defend any compromises they make on site selection by clearly articulating the advantages of integration of qualitative and quantitative methods.

Sampling Participants

In making decisions about the participants for their research, mono method and mixed methods researchers consider who will provide the data, how they will be sampled and recruited, and the number of participants needed to answer the research questions. These decisions also may require mixed methods social work researchers to balance tensions and prioritize decisions across quantitative and qualitative study components.

For mono method qualitative studies and the qualitative component of mixed methods studies, the researcher may use a variety of ***purposeful sampling*** strategies to recruit participants who can provide rich information. ***Maximum variation sampling*** involves selecting people who have different experiences and perspectives. For example, a study of an innovative policy might select policy makers, program administrators, frontline workers, and clients. The goal is to obtain a clearer line of sight through looking at the phenomenon under study from many perspectives, any one of which may be partially occluded. ***Extreme case sampling*** involves selecting participants who are unusual. Early researchers of resilience (e.g., Garmazy, 1985, 1993), for instance, identified protective factors (e.g., supportive relationships with an adult, sociability, physical health, and intelligence) by sampling children who were surprisingly resilient in the face of significant adversity (e.g., child abuse, parental alcoholism, or extreme poverty). *Homogeneous sampling* involves recruitment of participants who are similar, such as members of a distinct subgroup—for example, individuals from oppressed groups whose voices have been suppressed in policy debates.

Qualitative sampling may occur throughout data collection. As the study develops, it may be necessary to expand the sample, even using different purposive sampling strategies. For example, during the course of qualitative data collection, the social work researcher who has employed maximum variation sampling may become aware of another group of individuals affected by the policy under investigation and decide to investigate them more thoroughly using a homogeneous sampling strategy. Alternatively, during the course of qualitative data collection, the social work researcher who has employed a homogeneous sampling strategy may become aware that a few individuals seem to function worse following an innovative intervention and decide to examine these unintended negative consequences more thoroughly using extreme case sampling.

Sample size typically is not predetermined in qualitative research. The goal is to obtain an in-depth understanding. This usually requires obtaining a great deal of information from a smaller number of participants than is used for quantitative sampling. The more people studied, the less depth of understanding is acquired from each. Qualitative researchers sample until *saturation* is reached, in other words, until new participants are not providing additional information. The number of participants in a typical qualitative study may range from one to twenty or thirty.

For mono method quantitative studies and the quantitative component of the mixed methods study, *probabilistic sampling* may be employed, involving selection of a large number of individuals (typically larger than for qualitative sampling) who are representative of the population to which the researchers seek to generalize. This typically is accomplished through *random selection*, in other words, selecting participants by chance to represent the population using a systematic procedure such as consulting a random numbers table or drawing names from a hat. Sometimes the researcher wants certain characteristics represented in the sample out of proportion with the larger population. For example, a social work researcher investigating client responses to a particular parenting class may wish to compare the responses of Hmong and white parents. To make this comparison, the researcher would want to oversample Hmong parents relative to the general population. In this situation, the researcher first stratifies the population (Hmong and white) and then randomly samples within each stratum. In this way, an equal number of participants with the stratification characteristic can be represented in the final sample.

The sample size of a rigorous quantitative study typically is large to meet the requirements of statistical tests. It needs to provide a good estimate for the parameters of the population, reduce sampling error, and provide adequate power. To determine sample size, researchers can use sample size formulas such as sampling error formulas for surveys or power analysis formulas for experiments or quasi-experiments.

In addition to the decisions researchers make for any mono method qualitative or quantitative study, mixed methods researchers may integrate sampling strategies from qualitative and quantitative traditions. Although qualitative and quantitative sampling strategies are distinct, they can be complementary. For example, a probabilistic sample of children involved in child welfare could allow for a broad and generalizable description of the school achievement of these children. A purposeful sampling of a smaller number of children from this larger sample could allow for an in-depth understanding of the school engagement (e.g., enjoyment and investment in school) of children involved in child welfare who are achieving above, at, or below grade level expectations.

Sampling decisions made by the mixed methods researcher likely will involve compromises given the different aims of research from various traditions (e.g., in-depth understanding and generalization to a larger population). Mono method qualitative researchers may criticize quantitative sampling techniques as yielding a superficial understanding of the contents of social phenomena. Mono method quantitative researchers may criticize qualitative sampling techniques as yielding biased results. The responsibility of the mixed methods researcher is to explicate the strengths gained through any integration of sampling techniques.

Reflecting on the Role of the Researcher

In qualitative traditions, the researcher is considered to be the instrument of the analysis, interpreting and responding to participants as they interpret and respond to the researcher. Researchers reflect and write on how their own mental models affect the way in which participants perceive and respond to them (i.e., the data they collect and how they interpret their findings). Further, they spend significant amounts of time with participants not only to develop an understanding of their lives, but also to develop the rapport necessary for the sharing of significant stories, beliefs, and practices. In quantitative traditions, researchers assume a more neutral role, often following specific protocols to standardize their interactions with participants. In addition, their contact with participants typically is brief and may even occur remotely, for example, through online survey instructions.

Variations in the role of the researcher in qualitative and quantitative traditions can be integrated in mixed methods research. For qualitative components, researchers may spend significant amounts of time with participants developing trusting relationships with them and learning about the contexts of their lives. Other members of the research team may then administer quantitative instruments to minimize participant biases such as a desire to please the researcher with whom they have developed a relationship. Again, mixed methods researchers must carefully consider and justify compromises in their roles through connecting them to the primary research aims and the value of the integration of qualitative and quantitative traditions.

Regardless of the type of social science research (qualitative, quantitative, or mixed), however, considering the role of the researcher is basic because the presence of the researcher perturbs the context in particular ways that may critically influence the data. Participants in social science research address themselves to particular audiences and their cognitive constructions of that audience can influence their responses. For example, an African American mother involved with child protection may respond to a quantitative survey of her beliefs regarding punishment differently depending on whether or not she perceives the administrator of that survey to be black or white or to have the power to sanction her. Thus, careful reflection on how characteristics of the researcher (actual or perceived in the case of online surveys) may affect the data collected is an important step in the design of all research.

Selecting Instruments/Measures

Researchers carefully define the concepts of interest in their quantitative research or the quantitative component of their mixed methods research. If, for example, a social work researcher wishes to study a program to reduce aggression in children, then the program (independent variable) needs to be carefully defined as does the dependent variable (e.g., aggression) and any other variables of interest, such as mediating or moderating variables. Once the variables of interest have been defined, then the researcher will choose instruments or measures to assess those variables. These instruments or measures may include surveys, standardized clinical assessments, and structured interviews and observations. In the above example, the researcher may choose among any number of standardized assessments of children's aggression. Decisions about which instrument to choose will be affected by any available research on the reliability and validity of the instrument. In brief, the *validity of an instrument* or measure refers to how well it actually reflects the concept that it's intended to measure. Does it, for instance, produce results that converge with other measures of the same concept/construct and diverge from those measuring related concepts/constructs? The *reliability of a measure* refers to its stability. For example, how similar are the observations of two separate researchers using a particular observation protocol, or how similar are participants' answers on the same questionnaire items at different points in time (e.g., today and tomorrow) or on similar items on different parts of the same standardized assessment?

Qualitative researchers are less focused on variables per se. Within qualitative traditions, human functioning is viewed as interpretable only in its context. Thus, a particular variable such as hitting, intended to operationalize children's aggression on a behavioral protocol or standardized assessment, may actually have various meanings within different contexts (e.g., during rough and tumble play versus physical disputes at school). The same behavior also may have different meanings in various cultural communities, for example, appropriate self-defense against bullies in the neighborhood versus unacceptable physical aggression within the school. Furthermore, qualitative researchers may purposely avoid specifying particular variables prior to engaging in the research. Ethnographers, for example, may leave open the specific concepts under study until they obtain a holistic perspective on the community in order to avoid prematurely focusing on less culturally relevant issues. Instead, they may focus on developing a ***thick description*** (Geertz, 1973) of human behavior, that is, an in-depth and detailed account of the behavior of interest in sociocultural and historical context necessary to elucidate its meaning. The instruments used by a qualitative social work researcher may include open-ended interviews, field notes, observations of naturally occurring behavior, and review of historical documents.

There are, however, many instances in which qualitative and quantitative instruments or measures may be integrated in mixed methods inquiries. Indeed, ethnographers and other qualitative researchers routinely make use of demographic and other quantifiable data. Likewise, primarily quantitative social work researchers may integrate qualitative approaches to measurement. For example, they may wish to explore the validity of particular quantitative instruments in various cultural contexts by including qualitative interviews along with the quantitative assessment of interest to discern its meaning to particular groups and contexts.

Decisions about instruments made by mixed methods researchers likely also will involve compromises. Qualitative researchers likely prefer relatively flexible measures designed within particular cultural contexts. Quantitative researchers likely will prefer structured measures with established reliability, validity, and national norms. The mixed methods researcher, once again, must carefully consider study aims and research questions, as well as the value of integrating quantitative and qualitative measurement traditions.

Planning Procedures

Procedures refer to how quantitative or qualitative data were obtained and what the participants experienced. Where, for example, were qualitative and quantitative measures employed; how were they sequenced and over what period of time; and how long did each session take participants to complete?

As with other components of the method, procedures for qualitative and quantitative components likely are not inherently incompatible, but planning for their integration and sequencing is essential, especially if the same participants are used in both the quantitative and qualitative study components. Qualitative research traditions such as ethnography, for example, require prolonged engagement in the communities under study. During ethnography, researchers act as participant observers. They actually engage in the ongoing activities of a group usually over an extended period of time in order to understand the issue of interest from a cultural insider's perspective. During such activities, participants also form opinions of the researcher that can affect their behavior, including responses to quantitative study components.

Even in relatively short-term qualitative inquiries, sequencing of qualitative and quantitative components can be important to consider. Participants' experiences in the qualitative component may affect their responses to the quantitative component and vice versa. For example, beginning the procedures with a long short-answer quantitative survey may inhibit participants' elaboration of their experiences during the subsequent open-ended qualitative interview. Alternatively, some brief quantitative measures employed at the outset can allow the researcher an opportunity to establish rapport that is helpful in eliciting in-depth responses to subsequent qualitative measures.

CONSIDERING ETHICAL ISSUES

Before any mono or mixed methods can be deployed, including recruiting participants, researchers must obtain permission from institutional review boards (IRBs). Institutional review boards play an essential role in the ethical treatment of participants in modern research. Prior to the implementation of IRBs, some research raised troubling ethical issues. During the Nuremberg war crime trials, for instance, horrific biomedical experimentation by Nazi physicians and scientists on prisoners in concentration camps was made public. In the United States, unethical research included the Tuskegee syphilis research. From 1932 to 1972, the U.S. Public Health Service studied 400 black male sharecroppers with syphilis. Their goal was to observe the development of the disease. The men were not told they had syphilis, warned of its effects, or given medical treatment. At the end of forty years, more than 100 men had died from syphilis or related complications despite the fact that new drugs had become available to combat the disease (Jones, 1993).

In 1974, the U.S. signed into law the National Research Act (PL 93-348). This act created the National Commission for the Protection of Human Subjects of Biomedical or Behavioral Research. Members of the commission were charged with identifying basic ethical principles that should underlie all research involving human participants and then to develop guidelines to ensure that research is conducted in an ethical manner. *The Belmont Report* (U.S. Department of Health and Human Services, 2003) summarizes three basic principles and their implications for practice:

1. *Respect for persons*. Research participants must be treated as autonomous individuals capable of making their own decisions to participate or not in the research. Researchers must provide potential participants with information needed for them to provide their informed consent. This information includes exactly what their participation will entail, as well as any risks to their health or well-being. In addition, researchers must discuss confidentiality with potential participants as well as its limitations; for example, researchers may be legally required to report disclosures of child abuse. Even after providing consent, individuals have the right to discontinue their participation at any time.

2. *Beneficence*. Beneficence refers to acts of kindness or charity that go beyond strict obligation. In research, beneficence is an obligation. Researchers must not only avoid harming participants, but must also maximize potential benefits to participating in research; for example, a participant might experience educational benefits from discussing important topics with an informed researcher. Beneficence also may relate to benefits to society as a whole from the research, for example, evidence that particular interventions generally are effective in reducing certain mental health problems.

3. *Justice*. This principle emphasizes that those who bear the burdens of the research should also receive its benefits. This means that individuals may not be used for research just because they are convenient or can be manipulated. For example, research with individuals who are in hospitals, incarcerated, or in public schools may occur only if the research is directly relevant to individuals in these settings.

Federal regulations require that every institution seeking federal funding using human participants must have an institutional review board. Institutional review boards at universities and other institutions review and approve all research proposals before any contact with potential participants occurs. These IRBs consist of researchers and practitioners from diverse fields (for example, medicine, psychology, sociology, public health, and social work) to ensure that ethical standards are upheld. Members of the IRB may ask researchers to clarify or change their procedures or even decline to approve their research.

Ethical standards outlined in the *Belmont Report* may be expanded by professional organizations. The NASW Code of Ethics (2008), for instance, requires that social work researchers should take steps to ensure that research participants have access to appropriate supportive services.

RESEARCH EXAMPLE: APPLYING CONCEPTS—A MIXED METHODS EVALUATION OF A LAW SCHOOL CLINIC REPRESENTING PARENTS ACCUSED OF CHILD MALTREATMENT

In 2013, Wendy Haight was approached by Joanna Woolman, the director of a local law school clinic, about collaborating on an evaluation of the Child Protection Clinic (hereafter, the "Clinic"). In 2009, a state Supreme Court justice had approached law school faculty members about starting a legal clinic designed to provide representation to parents involved with child protective services (CPS). Her intent was to create a model that could be replicated around the state and country to provide high-quality individual representation to parents and to educate attorneys. She had observed firsthand the human and financial costs of unnecessary separations of families resulting from poor quality representation of parents in court: Children and parents were traumatized by forced separation and the state bore such costs as those for foster care and court. The judge also was aware that U.S. law schools have a tradition of closing the justice gap for people with low incomes by training law students to represent vulnerable clients. Law school students are certified under student practice rules and perform all of the tasks for a client that a fully licensed attorney may perform. They do so under the supervision of fully-licensed supervising attorneys.

Thus, law school clinics in the United States have the dual purpose of providing greater access to quality legal services to clients with low incomes and practical legal education to students. Clinic faculty members and other supervising attorneys must balance the educational needs of student attorneys to fully experience representing clients with their obligation to provide the highest quality legal services to clients (Joy & Kuehn, 2002). Students may be enthusiastic and highly motivated, but struggle to handle complex, high-stakes, and emotionally sensitive cases. Some practicing attorneys indicate that it takes years to gain an understanding of CPS and how to best work with families to have the safest and best outcome for children.

At the time of her discussion with Haight, Woolman was seeking both an in-depth analysis of Clinic services that could be used to strengthen it and an outcome analysis of how well the Clinic was meeting its goals that could be presented to funders and other stakeholders. Haight became intrigued by the Clinic's model of supporting families involved with CPS through direct legal practice. Her experience was that most child welfare research has focused on issues of policy and direct social services. Very little previous research had explored the use of legal services in supporting families involved with child welfare. Before you read about the resulting practice-based research (Haight et al., 2015), consider the questions posed in Box 6.1.

••

BOX 6.1
Guide to the Research Example

1. What various decisions and trade-offs, especially between qualitative and quantitative components, do you discern in this research with respect to site selection, sampling, instruments, and procedures?
2. In your opinion, what has been the value of the integration of qualitative and quantitative components with respect to site selection, sampling, instruments, and procedures for this research project?
3. What do you see as the drawbacks of the integration of qualitative and quantitative research components with respect to site selection, sampling, instruments, and procedures for this research project?

••

Questions and Hypothesis

In the law clinic example, we examined a qualitative research question and a quantitative hypothesis (Haight, Marshall, & Woolman, 2015). We sought to evaluate Clinic outcomes for families, but we first needed to establish their goals. Rather than imposing external standards, in the tradition of qualitative research we began with a qualitative analysis of what *participants* were intending to achieve through the Clinic. We then used these goals (as dependent variables) to test a quantitative analysis of outcomes. The second research question regarding participants' experiences in the Clinic was qualitative. The specific research questions and hypothesis were the following:

1. How successful is the Clinic in achieving child outcomes desired by participants? (We hypothesized that cases handled by fully licensed attorneys would be more likely to achieve these positive outcomes desired by participants than those handled by student attorneys.)
2. What are the strengths and challenges of the Clinic's parent representation from the perspectives of parent clients, clinic staff, and court professionals?

Design

We approached our research questions and hypothesis by integrating observational and cause-probing designs. The observational design was used to describe the clinic's strengths and challenges. The cause-probing design was used to assess outcomes for children. More specifically, we used a sequential, primarily qualitative mixed method design (QUAL → quant) for the general purpose of complementarity and expansion (Greene, 2007); that is, we used different social perspectives (e.g., those of clinic staff, court professionals, and clients) and different methods (qualitative interviews and quantitative analysis of administrative data) to more comprehensively study the Clinic's strengths and challenges and children's outcomes.

The qualitative component of our study was ethnographic in design. The quantitative component is a quasi-experimental, post-test only design with multiple post-test observations (Shadish et al., 2002). We used quantitative analyses of administrative records to test our hypothesis that fully licensed attorneys would achieve more positive outcomes than student attorneys using child outcomes identified by participants as desired during qualitative interviews. To interpret the results from these outcome analyses, as well as to support the further development of the Clinic, we examined Clinic strengths and limitations using qualitative interviews contextualized by participant observation and document reviews.

Site

Our selection of site reflected our primarily qualitative research emphasis. We sought an in-depth understanding of a particular innovative clinic. Future mixed or mono method research could include a selection of sites across diverse locales.

In brief, the Clinic is part of a small, private, independent law school known for its emphasis on practical legal education. It serves two urban counties in the upper Midwest. It uses certified student attorneys under the close supervision of two fully licensed, experienced attorneys. Student attorneys were enrolled in law school for a minimum of two semesters, were in good academic standing (minimum GPA = 2.0), and were enrolled in a class on child welfare law and practice. The clinic also includes parent mentors, former CPS clients, who provide practical and emotional support to parent clients. During the period when we evaluated the Clinic, it represented fifty-three clients; all but four were single mothers and most were from communities of color (about 60%). They were receiving a variety of services including chemical dependency treatment, therapy, anger management, parenting skills classes and domestic violence counseling.

Participants

Participants were sampled using a combination of qualitative and quantitative processes. Participants in the qualitative portion of the study were purposefully sampled to provide rich information on the Clinic from a variety of perspectives. They consisted of 39 individuals who had direct sustained contact with the Clinic: court professionals such as prosecuting attorneys and judges ($n = 12$), law school faculty including supervising attorneys ($n = 5$), parent mentors ($n = 2$), former and current student attorneys ($n = 11$), and parent clients ($n = 9$).

Participants for the quantitative portion of the study were sampled from secondary administrative data. They included children whose parents received the Clinic's legal representation services, and a propensity score matched group of children whose parents received representation from other fully licensed attorneys. Although assignment to group by the court appeared random, we did not control this process. Thus, we could not assume that treatment and comparison cases did not differ prior to the treatment groups' involvement in the Clinic in ways relevant to our outcomes. To minimize any selection bias, we used *propensity score matching* (PSM). This is a statistical technique used to better equate treatment and comparison groups by matching on a composite of participant characteristics. It often is difficult to find individuals who are similar across a variety of key covariates even when there are only a few background covariates of interest. Propensity score matching solves this issue by using logistic regression to control for several background covariates simultaneously, by matching participants on a single scalar variable (each participant's propensity score) (D'Agostino, 1998). We used matching variables that were significant predictors of reunification and other permanency outcomes such as prior entries into foster care, race, type of maltreatment, and age at removal from parent.

Procedures

In this study, issues of integrating qualitative and quantitative procedures were minimal given that the quantitative data were obtained from secondary administrative data sets. Thus, we did not have to consider, for example, how the sequencing of qualitative and quantitative data might have affected participants' responses because different participants were used in the qualitative and quantitative components of the study.

Qualitative Procedures

Document Reviews. We reviewed all written and electronic materials describing the law school and Clinic, including annual reports from the Clinic, course syllabi, and student evaluations.

Participant Observation. We attended nine of twelve class meetings over one semester, nine hearings in which four different students represented clients before the court in admit/deny hearings, pretrial hearings, review hearings, and a Permanency Review and Intermediate Dispositional Hearing. We also observed a variety of other hearings in which fully licensed attorneys represented CPS-involved parents.

Interviews. We conducted semi-structured face-to-face interviews at private locations convenient for participants including their homes, offices, or law school. Interviews lasted from 30 to 120 minutes and were audio-recorded. Interviews probed participants' experiences and perceptions of the strengths and limitations of the clinic including the quality of client representation and student education and perspectives on what constitutes positive case outcomes.

Quantitative Procedures

We obtained child outcomes from linking statewide administrative data sets received from the state departments of Health, Education, and Human Services.

Human Research Concerns

This study underwent university IRB review. Voluntary participation was an important issue to consider. Parents involved in complex legal cases that could result in loss of their children clearly are in a vulnerable position. It was especially important that they not feel pressured to participate, especially by those clinic staff providing them with services. Likewise, student attorneys were in vulnerable positions due to their student status, and it was important that they not be pressured to participate. The clinic director provided university researchers with a list of former and current clients and student attorneys as well as a written introduction of the project to these potential participants. We contacted them directly and made it clear to them that we would not inform clinic staff of their decisions to participate or not.

Confidentiality also was an important issue. To obtain meaningful responses to our questions, we needed participants to freely discuss their experiences, positive and negative. We promised them that their individual identifiable views would not be disclosed to others, especially others in positions of power. Confidentiality, however, does have limits. Parents, for instance, were cautioned that, as mandated child abuse reporters, we would report any new instances of child maltreatment they disclosed to us.

Mixed Methods Data Analyses

Our mixed methods data analyses occurred in three phases. First, we analyzed the qualitative data. Recorded interviews were transcribed verbatim with notes on paralinguistic cues including laughter and sarcastic tone. Through repeated readings of the transcripts and listening to recorded interviews, emic codes were induced (see Schwandt, 2003) by two independent researchers. (***Emic*** refers to the perspectives of people from the group under study. In contrast, ***etic*** perspectives are imposed from outside of the group.)

A coding scheme was created through discussion, critiqued by a local legal professional, and revised as needed. All interviews were coded by at least two independent researchers and any disagreements were resolved through discussion. To strengthen the credibility of our subsequent interpretations, we conducted ***member checks*** with some participants where we asked them to confirm our interpretations of their responses and if necessary to clarify or elaborate them.

Second, to describe the prevalence of various perspectives, we quantified qualitative data. Specifically, we indicated the presence or absence of each code for each interview for clinic staff, court professionals, and parents.

Next, we coded case outcomes desired by participants from qualitative interviews. We used these case outcomes to identify dependent variables for the quantitative analyses of administrative data. We used Fisher's Exact Tests to compare treatment and comparison groups.

Results

Case outcomes identified by participants as desired during qualitative interviews included family reunification, timely case closure, and children's placement with relatives. Contrary to our hypothesis, outcomes for children whose parents were represented by student attorneys did not differ significantly from those of a propensity-score-matched comparison group of children whose parents were represented by fully licensed attorneys. Participants described Clinic staff as providing strong legal counsel to parents, building positive attorney-client relationships, possessing positive personal characteristics, and providing a needed service to the broader community. Participants also identified areas for improvement including educating parents around court procedures and better cross-system collaboration between child welfare and legal professionals. Thus, this early research suggests that the Child Protection Clinic may be a promising model for providing quality legal representation to parents involved with child protection in order to support child well-being. The model deserves further research.

CONCLUSION

In this chapter we have focused on integrating qualitative and quantitative methods including any necessary decisions about balancing qualitative and quantitative priorities for site selection, sampling participants, selecting instruments/measures, and planning procedures. We also discussed ethical issues in research involving human participants. Many individuals participating in social work research projects, like those parents with low incomes accused of child maltreatment highlighted in the research example, are in highly vulnerable positions. Social work ethics directs us not only to follow federal guidelines on which IRBs are based, but also to take steps to ensure that research participants have access to appropriate supportive services. In chapter 8 we will return to the issue of design, focusing specifically on mixed methods components of observational and cause-probing designs.

Box 6.2 provides guidance for planning the methods after the research questions or hypotheses, purpose for using a mixed methods design, and research design have been identified.

••

BOX 6.2
Building a Mixed Methods Social Work Research Project: Planning Your Methods

1. Describe your site, participants, instruments/measures, and procedures. What are the trade-offs that you expect to make to incorporate an integrated approach? Do the benefits outweigh the costs of mixing methods?
2. How are you positioned vis-à-vis this research project? How might that social position affect the data you collect and how you will interpret it?
3. What are the potential risks, psychological and otherwise, to your study participants? How can you minimize these risks and increase the benefits? Do the risks outweigh the benefits?

••

SUGGESTIONS FOR ADDITIONAL READING

Jones, J. H. (1993). *Bad blood*. NY: Simon and Schuster.

      Historian James H. Jones describes the Tuskegee Syphilis Study conducted on black sharecroppers from 1932 to 1972. It provides compelling evidence of the importance of our modern institutional review boards. This book is appropriate to assign to MSW or PhD students.

U.S. Department of Health and Human Services. (1979). *The Belmont report: Ethical principles and guidelines for the protection of human subjects of research*. Washington, DC: U.S. Department of Health and Human Services.

      This report outlines standards for the ethical conduct of research involving people. It is accessible both to MSW and PhD students.

Integrating Analyses and Enhancing Rigor
Spirituality and Recovery from Addiction

Yvonne, a 52-year-old recovering from alcoholism, found that without alcohol to mask them, she increasingly struggled with negative feelings. Even before she had begun drinking, she had experienced depression, and her early life had been marred by child abuse and other troubles. Now, after withdrawing from alcohol, she still had to contend with health problems and the relationships fractured during her drinking days. For Yvonne, it was difficult to move past daily disappointments and face the future with any sort of optimism.

Yvonne found participation in the Three Good Things research help-ful. The daily rating of feelings highlighted just how bad she was feeling each day, bringing about the realization that she needed to work on finding more positives in life. This realization was strengthened as she worked to support her son through his own substance abuse recovery. Her gratitude for his recovery and the chance she had to be there for him motivated her to begin working on decreasing negative feelings, using the Three Good Things exercise to remind herself that good things happen even in the gloomiest of days. Yvonne experienced this herself during the course of the study, as she looked for positives even while enduring a series of health crises.

With gratitude reinforcing her recovery and brightening her mood, Yvonne wanted to model the same for others who were struggling. She sought ways to show hope for others who were coping with the un-numbing of negative feelings and other challenges after withdrawing from alcohol. However, it also brought her closer to the realization of how much she needed to continue working on her own recovery, and how much of a daily job it was to pull herself out of negative feelings and arrive at positive ones. (A. Krentzman, personal communication, May 7, 2014)

Addiction causes suffering to millions of people each year, both those who are addicted and their families, as well as lost productivity and increased health care costs to society. Each year in the United States many adults struggling with alcohol addiction enter into treatment. They may choose a variety of programs including self-help groups and treatments administered by physicians and other professionals. Most of these programs, however, have been influenced by Alcoholics Anonymous (AA). Alcoholics Anonymous was started in 1934 by Bill Wilson, a recovering alcoholic. Currently, AA meetings can be found around the world. In the United States, 1.2 million people belong to one of AA's approximately 55,000 meeting groups. Yet we know relatively little about how such programs work, especially the efficacy of various program components including the role of gratitude that was so important to Yvonne. Indeed, the rigorous study of addiction is fraught with methodological challenges. In addition to attending to issues of design, sampling, measurement, and analyses, for example, researchers must be vigilant about their own biases as members of a society that stigmatizes those suffering with addiction. In addition, they must convince marginalized individuals to engage with them in their study, and they must maintain contact with those who may be homeless or otherwise lead unstable lives filled with stress, trauma, and illness. In this chapter, we will first discuss the integration of quantitative and qualitative analyses and then issues of quality in mixed methods research. Finally, we will use Amy Krentzman's program of research to illustrate how a mixed method approach strengthened the quality (relevance and validity) of her inquiries into adults' recovery from alcoholism.

INTEGRATING ANALYSES

In some mixed methods studies, qualitative and quantitative data will, appropriately, only be analyzed separately (for example, when qualitative and quantitative data are collected for the primary purpose of triangulation). Indeed, Bryman (2008) noted in his review of mixed methods social science research that nearly half of 232 articles did not integrate findings. Their side-by-side treatment of quantitative and qualitative results differed little from the treatment of these separate components in mono method studies. Such mono method data analyses are described in any number of excellent texts and will not be repeated here, but Onwuegbuzie & Combs (2010) provide a concise overview of mono method quantitative and qualitative data analysis techniques frequently used in mixed methods research. In these studies, integration of qualitative and quantitative data occurred during the interpretation of completed analyses, usually in the Discussion section of the paper, or over a series of papers.

In other studies, the full potential of mixed methods social work research is achieved through the integration of qualitative and quantitative data *during* analyses, the focus of this chapter. At its best, such integration allows new ways of exploring an issue when mutually informing data are combined or converted from one form to another. Yet many mixed methods researchers report difficulty in bringing together qualitative and quantitative data during data analyses (Bazeley, 2012). Indeed, planning and meaningfully analyzing diverse types of data to include some back-and-forth *conversation* among qualitative and quantitative data *during* analysis remains an ongoing challenge (Greene, Sommerfeld, & Haight, 2010). There are no set recipes or prescriptions for such integrated data analyses any more than there are set recipes for mixed methods designs. Integrated data analysis plans are tailored to the purpose of the inquiry and to a greater or lesser extent are emergent as findings from qualitative and quantitative data raise questions and issues to be pursued in subsequent phases of data analyses. Such mixing requires the active problem solving, interpretation, and creativity of the mixed methods researcher. As Greene (2007) explained,

> Statements of inquiry conclusions, interpretations, or warranted assertions arise from the mind of the inquirer, not directly from the output of a statistical or thematic analysis. Inference and interpretation are fundamentally human cognitive processes. . . . So it is with mixed methods data analysis, and, in particular, with the mixing part of mixed methods data analysis. . . . the interpretations of the meanings of the mix . . . reside in the cognitive processes of the inquirer. As such, the mixing part of mixed methods social inquiry will always defy complete codification and will always resist inflexible prescriptions. (p. 143)

There is, however, a common general framework that can help organize the analyses of many mixed methods social work research projects. In this chapter we will focus on five general phases of planning for the integration of qualitative and quantitative components during data analysis relevant to many mixed methods analyses: the processing of quantitative and qualitative data; sequential analyses; and initial, midstream, and final integrated analyses (*see* Box 7.1). This discussion of integrated analyses will draw heavily on Greene's framework (2011). For purposes of discussion, we will take the individual as the unit of analysis. Note, however, that our strategy for analyzing mixed methods data also can be applied to larger units such as families, social service organizations, communities, or nations.

••

BOX 7.1
General Framework for Integrated Analyses in Mixed Methods Social Work Research

1. Process the quantitative and qualitative data.
2. Perform sequential qualitative and quantitative analyses.
3. Conduct initial integrated analyses: data transformation (i.e., converting or consolidating one form of data into the other to enable joint analyses).
4. Conduct mid-stream integrated analyses: data comparison and correlation to find patterns (e.g., extreme case analyses, integrated data displays, typology development).

5. Conduct final integrated analyses. The goal is to generate inferences and conclusions (e.g., warranted assertion analysis).

••

Process the Quantitative and Qualitative Data

Prior to any data integration, raw quantitative and qualitative data must be processed in preparation for subsequent analyses. During this first or preparatory phase of the data analysis, it is essential to budget sufficient time for training and data processing. Errors or failure to plan carefully at this phase will undermine all subsequent phases of analysis.

Qualitative data processing is an interpretive process and thus reflects the first step in the analysis. In many mixed methods social work inquiries, individual or group interviews must be processed for subsequent analyses. This process often involves the verbatim transcription of audio or video recordings and integration with notes describing the social and physical contexts of the interview. Such transcription is not an automatic process, but requires active interpretation for which transcribers must be trained. For example, conventions must be established for consistently representing local dialects and noting paralinguistic cues that affect meaning such as a sarcastic tone or reflect intensity of emotion such as laughing or pausing. In addition, there may be field notes and documents (e.g., newspaper articles or historical documents) that must be organized and prepared for analysis. This, too, is an interpretive process as decisions are made about which materials are included as significant to the inquiry and how these materials are conceptually organized.

The processing of quantitative data likewise is apt to be meticulous, time consuming, and essential. Any interview, questionnaire, or standardized instrument (developmental, mental health, or other) must be carefully scored and then checked for accuracy. In studies drawing on administrative or other secondary databases, variables relevant to the research question must be identified and understood and their quality considered. For example, caseworkers may have the option to enter information on a youth's interpersonal relationships, but may not do so consistently or may not have the knowledge to provide valid information. A host of other decisions may be made in preparing quantitative data for analysis including how to handle missing data and how to consolidate related variables to reduce the number of variables in subsequent analyses. Clearly, this preparatory phase of quantitative data preparation also involves considerable judgment.

Perform Any Initial Sequential Analyses

Many mixed methods inquiries will include an initial phase of separate analyses of qualitative and quantitative data prior to integrated analyses. Here, analyses proceed as they would for mono method qualitative and quantitative studies. Preliminary analyses then may be used to inform subsequent analyses of each data set or further integrative analyses. These preliminary analyses may be descriptive variable-oriented analyses (Ragin, 1987), organized by variable and method. The initial phase of separate quantitative analyses, for instance, may provide descriptive information about study participants including indicators of central tendency and dispersion, as well as where participants are located in the broader population for various instruments (e.g., measuring youths' substance misuse, mental health, and educational achievement).

The initial phase of separate qualitative analysis may involve inducing content codes from transcribed text, video-recorded observations, field notes, and/or documents. Typically, multiple researchers will view and review video recordings, and read and reread textual materials using ***analytic induction*** techniques (Shwandt, 2007); that is, they will develop a conceptual framework based on the participants' perspectives rather than imposing an external conceptual framework. These researchers may generate a list of descriptive codes relevant to the research question and then through discussion, for example, with study participants or colleagues, finalize the coding system. The coding system is then applied to textual materials, oftentimes by a different set of researchers. In making coding decisions, these researchers will refer both to transcribed texts and to audio or video recordings. All or a subset of these materials can be coded by more than one researcher, with disagreements resolved through discussion.

There are a variety of analytic procedures that may be applied to talk and behavior in addition to describing the actual verbal content or behaviors. For example, analyses also may describe systematically the language participants choose to express their ideas. Kayama, Haight, Gibson, and Wilson (2015), for instance, described the language African American youths, their caregivers, and educators used when describing the events surrounding the children's out-of-school suspensions. They found widespread use of vocabulary associated with the criminal justice system in reference to youths' misbehaviors (e.g., misdemeanors or felonies). Youth used such language when referring to themselves (e.g., as feeling like prisoners), educators to defend their punitive actions (e.g., as legally mandated), and caregivers/parents to defend against educators' punitive actions (e.g., as illegal). These researchers then considered the implications of such language and its usage for young black males developing self and social identities.

The final step in this phase of the analysis may involve examination of any patterns of correlation and relationship among qualitative codes and quantitative variables in the study. These may include simple bivariate correlations among quantitative variables (e.g., measures of mental health and substance misuse) and analyses assessing co-occurrence of qualitative codes (e.g., codes describing beliefs about violence and about power).

Conduct Initial Integrated Analyses

The first step in conducting an integrated analysis often involves preparing the data to enable joint analyses. ***Data transformation*** involves converting one type of data into the other to allow for simultaneous analysis of both data types together. Quantitative data may be *qualitized* and included with qualitative data in thematic analyses; for example, children's numerical scores on a mental health instrument may be qualitized as clinically significant, borderline clinically significant, or not clinically significant and integrated with qualitative analyses of challenging school experiences coded from interviews. A risk of this procedure is that detail and fine-grained distinctions in the quantitative data may be lost.

Likewise, qualitative data may be *quantitized* and included with quantitative data in statistical analyses. For example, the presence or absence of particular perspectives or experiences described in qualitative codes may be indicated. The intensity or primacy of these perspectives or experiences also may be ranked or rated. An advantage of quantitizing qualitative data is that researchers can avail themselves of statistical techniques that can aid in detecting patterns in complex mixed methods data sets. A risk is that the complexity and richness of qualitative data may be lost.

Data also can be transformed through the creation of new variables expressed in quantitative or qualitative form or a mix. This process involves the review of both qualitative and quantitative data sets to form new variables that are then used in further analyses. For example, results from a quantitative teacher rating scale of child behavior might be combined with qualitative interviews with teachers about children's families and neighborhoods to form a new variable capturing teachers' understanding of children's culturally normative behaviors. The creation of such new variables can furnish critical information not apparent from the independent analysis of either quantitative or qualitative data alone. In the above example, the new variable can be examined in relation to various outcomes such as quality of teacher-child interactions, number and type of disciplinary actions, and child achievement and school engagement.

Data consolidation involves merging of multiple data sets into one. There are a number of software programs that allow entering both qualitative and quantitative data to organize text and numbers. Bazeley (2010, 2012) divided these programs into three groups. First, there are general purpose spreadsheets and databases that allow the recording of both text and numeric data and can be useful for the synthesis of various data forms. Second, there are programs that are designed primarily for qualitative or quantitative data analysis but provide for combination or conversion of data. Some tools developed initially for qualitative analyses have now developed specific capacities for integrative analyses (e.g., NVIVO (http://www.qsrinternationala.com) and MAXQDA (http://www.maxqda.com). Some tools developed initially for quantitative analyses (e.g., SPSS) now have add-on text-analysis modules that have some limited ability to categorize text data and then combine it into statistical analyses (e.g., SPSS Text Analysis for Surveys, http://www.spss.com). Finally, there is software developed for specific purposes that often reflect mixed methods. These programs support particular types of analyses that are inherently mixed. For example, software for geographic information systems (GIS) links physical, demographic, statistical, and social data by plotting them onto maps.

Perform Midstream Integrated Analyses

Midstream integrated analyses are typically exploratory. The goal is to apply the results from one data set to another to generate new insights. Greene and colleagues (Caracelli and Greene, 1993; Greene et al., 2010) described a number of strategies for midstream integrated analyses. These strategies are not necessarily independent of one another, and any study may employ a number of approaches sequentially or iteratively. Some examples are listed below:

- *Extreme case analysis* involves the identification of extreme cases for further analysis. There are a variety of reasons why identification of extreme cases may be important. Extreme cases may provide disconfirming evidence for the hypotheses under investigation, leading to refinements of the hypothesis, or they may deepen qualitative interpretations. Extreme cases identified from the analysis of one data type may be pursued via analysis of data of the other type, with the intent of testing and refining the initial explanation for the extreme cases. For example, extreme cases in the form of high residuals from a regression analysis of quantitative data may be pursued via analysis of qualitative data, the results of which are used to refine the original explanatory model. Alternatively, extreme cases identified from constant comparative analysis of qualitative data are further examined via analysis of quantitative data, the results of which are used to refine the original interpretation. Similar to the other integrative analysis techniques, negative case analysis also has an iterative potential.
- *Integrated data displays* can enhance the mixed method researcher's holistic understanding and development of a coherent narrative. Integrated data displays or cross-method matrices (Miles and Huberman, 1994) can be used to present information from multiple methods together. Such a presentation allows a joint display of different kinds of data and invites analytic integration and imagination. Such integrated analyses may be informed by typologies, or they may be more open ended. They may be case based or variable

based. In a case-based integrated analysis, a descriptive portrait is developed and organized by case (for example, person, family, or organization). In a variable-based integrated analysis, the descriptive portrait is organized by quantitative variable or qualitative code (for example, indices of marital conflict and experiences of anomie). Such holistic analyses may reorganize and integrate the descriptive data from the sequential phase into comprehensive narratives. (The research example presented in chapter 8 will include a number of integrated data displays.)

• *Typology development* involves the analysis of one data type to identify dimensions of interest and create a set of substantive categories or typology. This typology is then incorporated into the analysis of the contrasting data type. In essence, analysis of one type of data yields a set of substantive categories that is used as a framework and applied to analyzing the other data type. For example, quantitative analyses of children's psychological and behavioral functioning may provide a conceptual framework that is incorporated into qualitative analyses of their personal narratives of interpersonal conflict. A set of conceptual dimensions resulting from one set of analyses (e.g., various clinically significant mental health issues) may be incorporated into the analysis of the other data (e.g., children's narratives of physical aggression). As Caracelli and Greene (1993) point out, typology development has an iterative potential. A typology created from one data type can be applied to analysis of the other data type, and the results can be used to refine and elaborate the original typology.

Conduct Final Integrated Analyses

The final phase of integrated mixed methods analyses focuses on the generation of defensible inferences from review of data from qualitative and quantitative sources. These analyses may involve integrated data displays or typology development. They also may include *warranted assertion analysis*. In warranted assertion analysis, the researcher repeatedly rereads the qualitative and quantitative data sets as a whole, working inductively toward claims grounded in all the data. Next, evidence for each claim is assembled. Then, the researcher iteratively refines each claim through vigorous searches for disconfirming evidence.

ENHANCING QUALITY

In this section we will turn our discussion to criteria for assessing the quality of mixed methods inquiries. As with any research tradition, mixed methods studies vary in quality. In literature reviews and decisions about social programs and policies, the findings from higher quality studies are more heavily weighted than those from weaker studies. There are, however, challenges to assessing the quality of mixed methods studies. Although criteria for quality research overlap in quantitative and qualitative traditions, they also vary somewhat. For example, both quantitative and qualitative social science research traditions generally value careful empirical observations and logical argumentation. Quantitative research, however, focuses on issues such as the representativeness of samples and generalizability of findings whereas qualitative research generally prizes richness of samples and contextualization of findings. How does one mix quality criteria for both quantitative and qualitative research? In addition, because both quantitative and qualitative components of the mixed methods project bring their own set of challenges, how does one minimize either additive or multiplicative threats to rigor? Finally, are there quality criteria specific to mixed methods studies, for example, quality of the integration of qualitative and quantitative components?

From our perspective, there is no single checklist of strategies for enhancing rigor that are applicable across all mixed methods inquiries. Assessing the quality of any study, mono or mixed methods, is an exercise in the application of critical thinking to particular studies. There are, however, grounds for distinguishing and designing studies that are more or less credible and useful. Alicia O'Cathain (2010), among others, has developed a detailed framework to help researchers undertake and assess good mixed methods research. In this chapter, we will present a general framework for thinking about the quality of mixed methods social work studies organized around the central concepts of validity and relevance.

VALIDITY OF MIXED METHODS RESEARCH

A Theory of Validity

In their classic text, Shadish and colleagues (2002) characterize **validity** as relative, as the "approximate truth of an inference" (p. 34) or knowledge claim. They make two critical and related observations about validity. First, validity judgments are not absolute. When we say that something is valid, we are making a judgment about the extent to which the evidence supports the inference or knowledge claim. Typically, that evidence comes from empirical findings and the consistency of those findings with other sources of knowledge such as past findings and theories. Assessing validity always involves fallible human judgments and we can never be sure that all of the inferences drawn from a single study are true or that other inferences have been conclusively falsified.

Second, no particular research design or method guarantees the validity of an inference. As Shadish and colleagues (2002) explain, "validity is a property of inferences. It is *not* a property of designs or methods" (p. 34). For example, employing a randomized controlled trial, a design characterized as the "gold standard" by some, does not guarantee that the researcher will make a valid inference about the presence of a causal relationship. For example, the researcher may fail to consider that differential attrition may vitiate randomization, power may be too low to detect the effect, or improper statistics may be used to analyze the data. In short, validity judgments are not context independent properties of methods; they have to be assessed in relationship to the implementation of the research (Maxwell, 2004, 2010).

Shadish and colleagues (2002) recommended that in designing studies or assessing the rigor of any given study, we consider ***threats to validity***, i.e., reasons why we can be partly or completely wrong in our inferences and knowledge claims. These threats may be conceptualized as alternative explanations or rival hypotheses. As a component of research design, validity consists of strategies used to identify and rule out these threats.

Shadish and colleagues recommended protecting against threats to validity using design features such as comparison groups and pretests and posttests. The goal in quantitative, qualitative, or mixed methods research is not to rule out all possible threats to study interpretations and conclusions, but to rule out *plausible* alternative explanations.

As Maxwell (2005) described, quantitative researchers generally attempt to design, in advance, controls that will deal with both anticipated and unanticipated threats to validity such as framing of explicit hypotheses prior to data collection, randomized sampling and assignment to experimental (treatment) and control (comparison) groups, use of reliable and valid instruments, standardization of procedures, and appropriate tests of statistical significance. These prior controls deal with most validity threats in a generic fashion. For example, random assignment of participants to experimental and control groups "purports to control an infinite number of 'rival hypotheses' *without specifying what any of them are*" (Campbell, 1984, p. 8, as cited in Maxwell, 2005, p. 107). In this case, the experimental and control groups are equivalent, probabilistically, prior to the application of the experimental condition (e.g., the social work intervention under evaluation). Threats to validity are equally likely to affect experimental and control groups and so cannot be a source of rival hypotheses explaining any observed differences between the groups subsequent to the intervention.

In contrast, qualitative researchers rarely have the benefit of previously planned comparisons, sampling strategies, or statistical manipulations that address plausible threats to validity. Qualitative researchers must try to rule out most validity threats after the research has begun, using evidence collected during the research itself to make these alternative explanations implausible. This approach requires that the researcher identify *specific* threats and develop ways to rule them out. In qualitative research, specific practices to strengthen the credibility of inferences include intensive extended engagement with the community under study, thick description of behavior in context, member checks on researchers' interpretations, searching for **negative cases**, investigator **reflexivity** regarding the effect of his/her own biases on the research, and triangulation (*see* Lincoln & Guba, 1985, for one influential perspective on establishing trustworthiness in qualitative research).

Establishing Validity in Mixed Methods Research

Quality of Quantitative and Qualitative Study Components

The validity of inferences in mixed methods inquiry is dependent on the quality of the quantitative and qualitative design components, methods, and resulting data on which they are based. Clearly, quantitative and qualitative components of the mixed method design should maintain high standards relative to their particular qualitative and quantitative traditions. Thus, an initial step in assessing rigor in mixed methods research is to consider the appropriateness and quality of the research design in relation to the qualitative and quantitative research questions or hypotheses, as well as the quality of the data derived from the quantitative and qualitative methods (i.e., site selection, sampling, measures, procedures, and analyses). Quantitative strands should adhere to criteria for enhancing rigor in quantitative traditions, and likewise qualitative components need to adhere to criteria for enhancing credibility in qualitative traditions. For example, the quantitative component of a mixed methods evaluation of a social work intervention might address causal hypotheses pertaining to the effectiveness of the intervention by employing an experimental design in which researchers (1) randomly select a sample of participants from the broader population to which they intend to generalize, (2) randomly assign these participants to experimental and control groups, (3) administer treatment to the experimental group in a standardized fashion, (4) measure participant characteristics via valid and reliable assessments, and (5) employ appropriate statistic tests. In the qualitative component designed to enhance understanding of the experiences of the intervention by participants from diverse cultural communities, researchers might seek sustained engagement at the research sites where, for example, they observe and participate in a variety of contexts; hold in-depth, repeated conversations with participants occupying a variety of social roles; and review historical documents.

Quality of Mixed Methods Integration. In addition to adhering to best practices in the traditions of each qualitative and quantitative component, there are unique issues to consider when judging validity in mixed methods research. Researchers not only make inferences from separate quantitative and qualitative components, they also make **meta-inferences** from their integration in the whole study. Onwuegbuzie and Johnson (2006) outlined a number of issues specific to quality of integration of qualitative and quantitative components in mixed methods research. They described a number of legitimation (validity) types including *inside-outside legitimation*, which refers to the extent to which the research has adequately presented the insider perspective from the qualitative component and the outsider view from the quantitative component to describe and/or explain the phenomenon of interest. *Weakness minimization* refers to the extent to which weaknesses from one approach are compensated for by the strengths of the other approach. *Commensurability* refers to the extent to which the inferences drawn from the mixed data set reflect a mixed worldview, moving back and forth from a qualitative to a quantitative lens. Onwuegbuzie and Johnson note that, "through an iterative process, a third viewpoint is created, a viewpoint that is informed by, is separate from, and goes beyond what is provided by either a pure qualitative viewpoint or a pure quantitative viewpoint" (p. 59).

Establishing Relevance in Mixed Methods Research

Regardless of how methodologically rigorous a study from any mono or mixed method tradition is, judgments of its quality most critically hinge on its relevance. Does the research address an issue of substance with respect to theory, practice, or policy? Rigorous designs and methods are irrelevant if the research question is trivial. With respect to mixed methods studies in particular, is the product of the integration of qualitative and quantitative components more than the sum of the quantitative and qualitative parts? Would resources have been better spent in two separate qualitative and quantitative studies? As with validity, there is no recipe or checklist to determine relevance, and reasonable scholars may differ in their judgments. Nonetheless, before embarking on any complex and rigorous research project, researchers would be well advised to ask themselves the *so what?* question: What difference will the information I obtain from my study make for our general understanding of the phenomenon of interest, social work practice, or policy?

In addition, it is essential to consider the quality of reasoning, from the design and methods to the conclusions and recommendations. Are the conclusions and recommendations supported by the design? For example, a quantitative social work researcher may implement a correlational design with methodological rigor, but then make recommendations for policy as if the design and methods confirmed a causal inference. Are the conclusions and recommendations appropriately tempered by study limitations? For example, are strong recommendations for practice made on the basis of weak data? Box 7.2 summarizes our general framework for thinking about the quality of mixed methods research.

••

BOX 7.2
A Framework for Thinking about the Quality of Mixed Methods Research

1. *Is the design appropriate given the research question or hypothesis?*
2. *What strategies are in place to enhance validity?*

Quantitative component	Qualitative component	Integration
(*may* include)	(*may* include)	(*may* include)
Random sampling from population	Extended community engagement	Inside-outside legitimation
Random assignment to groups	Thick description	Weakness minimization
Reliable, valid measures	Member checks	Commensurability
Standardized procedures	Negative case analysis	
Tests of statistical significance	Triangulation	
	Reflexivity	
etc.	etc.	etc.

3. *How relevant is this research?*
   Does the research address an issue of substance with respect to theory, practice or policy?
   Do recommendations for practice and policy follow from data collected from the particular study design and methods?

••

RESEARCH EXAMPLE: APPLYING CONCEPTS—A MIXED METHODS RESEARCH PROGRAM INVESTIGATING SPIRITUALITY AND RECOVERY FROM ADDICTION

Amy Krentzman studies addiction recovery through the lens of *positive psychology*. Positive psychology is the scientific study of strengths that allow individuals and groups to flourish. Her interest in the area of substance abuse research grew out of her second year MSW internship. At that time she worked in a residential program with men who were formerly homeless; many of them were dually diagnosed with addiction and mental illness. She was inspired as she watched a large number of clients recover from substance addiction and wanted to better understand why the program was successful. Her interest in gratitude, spirituality, and positive communication grew as she became increasingly interested in factors that allowed people in recovery not only to obtain sobriety, but to achieve personal fulfillment and joy. During our interview, Krentzman explained her focus on positive psychology rather than pathology: "My rationale is that a new sober life must be rich enough to compete with the powerful effects of drugs and alcohol in order to offer a compelling alternative." (A, Krentzman, personal communication, May 7, 2014). Before reading about Krentzman's research, consider the questions in Box 7.3.

••

BOX 7.3
Guide to Krentzman's Research

As you read about Krentzman's research, you may wish to reflect on the following:

1. How does Krentzman enhance the validity of inferences drawn from qualitative and quantitative components of her research program? From their integration?
2. To what extent and how does the integration of quantitative and qualitative components enhance the rigor of her research program in terms of validity and relevance?
3. To what extent does Krentzman's mixed methods approach yield results (data, understanding, implications) that are more than the sum of their constituent qualitative and quantitative components? What is gained by the integration of qualitative and quantitative components in this research program?

••

In a program of research spanning several years, Krentzman began with observational and cause-probing designs to better understand the processes that lead to a fulfilling and sober life for those recovering from addictions. Then, she and her colleagues used that understanding to design, implement, and evaluate a gratitude intervention. A strong critical thinker, Krentzman prioritized issues of relevance and rigor in her research. The use of strong designs, including experimental mixed methods designs, supported the rigor as well as the relevance of her research. Her ongoing research is published in a variety of high-quality peer-reviewed journals. Several recent articles include Krentzman, Cranford, & Robinson (2013); Krentzman et al., 2015; and Krentzman, Higgins, Klatt, & Staller (2015).

Krentzman began her research career in an environment dominated by quantitative methods. Her training and education, along with her love of statistics, led her to focus a great deal of her early work on quantitative analyses of secondary data. She used strong statistical tools to enhance the rigor of the longitudinal studies she employed to examine pathways to recovery for adults with alcohol dependence. Although it yielded important insights, Krentzman was dissatisfied with this mono method design. She sought an approach that would allow her to explore the many insights she had gained from providing services to individuals in recovery as a social worker. She began to consider how the integration of qualitative methods into her quantitative research program might enhance the relevance and validity of her studies. Krentzman described her shift from mono method quantitative to mixed methods research to enhance the relevance of her research:

> Previously I worked in a very quantitative environment where they almost thought qualitative methods were like reading tea leaves at the bottom of a cup. They thought, *how do you know that . . . how is that valid?* But I was able to structure my time and I found myself taking qualitative methods classes in sociology and in social work. Sitting in on these classes I felt strongly about that way of knowing and bringing these ideas back to my colleagues. I remember also doing a quantitative data analysis and seeing that if you're doing longitudinal alcoholism research, the people who are unavailable for follow-up are the people who are the clients of social workers. So the people who drink more, the people who become incarcerated, the people who become homeless, they're not available for follow-up waves because you can't find them. So we need other methods than longitudinal quantitative methods to hear and understand that population. Qualitative studies can capture the experiences of the people who [would be] unable to be retained in a year-long follow-up study because their lives are such that they don't have a consistent address. A lot of research is done where those people, their experiences, their voices, their data points are not taken into account in the results that are cranked out through the statistical model because those are the people who dropped out. (A. Krentzman, personal communication, May 7, 2014)

Krentzman also articulated some of the important ways that mixed methods served to enhance the validity of her inferences. For instance, in the previous example, she highlighted some of the threats to validity within large-scale longitudinal studies and how they might be reduced through the incorporation of qualitative methods. She noted that, in one quantitative study, nonrandom attrition was exacerbated by the longitudinal design. The validity of her inferences about population characteristics or about factors leading to recovery was compromised when those participants who were struggling most were lost from the study. Incorporating a qualitative component made it possible to obtain in-depth cross-sectional data from participants for whom longitudinal follow-up would likely be difficult (e.g., the homeless and those struggling with multiple relapses). She also described how the intentional integration of a qualitative component led to new discoveries and insights to strengthen an intervention built from the integration of quantitative and qualitative methods:

> We discovered two things in my gratitude study when we interviewed [participants] in in-depth [qualitative] interviews. They told me that part of their experience of alcoholism was that it left them with a persistent habit of negative thinking—almost obsessive ruminating about negative things that happened and negative ways they felt. And person after person shared that with us. We know that negative mood is a predictor of relapse, but hearing it in this way from them made me realize, wow, what they're telling me is that this negative thinking is a deeply engrained pattern that over a career of alcoholism ends up this way—the way chronic drinking changes the brain in different ways—it's hard to feel pleasure after a career of addiction. Somehow it's leaving them with this persistent habit of focusing on negative thoughts.
>
> Now this gratitude intervention was an intervention that helped people intentionally focus on three good things that happened. So I realized, wow, this really can help them cognitively restructure the way they think by intentionally focusing on what happened that was good. And then the next day looking for the good thing and then noticing it and saying, "Oh that's one of the things I'll write about tonight." So then it's not only a 10 minute activity they do at night when they write about the three good things, but every day there's a scanning of the environment to find the good thing and say, "Oh yeah that's going to count tonight." And that changes [things] because they were telling us, "I tend to think about the negative. It's easy for me to think about the negative. That comes easily to me, but thinking about the positive is hard for me, and this exercise helped me to do that." So that was, to me, a big discovery.
>
> [In addition] we had a [quantitative] assessment instrument designed to measure their mood. So it was 20 mood items. They were asked to rate to what degree they felt angry or calm or energized [etc.]. And that was just meant to be neutral, to capture how they felt after they did the exercise. It was a measurement instrument and that was it. But what they told us [qualitatively] both in the treatment and in the control group is that they thought *that* was an intervention and they thought it was really helpful. And there's this thing with addiction called alexithymia, which means an inability to put a word to a feeling, an inability to define or to articulate or to know what you're feeling. And for them because they experienced this alexithymia, they thought [that measurement instrument] was helpful because it helped them realize what they were feeling. So we may be right here finding or discovering a new intervention that people feel [is] helpful. It was interesting that this instrument [was] just designed as a [quantitative] measurement; they thought it was therapeutic. And one person even took it to their therapist and said, "Look what we're doing in the research study; isn't this awesome? Let's talk about this." Because they would tell me that they would take that questionnaire and they would realize, "Oh I don't feel that good, I need to do something. Oh, I now realize I'm not doing that well and now I have to

do something to fix things, I have to do something to soothe myself or change things or make myself feel better." But they didn't even realize they were [upset] emotionally until they took the assessment. Well, we'd be able to intervene, because intervention improved their mood and we have that data at the quantitative level. So we're on to something with an intervention, but this surprise from the qualitative data tipped me off to it a whole other kind of intervention that wasn't even on my radar. (A. Krentzman, personal communication, May 7, 2014)

Indeed, the new discovery that resulted from the qualitative components seemed especially salient to Krentzman not only during descriptive phases of her research program, but also into intervention phases. She described the intervention that they had designed as a "castle" that she and her colleagues spent two years building. They then used qualitative techniques to invite the consumers of the intervention to describe their experiences resulting in yet more discoveries:

I was so fascinated to hear what they thought, what their experience was in this thing that we spent two years designing. So first of all that was just fascinating, but it's almost like they provided me with [gift] boxes and I had no idea what I was going to find inside the boxes until I opened them. And so in that one case it was like, *Oh, an idea for a new intervention*, and in another case it was like, *Oh, insight into the experience of addiction's persistent negative thinking* that helps me understand addiction better. So I didn't know what prizes I was gonna [get]—it's like those children's toys where you open it up and you don't know what the prize is gonna be inside. So you don't really know what you're gonna find, but you're gonna find stuff that could be really helpful. (A. Krentzman, personal communication, May 7, 2014)

Krentzman also elaborated how her education in qualitative research helped her to better appreciate the role of the self in research. By integrating a qualitative perspective into her quantitative research, she more broadly considered what information is relevant to the inquiry (i.e., the observations and responses of the researcher) and increased the rigor of her quantitative methods (i.e., she considered how her own appearance and demeanor could impact participants' responses to a computerized, quantitative instrument):

Qualitative [approaches] let you use yourself as an instrument in the research process and I think that's what draws me to it a lot. And I can give you some examples and also just the simple fact that you miss a lot if you don't have mixed methods. If you have just a quantitative study there's an enormous [amount] of great stuff that is off the radar that you never get. And that stuff is the stuff that could be groundbreaking, that could be innovative, that could be something no one else has ever been able to document. And that's happening in my current study. I learned two things that I never would have learned if there was not a qualitative component in my study. . . . So with the gratitude study, the participant would come to the office face-to-face and we'd do the informed consent and [then] I'd say, "Ok the first part is you go to that computer and you do a 40 minute online baseline assessment and I'm gonna sit right next to you in this room and so if you have any questions at all, I'm right here and just tell me and I'd like to answer your question." So they would face that wall and I would face here. So I didn't wanna like lean over their shoulder. But, I noticed that without using my eyes I was actually collecting a lot of data because different people would interact with the keyboard differently . . . some people were like very tentative and quiet and other people were very noisy and rambunctious. And I'm thinking, Wow I am collecting data with my ears and I'm getting, I'm collecting something that might even be meaningful. . . . I knew that that was legitimate and important. It was interesting, I made notes about it. And then I also thought . . . about other things that I would have thrown in the rubbish heap if I didn't know about qualitative methods. Like I thought about what do I wear on the days when I'm bringing a participant into the office? And I would dress up more. And I thought about my choice of clothing and I thought about my choice of reading material. I'm not reading *People Magazine* because I wanna encourage a sense of legitimacy. So I would bring these statistical texts. I was like a librarian quietly turning the pages and I realized, well I'm choosing material that will support the idea that I'm studious, that I'm serious, that this is not frivolous—the whole experience I realized all of that is important, it's all relevant and it's legitimate. The qualitative training I got told me that. (A. Krentzman, personal communication, May 7, 2014)

CONCLUSION

A number of mixed methodologists (e.g., Bryman, 2008) argue that the sum of a mixed methods study should be more than its constituent quantitative and qualitative parts. In addition to attending to rigor, that is, validity and relevance for qualitative and quantitative components, something must be gained from their integration. In the example of Krentzman's research, the integration of qualitative components into a primarily quantitative program of research enhanced the relevance and validity of the research and led to new discoveries.

Realizing the potential of mixed methods social work research does not stop at the integration of concepts, questions, and methods. One of the areas in which some mixed methods researchers struggle is the integration of data analyses. At their best, mixed methods data analyses are complex and creative integrations of qualitative and quantitative data requiring a flexible and pragmatic stance. Perhaps the most challenging aspects of mixed methods social work, integrated analyses are tailored to the goals and characteristics of each individual research project and so by their very nature resist codification. There are, however, a number of general approaches and strategies common to many mixed analyses. The integrated data analysis strategies outlined in this chapter are not independent of one another, and any study is likely to embrace a range of approaches. As Krentzman's analyses of recovering adults' responses to an innovative gratitude intervention illustrated, mixed methods analyses exploit the integrative potential of quantitative and qualitative data to fully address the research questions and raise even more.

As you continue to design your own mixed methods projects, Box 7.4 provides a guide to planning your analyses and enhancing the quality of your study.

●●

BOX 7.4
Building a Mixed Methods Social Work Research Project: Planning the Analysis and Enhancing Quality

1. Planning the data analysis is a critical part of any research proposal. What quantitative data will you collect? What qualitative data? Will these data be integrated? If so, outline your plan using the general framework described in this chapter as appropriate: processing the data, sequential analyses, and initial integrated analyses, mid-stream integrated analyses, and final integrated analyses.

2. How will you enhance the quality of your proposed research project? You will have made a strong case for the relevance of your project in your introduction. In the Methods section of your proposal, describe how you will strengthen the validity of your quantitative component, the credibility of your qualitative component, and your meta-inferences from their integration. What are the trade-offs you will make as you balance the demands of qualitative and quantitative components and what is the rationale for your decisions?

●●

SUGGESTIONS FOR ADDITIONAL READING

Bazeley, P. (2010). Computer assisted integration of mixed methods data sources and analyses. In A. Tashakkori and C. Teddlie (Eds.) *SAGE handbook of mixed methods in social and behavioral research* (pp. 431–467). London: SAGE.

    This article by Bazeley can be particularly useful to PhD students as it describes software programs helpful to mixed methods analyses as well as strategies for integrating qualitative and quantitative data.

Greene, J., C., Sommerfeld, P., & Haight, W. L. (2010) Mixing methods in social work research. In L. Shaw, K. Briar-Lawson, J. Orme, & R. Ruckdeschel (Eds.), *The SAGE handbook of social work research* (pp. 315–331). Thousand Oaks, CA: SAGE.

In this chapter that is written for social workers, the authors' discussion includes strategies for integrating qualitative and quantitative data. It is appropriate to assign to MSW and PhD students.

O'Cathain, A. (2010). Assessing the quality of mixed methods research: Toward a comprehensive framework. In A. Tashakkori & C. Teddlie (Eds), *SAGE handbook of mixed methods in social and behavioral research* (pp. 531-555). Thousand Oaks, CA: SAGE.

This chapter provides a framework to help researchers undertake and assess good mixed methods research. It is appropriate to assign to PhD students.

Onwuegbuzie, A. J., & Combs, J. P. (2010). Emergent data analysis techniques in mixed methods research: A synthesis. In A. Tashakkori & C. Teddlie (Eds), *SAGE handbook of mixed methods in social and behavioral research* (pp. 397-430). Thousand Oaks, CA: SAGE.

This article on mixed methods data analysis can be helpful to PhD students.

Onwuegbuzie, A. J., & Johnson, R. B. (2006). The validity issue in mixed research. *Research in the Schools, 13*, 48-63.

This article conceptualizes validity in relation to mixed methodology. It is appropriate for MSW and PhD students.

8

Mixed Methods Designs
Children from Rural Methamphetamine-Involved Families

I first met Kim when conducting a qualitative interview and administering quantitative developmental assessments to her as part of a mixed methods study of the impact of parents' methamphetamine misuse on their children. Kim was eight years old. Her parents were addicted to methamphetamine and also abused alcohol and marijuana. As a young child, Kim observed physical violence between her parents and also between their adult friends. At the age of six, Kim was sexually abused by the teenage son of one of these friends during a drug party when she and her siblings were left unsupervised for several days. After bouncing around to various relatives for nearly a year, Kim was eventually placed in a stable foster home. After several months, she was beginning to adjust to her new home. She was clean, safe, well-fed, and attending school regularly for the first time and enjoying some academic success. Unfortunately, her foster family would be moving to another state so Kim would soon be transferred to another foster home. I left the session with a variety of concerns regarding the quality of Kim's interpersonal relationships, working models of attachment, and vulnerability to further abuse. Indeed, after our two-hour session Kim declared that she loved me and wanted to go home with me.

I next met Kim four years later. At the age of twelve, she was often truant from school, hanging out with an older group of teenagers, and had been involved in physical altercations both in her community and at school. Psychological assessments indicated clinically significant levels of externalizing behaviors, including aggression, as well as anxiety and depression. Her caseworker and her teachers reported that presumably well-functioning families had stopped inviting Kim to birthday parties, play dates, etc. and even encouraged their children to avoid her at school. During one of our interviews, Kim declared that she liked to fight —that it "relieved" her. Kim's case workers described feeling disturbed by her behavior and pessimistic about her future. (Wendy Haight's reflections on "Kim." Note that, to protect confidentiality, all participant names are pseudonyms and some case details have been altered.)

Wendy met Kim and other rural children from methamphetamine–involved families while on the faculty of the University of Illinois, Urbana-Champaign

(UIUC) School of Social Work. At the time, the abuse of methamphetamine, a highly addictive central nervous system stimulant, had become a growing and urgent public health, criminal justice, and child welfare problem across the United States including the rural Midwest. A land grant university, the UIUC historically has been committed to engaged research of relevance to the community. Haight, together with social work faculty, community colleagues, and PhD students, embarked on a six-year-long odyssey to understand and then bring positive change to the lives of rural children from methamphetamine-involved families.

Mixed methods designs proved to be essential in the conduct of this research program. Mixed methods allowed us to explore research questions that addressed complex social issues affecting Kim and other children through observational designs, as well as to understand the outcomes of an intervention through cause-probing designs. For example, in our investigation, the quantitative component (scores obtained through standardized psychological assessments) was designed to assess the psychosocial functioning of children from rural, methamphetamine-involved families in relation to normative developmental expectations using an observational design and assess outcomes of our intervention using cause-probing designs. The qualitative component was intended to provide insight into families' experiences and perspectives in order to design and then to understand our intervention using an observational design. The integration of qualitative and quantitative designs and methods provided a depth and breadth of understanding not possible in mono method inquiry, whether qualitative or quantitative in nature.

In this chapter we will focus on components of research designs specific to mixed methods research. After determining whether to use a general observational or cause-probing design or some combination, mixed methods social work researchers then consider how specific quantitative and qualitative components are integrated. In this chapter, we will first describe a number of design dimensions specific to mixed methods research. Next, we will provide examples from John Creswell and his colleagues, who have used some of these dimensions in creating mixed methods design typologies. Then, we will use our study with rural families involved with methamphetamine misuse and child welfare to illustrate dimensions of these typologies in a multiphase (or multi-strand) mixed methods program of study. We will conclude this chapter with excerpts from an interview with a child protection worker who served as a community-based coinvestigator on this project. She reflects on her experiences with this research project, including the strengths and challenges of mixing methods. As we will elaborate in this chapter, the collaboration between university-based and community-based social workers was essential to the success of this mixed methods inquiry.

TABLE 8.1
Five Design Dimensions to Consider When Planning Mixed Methods Research

1. *Purposes* for mixing (Why choose a mixed methods over a mono method design?)
2. *Priority of methods* (What is the relative importance of qualitative and quantitative components?)
3. *Sequence* (How are quantitative and qualitative components ordered: sequentially or concurrently?)
4. *Integration* (When in the research process do quantitative and qualitative components interact and when do they remain separate?)
5. Number of *strands (phases) of research* (Are methods mixed within a single study and/or across several studies in a larger research program?)

MIXED METHODS DESIGN DIMENSIONS

Once mixed methods social work researchers have identified a descriptive or cause-probing design (chapter 5), they plan how qualitative and quantitative components will be integrated within these general designs. As introduced in chapter 5, methodologists have identified a number of design dimensions specific to planning mixed methods research (see Table 8.1).

As we discussed in chapter 4, mixed methods researchers may consider at the outset of their projects their primary *purposes* for mixing. As described in chapters 5 and 6, there are always trade-offs to be made in designing any research project, mono method or mixed methods. Monetary resources, researchers' time, and participants' patience are just a few of the finite resources available for any given project. Designing a research project requires weighing the relative advantages and disadvantages of adding any particular design feature while keeping the purposes for the research in mind. For example, the primary purpose of a particular qualitative research component may be to observe cultural practices and secondarily the meaning of those practices to participants. Thus, the researcher may choose to focus resources on participant observations, but that focus may limit the number and depth of individual interviews to understand the meanings of the observed practices to the participants. Considering the purposes of the research may be even more important in designing mixed methods studies because resources are distributed over both quantitative and qualitative components. When designing mixed methods studies, researchers must carefully consider whether the reasons for mixing methods outweigh the limitations of distributing resources across both quantitative and qualitative components of the study rather than focusing on one method alone.

Second, the mixed methods researcher may consider the *priority of methods*, which refers to whether the quantitative or qualitative methods are more important to our understanding of the research problem or whether they contribute equally. It is not always clear at the beginning of the research project which method will be most significant. In our research example of parents' methamphetamine misuse in this chapter, quantitative and qualitative methods were given equal weight in planning the study, but as we will discuss later, unexpected findings from the qualitative data proved to be more important to shaping the direction of our subsequent analyses.

Third, mixed methods researchers consider the *sequence* or timing of quantitative and qualitative methods: whether they are concurrent or sequential. In the research example presented in this chapter, quantitative developmental testing and qualitative interviews were conducted concurrently. Typically, children were administered standardized assessments and interviews in the same session or in sessions only days apart. In other designs, the quantitative or qualitative component may be implemented first and used to inform the other component. For example, qualitative in-depth interviews may be conducted, analyzed, and interpreted and then used to inform the development of a quantitative survey instrument. Alternatively, quantitative surveys may be used to identify outliers who are then targeted for in-depth qualitative observations.

Fourth, mixed methods researchers consider the *integration* of quantitative and qualitative perspectives; in other words, when in the research process they will be mixed and when they will remain separate. For example, will there be interaction between the two throughout the study or will the two parts of the study remain separate until interpretation of the data? In our research example for this chapter, methods were mixed at the outset of the study and reflected an integrated approach throughout. The research questions incorporated qualitative and quantitative perspectives. Further, there was a deliberate decision made at the outset of the study to utilize quantitative methods in order to explore aspects of children's development and social functioning relative to a larger population of children and a qualitative approach to gain a deeper understanding of the children's experiences including how those experiences might be affecting the results captured within the quantitative analysis.

Finally, researchers may mix methods in a multi-strand (or multiphase) program of research or within a single study. In their design typology, Teddlie and Tashakkori (e.g., 2009) recognized that mixed methods perspectives may be implemented during various phases of a larger research program. In other words, mixed methods approaches may occur within a single study, or they may be used in a sequence of studies including mono method studies across a research program. In the example for this chapter, mixing occurred both within and across a multiphase program of research.

RATIONALE FOR CREATING MIXED METHODS DESIGN TYPOLOGIES

Methodologists have combined diverse design dimensions into typologies (or frameworks) that researchers may consider when planning studies.

Typologies can consist of any number of dimensions depending on their goals or purposes. In a well-known example from quantitative research discussed in chapter 6, Shadish and colleagues (2002) described a typology consisting of design dimensions intended to strengthen the validity of causal inferences in experimental and quasi-experimental designs. For example, the use of comparison groups, the random assignment of participants to those groups, and the use of pretests and posttests in quantitative evaluation studies can increase our confidence in our conclusion that the social work program was (or was not) effective in causing any observed changes in participants. They described the purpose for their typology: "We use these designs to illustrate how various validity threats operate with actual examples, for it is far more important to learn how to think critically about these threats than it is to learn a list of designs" (p.104).

Mixed methods scholars also have proposed design typologies that help us to think about how to integrate quantitative and qualitative traditions. It is important to remember that these design typologies are not intended to be exhaustive. Mixed methods designs are diverse, created to fit particular research questions, and emergent; that is, they may change as the study progresses. For example, new phases of research may be added during the course of the project, or changes in design and data collection may result as findings from quantitative components inform qualitative components or vice versa (Teddlie & Tashakkori, 2010).

Mixed methods design typologies are useful for a number of reasons. First, they provide exemplars for students and researchers new to mixed methods. They are starting points or viable options to think about and build upon when planning and implementing any given mixed methods study. Second, design typologies help in the development of the field of mixed methods research by advancing a common language. Third, they help to distinguish mixed methods designs from mono method designs. Such distinction highlights the unique contribution of mixed methods research to the social and behavioral sciences (Leech & Onwuegbuzie, 2009; Teddlie & Tashakkori, 2010).

MIXED METHODS DESIGN TYPOLOGIES

Mixed methods typologies focus on different design dimensions included in Table 8.1: the *purposes* for mixing, the *priority of methods*, the *sequence* of qualitative and quantitative components, the *integration* of qualitative and quantitative components, and the number of *strands* of research. There are multiple design typologies with different purposes to draw from in planning mixed methods research. Below, we present the typology of John Creswell in order to help the social worker new to mixed methods understand the nature of design typologies and what they might have to offer.

TABLE 8.2
Creswell's (2015) Design Typology

Basic Mixed Method Designs	Advanced Mixed Method Designs
Convergent design	Intervention design
Explanatory sequential design	Social justice design
Exploratory sequential design	Multistage evaluation design

Creswell's Typology

John Creswell and colleagues (e.g., Creswell, 2014; Creswell, 2015; Creswell & Plano Clark, 2011; Creswell, Plano Clark, Gutmann, & Hanson, 2003) have developed typologies that consider the sequencing, priority of methods and purposes of mixed methods (*see* Table 8.2)

Basic Mixed Methods Designs

Convergent Designs

These designs involve the separate collection and analysis of quantitative and qualitative data. The goal is to merge the results of quantitative and qualitative data analyses to yield a more complete understanding than would be obtained by either type of data analysis alone. The researcher first collects and analyzes the quantitative and qualitative data separately. Then, the two data sets are brought together or merged. Finally, the researcher examines the extent to which the quantitative results are confirmed by the qualitative results (or vice versa) and any differences are explained.

In these designs, qualitative and quantitative data are collected at the same time. Equal weight may be given to quantitative and qualitative components. For example, a researcher may collect both quantitative and qualitative data and then examine areas in which these data converge or diverge. In the research example presented in this chapter, social work researchers compared a quantitative clinical instrument assessing the mental health functioning of foster youth with youths' responses to qualitative clinical interviews. Youths' functioning as assessed by clinical instruments was examined in relation to their reported experiences and discrepancies were interpreted. Alternatively, priority may be given to either quantitative or qualitative approaches; in other words, one method may be nested within a study dominated by another method. For example, in a primarily qualitative study of the perspectives of professionals and experiences of clients, the social work researcher might conduct repeated in-depth interviews but nest within these interviews a short quantitative assessment of attitudes.

Explanatory Sequential Design

These designs begin with a quantitative component and then implement a second, qualitative component. The researcher first collects and analyzes the quantitative strand. Then, results from the quantitative strand are used to determine what results need further exploration in a second qualitative phase. Next, qualitative data are collected to help explain the quantitative data. Finally, the researcher considers how the qualitative results help to explain the quantitative results.

In the ***explanatory sequential mixed method design***, priority is given to the quantitative data. The qualitative data help explain and interpret the findings of the primarily quantitative study. For example, social work researchers might wish to observe and explain client behaviors and characteristics following an intervention. They could collect and analyze quantitative data from an experimental evaluation of intervention outcomes and then collect and analyze qualitative data focusing on the experiences and perspectives of a subsample of clients to consider why they responded differently. In other words, the qualitative component could be used to better understand or explain the quantitative component.

Exploratory Sequential Designs

In these designs, a problem is first explored through qualitative data collection and analysis. The results from the qualitative analyses are then used to design a quantitative component (e.g., new measures or interventions). The new measure or intervention is then tested (e.g., the validity and reliability of the new measure are assessed) or the new intervention evaluated. Finally, a report is made on how the new instrument or intervention improves upon the existing instruments or interventions.

In the typical ***exploratory sequential mixed methods design***, priority is given to the qualitative phase of the study. The focus of the research is on exploring a phenomenon. This design can be used to develop better measures (the example of Gilman's research in chapter 4) or to see if the data from a few individuals collected during the qualitative phase can be generalized to a larger sample (quantitative phase). For example, social work researchers may collect and analyze in-depth qualitative interview data exploring the experiences of clients and then use that information to design a quantitative survey to consider the generalizability of certain of these experiences to other clients.

Advanced Mixed Methods Designs

Advanced mixed methods design build on the three basic designs.

Intervention Designs

The goal of these designs is to conduct a quantitative experiment, for example, to evaluate an intervention, with a qualitative component. The researcher first must determine how qualitative data will be used: before (exploratory sequential), during (convergent), or after (explanatory sequential). Then the experiment is conducted and outcomes evaluated. Next, qualitative data are analyzed. Finally, the researcher considers how the qualitative results enhance or inform interpretation of the quantitative results.

Social Justice Designs

In these designs, the researcher adds to the basic design by threading a social justice perspective throughout. The researcher first identifies the basic design and then considers how the theoretical lens will inform the design. Finally, the researcher reflects on how the social justice lens helped to address the problem under study.

The distinguishing feature of these designs is their tie to a particular theoretical perspective. For example, social work researchers might take an explicitly feminist perspective beginning with a quantitative policy analysis followed by an ethnographic examination of how official policies actually affect and are experienced by the people they are designed to protect. Note that the role of conceptual frameworks may extend beyond the identification and formulation of research questions. Certain frameworks such as feminism and critical race theory also have implications for how the research is conducted and interpreted (Creswell & Plano Clark, 2011).

Multistage Evaluation Designs

Studies using these designs are conducted over a period of time to evaluate the success of a program or activities. The researcher identifies a program in need of evaluation, considers which basic design is needed for the evaluation, identifies the stages of the evaluation, determines at each phase whether quantitative and/or qualitative data are needed, and finally conducts the evaluation, revising the program and instruments as needed. The following research example can be described as a multistage evaluation design.

RESEARCH EXAMPLE: APPLYING CONCEPTS—A MIXED METHODS RESEARCH PROGRAM OF PARENTAL METHAMPHETAMINE MISUSE IN THE RURAL MIDWEST

The research example we will develop in this chapter uses a complex, multiphase (multi-strand) mixed method observational and cause-probing design. We will use this extended example to illustrate the evolution of a mixed methods project over a series of studies spanning a number of years. Because Haight was a principal investigator of this study, we take the opportunity to explain the reasoning behind our various design and method choices. This section will describe studies previously reported in a variety of publications. Readers interested in learning more about this program of research can refer to Black, Haight, & Ostler, 2006; Haight, Black, et al., 2010; Haight, Carter-Black, & Sheridan, 2009; Haight et al., 2007; Haight, Jacobsen, et al., 2005; Haight, Marshall, et al., 2010; Haight, Ostler, et al., 2009; Ostler, Haight, & Black, 2007; and Sheridan et al., 2011.

In launching our research, we began by reviewing some of the basic designs described by mixed methods scholars in their various typologies and then elaborated them to fit our research questions and evolving inquiry. We first considered observational and cause-probing purposes for our study. Then, we used a number of the design components from the mixed method design typologies we've discussed: the purpose for mixing, when the mixing occurs, the sequencing of quantitative and qualitative components, and the relative emphasis given to these components. Before reading about this program of research, consider the questions in Box 8.1.

•••

BOX 8.1
Guide to the Example

As you read this example of mixed methods research, you may wish to consider the following questions:

1. How did quantitative and qualitative design components build on one another throughout this program of research? To what extent to you think this design was emergent and to what extent was it fixed or preplanned?
2. Consider the data analysis. How did quantitative data analyses influence qualitative analyses and vice versa? How were qualitative and quantitative analyses integrated? To what extent do you think that the *conversation* between qualitative and quantitative data achieved more than analysis of either qualitative or quantitative data alone?
3. How did the researchers enhance the rigor (validity and relevance) of their project? (Consider quantitative and qualitative components as well as their integration.) How could rigor of this program of research have been strengthened?

•••

As with many other social work research programs, our problem and questions emerged from the field. In 2003, Haight was approached by MSW-level child welfare workers serving a rural, white, working class area of Illinois. The child welfare workers in this area had noticed an influx of children from methamphetamine-involved families onto their caseloads. Their parents and sometimes grandparents typically misused many substances including marijuana, prescription drugs, and alcohol, but had become quite impaired from their more recent drug of choice, methamphetamine. Hence, a more accurate description of these parents' substance misuse is *polysubstance misuse*. The reason these families came to the attention of authorities, however, was their methamphetamine misuse. Child welfare workers viewed these cases as more serious than others of their cases, including those of other children from substance-involved families. Many of the children whose parents misused methamphetamine appeared to be struggling with issues of trauma and from the impact of long-term isolation and neglect. Upon entry into care, many failed to form positive relationships and to adjust to their foster families. Child welfare workers asked Haight a seemingly straightforward question: What do we know about the psychological development of children from methamphetamine-involved families that will help us to respond thoughtfully and effectively to those who are struggling? We set out together to learn more.

Reviewing the Literature

Our first step was to review the existing literature on the impact of parental substance misuse on children (see Haight, Ostler, et al., 2009; Sheridan et al., 2011). We drew not only on social work research, but also on research in psychology, sociology, public health, and medicine. We learned that parent substance misuse places a significant strain on child welfare systems. A disproportionate number of children from substance-involved families enter the child welfare system and they stay for longer periods of time than children whose families are not involved with substances. Furthermore, when parents misuse drugs, children may be exposed to

- Drugs prenatally affecting brain development
- Criminal behavior including the use of illicit drugs, family attitudes accepting of substance misuse, and the availability of drugs in the home
- Compromised parenting including inconsistent discipline and inadequate parental monitoring
- Maltreatment including neglect and physical and sexual abuse
- Stigma from the public who view substance use disorder as indicative of a moral failure

Given these multiple stressors, it is not surprising that children whose parents misuse illicit substances are more likely to

- Misuse substances
- Experience mental health problems
- Drop out of high school
- Experience early pregnancy
- Become involved in criminal or other antisocial behavior

The children of special concern to the rural Illinois child welfare workers, however, were those whose parents had come to the attention of the state because of their involvement with methamphetamine. We learned that

- Methamphetamine is a powerful, highly addictive central nervous system stimulant.
- Methamphetamine is less expensive and more easily available than cocaine with a much longer high, which can last from ten to twelve hours.
- When using methamphetamine, the user experiences an initial rush or euphoria; decreased fatigue and appetite; and increased energy, alertness, and libido.
- With chronic use, the brain adapts and the user cannot experience a normal good mood, or energy level.
- Regular use may result in brain damage comparable to that seen in early dementia and schizophrenia.
- Death may result from secondary damage to the lungs, heart, and kidneys.
- Regular use is associated with a variety of psychiatric symptoms including psychosis, depression, rapid mood changes, irritability, and out-of-control rages and violent behavior.
- Because interpersonal violence is extensive among users, users also may suffer from posttraumatic stress disorder.
- Although methamphetamine misuse occurs in cities, it has primarily been a rural problem, especially in the Midwest and South.
- The highest rates of methamphetamine misuse occur among twenty- to twenty-nine-year-olds who often have children.

Developing the Initial Research Questions

From our review of the existing literature, we gained valuable insights into the possible impact of methamphetamine on the user and of parental substance misuse on children. We also learned about the possible impact of prenatal exposure to methamphetamine on the infant's physical development. We concluded, however, that very little was known about the impact of parents' methamphetamine misuse on children's psychosocial development, including mental health, important to the design of effective interventions. Thus, our initial research question was what are the effects of parents' methamphetamine misuse of children's psychosocial development?

Choosing a Mixed Methods over a Mono Method Design

Clearly, our community partners were facing a complex multidimensional set of problems. To design effective interventions they sought a holistic understanding of the contexts in which the children from methamphetamine-involved families on their caseloads had been reared, their experiences of those contexts, the experience of their parents and other family members, and their psychosocial (including mental health) functioning. Mono method qualitative or quantitative approaches alone appeared inadequate to address these research questions. Quantitative clinical assessments of children's development were essential to placing their developmental and mental health functioning within the broader context of normative expectations and other children involved in foster care. Qualitative examinations of the contexts in which children were reared, as well as the perspectives and experiences of these children and their family members, were essential to understanding the broader context of parental drug misuse as it related to children's development. Ultimately, information gained through both qualitative and quantitative approaches would be used in designing services that would be needs based and culturally sensitive to these families and children.

To approach the complex problem of the psychosocial functioning of children from rural methamphetamine-involved families, we settled on a multi-strand (multiphase) mixed methods design. The design was intended to evolve as we conducted the research program, and each step along the way was tailored to our emerging research questions. The design combined features of the typology of Shadish et al. (2002) (see chapter 5 discussion of descriptive or cause-probing designs), Greene's typology (purpose), and Creswell and colleagues' typology (sequence), as diagrammed in Figure 8.1 and explained, below. The first strand employed an observational mixed method design, and the second a cause-probing mixed method design.

Strand 1: Observational Concurrent QUAL Quant Design for the Primary Purpose of Complementarity and Secondary Purpose of Triangulation

The first strand of our design was observational. It emphasized the qualitative component, and qualitative and quantitative components were implemented concurrently including during analyses. Indeed, we mixed qualitative and quantitative methods beginning with our initial descriptive research questions. One research question was qualitative in focus: what are the contexts in which children from rural methamphetamine-involved families are reared? The other research question was quantitative in focus: how are children from methamphetamine-involved families in this rural community doing, psychologically, relative to other children in the United States including those in foster care? Our primary purpose in choosing a mixed methods design for the first strand of our research was complementarity. We combined qualitative and quantitative approaches to generate a deeper, broader, and more comprehensive portrait of rural children whose families

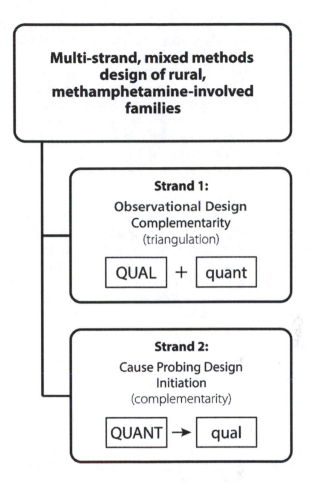

Figure 8.1
Design

were involved with methamphetamine misuse and child welfare. Our secondary purpose was triangulation. We employed some quantitative and qualitative measures of the same constructs to strengthen our interpretation based on the convergence of different methods with nonoverlapping strengths and limitations or to generate new insights through divergence of findings.

Given the challenges of integrated data analyses, we developed a plan for analyzing the data during the initial phases of the research. As we described in chapter 6, our overarching analysis plan consisted of several stages. We began by processing the data including transcribing qualitative interviews and scoring standardized assessments. Next we generated codes (described below) to describe the primary themes expressed in the interviews. Then we conducted a variable-oriented analysis of the themes from interviews and scores on standardized instruments. We also conducted integrated bivariate analyses of the relations between interview themes and scores on standardized instruments. In addition, quantitative and qualitative analyses mutually informed and complemented one another to identify and then better understand potential protective factors. Quantitative and qualitative data also were integrated to form profiles of methamphetamine-involved families, and of especially vulnerable children.

Qualitative Component

We approached our first research question using ethnographic methods. Strengths of ethnography attractive to our mixed methods inquiry included its characteristic use of multiple methods. In this case, we conducted interviews and observations, reviewed case records and local news reports, and attended local community meetings. Each of these diverse methods has different strengths and limitations. They also tap into different aspects of the complex phenomenon of children's experience within rural methamphetamine-involved families (e.g., experiences of love and trauma). Furthermore, they allow examination of diverse and sometime conflicting perspectives, for example, of children's parents and of their child protection workers. Our goal in using ethnography was to strengthen our inferences and broaden our understanding. Below, we outline our methods:

- *Interviews*: We conducted in-depth audiotaped interviews with multiple informants including recovering parents, foster parents, children aged seven to fourteen whose parents misused methamphetamine among other substances, foster parents, and Department of Children and Family Services (DCFS) professionals, as well as other professionals such as police, lawyers, educators, and substance misuse counselors. We asked adults to describe their experience with (or within) methamphetamine-involved families, beliefs about the effects of methamphetamine on school-aged children, and appropriate support for children. Children were asked some open-ended questions such as "Tell me about your family" and a number of more specific probes about their experiences of parents' methamphetamine misuse. The primary purpose was to understand the various perspectives of individuals with differing experiences of parental methamphetamine misuse on the contexts in which children were reared.
- *Observations*: We completed ninety hours of participant observation shadowing DCFS child protection workers investigating rural

families suspected of methamphetamine involvement. We also conducted more focused observations in homes of a subsample of intact families involved with child protection because of methamphetamine misuse. The parents of many of these families were receiving outpatient substance misuse treatment and were closely monitored by and receiving services from child welfare while their children remained at home. The primary purpose of these observations was to allow us to see for ourselves the conditions in which children were reared. The physical conditions in many of the impoverished rural homes were substandard. Some had missing doors, holes in the walls, and were lacking basic household furnishing such as bed frames. Observations also allowed us to see interactions between parents, children, and siblings that might not be articulated during interviews. Our observations were systematically recorded in daily field notes.

• *Case record review:* To supplement our understanding of children's experiences, we also reviewed their DCFS case records. These case records provided additional longitudinal information about children's functioning from the perspectives of educators and child welfare and court professionals.

• *Other document review*: We also reviewed local newspaper articles dealing with methamphetamine and other documentation of methamphetamine use in rural Illinois.

• *Community meeting attendance*: To gain additional insight into perspectives on methamphetamine misuse held in the larger mainstream community, we also attended a number of community meetings including those of the Illinois Methamphetamine Task Force. We recorded our observations of these meeting in field notes.

Some Notes on Analyzing the Qualitative Data

Our qualitative analysis focused on participants' perspectives, understandings, and experiences of parental methamphetamine and its impact on children's lives. Beyond judgments of the degree to which participants were being open and truthful with us, for example, providing detailed and internally consistent accounts during interviews, we tried *not* to impose our own judgments of the veracity of their reports from some external standard. Rather, we tried to imagine ourselves walking in their shoes. To accomplish this objective, we developed emic codes or codes that refer to the perspectives of people living within a culture as opposed to *etic* perspectives that are imposed from the outside of the cultural group. To develop emic codes we repeatedly read transcripts of interviews and reviewed field notes to understand the perspectives of participants. All materials—transcribed interviews, field notes, and record reviews—were read by two individuals who independently and through discussion generated a list of descriptive codes characterizing participant responses. Then, we returned to the community to conduct member checks; that is, we asked a number of our research participants if they felt that our codes were consistent with and inclusive of their own experiences and observations. Member checks helped to ensure that descriptive codes characterized the meanings informants intended to convey in their initial responses (*see* Denzin & Lincoln, 2000; Lincoln & Guba, 1985; Miles & Huberman, 1994).

Once the coding scheme was developed, the transcribed interviews were coded by two independent researchers who resolved any disagreements through discussion. This step is important because all researchers approach the data with particular perspectives based on their own experiences and working models that can create blind spots in seeing participants' perspectives. The use of more than one coder, especially with different professional backgrounds and life experiences, can minimize the impact of any given researcher's limited perspective and biases. This step also helped to ensure consistency of coding and the adequacy of our coding descriptions. Sometimes, raters made random human errors and other times we found that our codes needed to be more fully described.

Results from the Qualitative Component

What consistently emerged from the ethnographic data—interviews, participant observations, focused observations in homes, and case record and document reviews—was a portrait of a rural drug subculture with some distinct antisocial beliefs and practices. In terms of triangulation, we saw a high degree of convergence across qualitative methods. Children's experience of this subculture often included exposure to environmental danger, especially from methamphetamine labs that contaminated the home and sometimes produced explosions and fires. Their family lives often were chaotic as their parents spiraled into addiction, and many experienced neglect, abuse, and loss of parents and other family members through lengthy prison terms or death. Isolation, secrecy, and suspicion of outsiders also were part of some children's experiences. Most children were exposed to adults' misuse of multiple substances: not only methamphetamine, but marijuana, other illegal substances, alcohol, and prescription medicine. Many children also were exposed to adult criminal behavior. In addition to abusing illegal substances, parents' drug seeking behavior often involved other illegal behavior such as stealing. Some children reported that they not only observed but also were brought into these activities by their parents. Many children were exposed to violence between their parents and between other adults frequenting the home to purchase or use methamphetamine. Children sometimes became involved in the violence, for example, protecting their mother or a younger sibling. Below, we use an excerpt from an interview with thirteen-year-old

Karen to illustrate how qualitative interview data can reflect a child's-eye view of the intersection of parental substance misuse and violence:

> When my mom and dad was living together, they used to fight a lot. And then one day my mom just decided to leave because she didn't want to get hit on anymore and stuff like that. So one day, the day before Christmas, she left, and she went walking in the snow. And then, a year or two later, she was up in Chicago and she was on the streets . . . and she was a prostitute and then my dad was taking care of us for 7 years. He did drugs too and alcohol, a lot. And one day my dad, he had this girlfriend named Kate, and one day him and her got in a fight and they were both high and I went to give her 7 and 7. And I went to give that to her and he took it out of my hand and threw it and he grabbed me by the throat and drug me in the house and started beating me . . . and I don't know why he did that. . . . One night Kate and my dad got into a fight and she threatened to kill me. I don't like her. And she threatened my mom that she was gonna take John (baby brother) and kill him. Some people say that they want my life and then I tell them that they shouldn't because it might look easy, but it's not because I have a lot of history that really hurts. And they say that they want my life and I tell them, "I'd rather have yours." (Haight, Jacobsen, et al., 2005, p. 960)

Quantitative Component

Implemented concurrently with our qualitative methods, our quantitative methods addressed children's psychosocial functioning. We used standardized assessments to place children's psychosocial functioning within the broader context of school-aged children and children in foster care. This component proved valuable in further investigating our community partners' informal assessments and our observation that many children were struggling with mental health issues.

Some Notes on Quantitative Data Analysis: Choosing Appropriate Measures

Quantitative data analyses are only as good as the data that come from our measures, in this case, standardized assessments. Choosing appropriate measures and interpreting them is especially complex when dealing with marginalized groups. We sought instruments that were culturally appropriate, and would make sense to these rural children, all of whom were from low-income families. We identified a variety of standardized assessments that had been used with children from a wide range of cultural communities. For example, we asked children's primary caregivers to complete the Childhood Behavior Checklist (Achenbach & Rescorla, 2001). It is a questionnaire that focuses on observable behaviors and has been successfully used in a variety of cultural contexts including rural areas. It yields standardized scores for

TABLE 8.3
Percentage of Children Scoring in the Clinical Range (≥98th percentile) on the CBCL: Quantitative Data Display

	Girls (*n* = 16)	Boys (*n* = 22)
Externalizing	75*	32
Aggression	31	23
Rule breaking	44	23
Internalizing	44	32
Total	75*	41

*Gender differences, $p \leq .05$, chi-square.

externalizing behaviors, such as physical aggression and rule breaking, and internalizing behaviors, such as anxious or depressed behaviors.

Some other instruments we tried proved to be problematic with this group of children. The Trauma Symptom Checklist for Children Revised (TSCC-R; Briere, 1996) provides information on a variety of trauma symptoms including posttraumatic stress disorder and dissociation. Approximately one-third of children in our sample scored high on the Underreporting scale of the TSCC-R, which means that the validity of their responses is questionable. Many denied common experiences such as bad dreams or angry feelings, suggesting that they were not responding openly. We also administered the American Drug and Alcohol Survey (ADAS; Oetting, Beauvais, & Edwards, 1985), which provides information on children's attitudes toward substance use and their own substance use. Even more children responded in problematic ways to this instrument, for example, by denying knowledge of any substance. One young boy refused any further participation in the study when shown the ADAS. Although these instruments did not yield valid information on attitudes and experiences with substance misuse, children's responses did provoke us to investigate further. We learned, for example, that many children had been taught by parents not to talk to outsiders about family or other personal business. Some children had even been physically punished for responding honestly to teachers' concerned questioning about their safety and well-being.

Results from the Quantitative Component

Quantitative components of this first phase of the research project did confirm (triangulate), complement, and extend our understanding of children's mental health functioning from qualitative study components. Table 8.3 describes the percentage of children in our sample who scored in the *clinical range*, that is, in the 98th percentile or above, on various scales and subscales of the Childhood Behavior Checklist (CBCL). Overall, children in our sample had multiple psychological and behavioral challenges. Many displayed high levels of externalizing behaviors including aggression and rule breaking. Many also displayed high levels of internalizing behaviors, such as sadness and anxiety and *total* problems. We also observed some gender differences in an unexpected direction. Girls were more likely than boys to display clinically significant levels of externalizing behaviors and total problems (*see* Haight, Marshall, et al., 2010).

Emergent Research Questions and Integrated Data Analysis

As in many mixed methods inquiries, features of our design emerged as we conducted our study. Both our qualitative and quantitative data raised questions we had not originally considered, but whose relevance to understanding the experiences and psychological functioning of children in our sample became apparent. Given the presence of violence in the contexts in which these rural children from methamphetamine-involved families were raised, as indicated by the ethnographic data, and the unexpectedly high levels of aggressive behavior in girls, as indicated by the quantitative data, we asked what are the characteristics of girls who display physically aggressive behavior? Analysis of this question included the construction of a profile of girls using qualitative and quantitative data. Given significant individual variation in children's psychosocial functioning on standardized assessments and reported experiences during interviews, we also asked what are potential protective factors for the psychological functioning of children from methamphetamine-involved families? This question was addressed through a back and forth process in which quantitative analyses informed qualitative analyses and vice versa.

Physical Aggression: Literature Review. As we approached each new question emerging in our study, we returned to the literature to review existing research. This is important during each phase of a mixed methods design due to the number and complexity of research questions. In other words, conducting mixed methods research involves an ongoing dialogue among the data, the design, *and* the existing literature.

To address the first emergent research question, we reviewed studies of physically aggressive girls. We found a substantial developmental literature on aggression. This literature indicated that, when children are physically aggressive, we need to be concerned. Physical aggression is one of the best social predictors of children's concurrent and future maladjustment. Many children in our sample had experienced multiple risk factors for aggression such as exposure to adult violence, including intimate partner violence, criminality, and substance misuse. Many of the children in our sample also had experienced trauma. Their own physical aggression could place them at risk for further trauma. Physical aggression also places them at risk for the initiation of substance abuse and involvement with delinquent peer groups

TABLE 8.4
Girls and Boys Producing Spontaneous Narratives of Physical Aggression: Integrated Display of Quantitative and Quantitized Qualitative Data

	Girls (%) (n = 10)	Boys (%) (n = 7)
QUANT CBCL clinical		
Externalizing	90	29
Aggression	40	14
Internalizing	50	0
Total	80	29
QUAL interviews with professionals		
Child most concerned about	60	0
QUAL child narratives		
Child initiates physical aggression	50	0
Child target of physical aggression	100	57
Violence appropriate retaliation	50	14
Violence emotionally gratifying	50	14

and the juvenile justice system. Relatively more developmental literature has focused on physical aggression in boys rather than girls. Given the paucity of research on physical aggression in girls, especially rural girls, we approached these emergent research questions with a curiosity about the context and meaning of physical aggression for the girls in our sample (*see* Haight, Marshall, et al., 2010 for literature review).

Integrated Data Analysis of Aggression. The next step in our data analysis was to integrate findings from our various data sources. Seventeen of thirty-six children spontaneously produced fifty-eight narratives of personal involvement in physical aggression. We integrated children's CBCL scores, their narratives of physical aggression, and qualitative interviews with the professionals who collected the data. We asked the professionals (master's level social workers and counselors) who had collected the data to sort the children into three groups. The first group consisted of children they viewed as relatively resilient. The second group of children had a number of significant psychological and behavioral issues. The small number of children they placed in the third group were those about whom they had grave concerns.

Table 8.4 summarizes quantitative and qualitative data for children who spontaneously provided narratives of physical aggression. It is an example of a very simple integrated data display. Nine of the ten girls who produced narratives of physical aggression had clinically significant levels of externalizing behaviors including four who had clinically significant levels of aggressive behavior. Many of these girls also had high levels of internalizing and total problems. Relatively fewer boys had clinically significant scores.

Note that professionals concurred that they were gravely concerned about 60 percent of the girls who produced personal narratives of physical aggression. The social workers explained that they were concerned because they observed these girls as ostracized from nondelinquent peer groups, and because the girls viewed others' continuing physical aggression against them as an inevitable part of their futures and described their own physical aggression as unavoidably driven by that violence.

Analysis of children's narratives of physical aggression indicated that they primarily occurred at home and involved adults. Children attributed physical aggression to anger and adult substance misuse and described negative outcomes of the aggression: people got hurt and relationships were broken. Half of the girls described themselves as initiating physical aggression, all described themselves as targets of physical aggression, and half of the girls characterized their own physical aggression as appropriate retaliation with emotionally satisfying consequences.

Profiles. Our integrated data analysis included the construction of individual profiles of the girls who spontaneously produced narratives of physical aggression. These profiles allowed us to identify a small cluster of five girls who were of the highest overall concern based on clinically significant CBCL scores and interviews with professionals. All five girls described initiating physical aggression and being the target of physical aggression, and they viewed violence as appropriate retaliation and emotionally gratifying. Perhaps most striking are the positive emotional responses or outcomes described by these five girls as resulting from their own physical aggression. Violence is portrayed as providing a release from intense pent-up anger and/ or hurting someone is fun. In the following narrative fragment, twelve-year-old Kasey, one of the five girls, described her own feelings about her physically aggressive behavior:

> Sometimes when I'm mad at a person . . . I think bad thoughts about 'em and want to hurt 'em sometimes. . . . I like getting into fights, when I can—that's all of the time—'cause I just like to see the blood pour from people. . . . My brother, because he took my purse and kept running all over the house, so I kept on punching him until he was bleeding because I just get sick of him doing things and doing it and doing it and doing it. . . . So I finally just punch him until he stops. (Haight, Marshall, et al., 2010, p. 1229)

Protective Factors. Given our goal of assisting social workers in designing effective interventions, we also were interested in identifying potential protective factors we could build upon. A review of existing research indicated the following (*see* Sheridan et al., 2011, for literature review):

- Supportive relationships with extended family members may be particularly important for rural drug-involved families.
- Healthy extended family members can serve as nonthreatening family insiders who provide children with help and visible alternatives to parents' drug-involved lifestyles.

TABLE 8.5
Positive Grandparent Involvement: Clues to Protection (integrated display of quantitative data and quantitized qualitative data)

1. Spontaneous mention of positive relationship with grandparent: (50%)
2. Mean CBCL scores by child's mention of a positive relationship with a grandparent

	Positive grandparent?	
	No	Yes
CBCL externalizing	66.32	57.00*
CBCL aggression	15.40	7.75**

*$p < .05$; **$p < .01$ (*t*-tests. $N = 39$).

3. How grandparents protect:
   Shelter, material support (15%)
   Psychological support (13%)
   Leisure (38%)

- There is a high rate of kinship placements in drug-involved families.
- Children in kinship care placements have fewer social and behavioral problems than those in traditional foster care placements.
- Increasing numbers of grandparents are serving as primary caregivers for children involved in the public child welfare system.

In the next and final step of data analysis from strand 1 of our research design, we once again integrated qualitative and quantitative data to provide some clues to possible protective processes. First, quantitative findings revealed that, as a group, children showed very high levels of externalizing behaviors including aggression; however, a number of girls and boys showed few behavioral problems. Emic coding of child interview narratives revealed, for a number of children, the presence of a positive grandparent. We wanted to examine this connection in order to explore the role of grandparent involvement as a potential protective factor for children from methamphetamine–involved families. Table 8.5 shows the results from our integrative qualitative and quantitative analyses, and illustrates the back and forth conversation of the quantitative and qualitative data.

First, qualitative data from the interviews indicated that half of our children spontaneously described a positive supportive relationship with a grandparent. As a group, children who described such relationships scored significantly lower on CBCL externalizing including the aggression subscale than children who did not mention a positive grandparent. Next, we returned to the qualitative data to better understand this relationship. Children's interviews provided some clues as to how grandparents may support children. As you might expect, children described that grandparents provided shelter and material support when their parents were incapacitated because of substance abuse; some provided psychological support. Interestingly, the largest subcategory of support mentioned by children was leisure.

When we returned to a review of the developmental research, we learned that leisure is an important developmental context for school-aged children and adolescents. Some children in our study described a variety of activities with their grandparents including mushroom picking, fishing, walking in the forest, swimming in ponds, going to fairs, raising animals, and participating in church and youth sports. These leisure activities provided alternatives to parents' drug parties, helped children to develop healthy skills they could use to enjoy their spare time, and also exposed children to nondelinquent peers and other presumably well-functioning adults.

Discussion

Returning to the initial impetus for this research project—to assist practitioners in better understanding the complex needs of the target population in order to build more effective interventions—we were able to use results from our first strand of research to identify a problem area and associated risk factors for child maladjustment. Additionally, we were able to identify a group of high-risk girls for whom mental health intervention should be of highest priority. In line with strengths-based social work practice, the next step involved the identification of protective factors in order to begin to build preventive interventions.

Strand 2: Cause-Probing, Sequential QUANT → qual Design for the Primary Purpose of Initiation and Secondary Purpose of Complementarity

Prior to beginning strand 2 of our research program, we used what we had learned in strand 1, in combination with evidence-based practice in children's mental health, to design an intervention tailored to the needs of rural children from families involved with child protection and methamphetamine abuse. In the second strand of our mixed methods research program, we evaluated our intervention using an experimental design elaborated using qualitative data. This strand emphasized the quantitative component to confirm or disconfirm the effectiveness of the intervention, but had a significant qualitative component used to explore the experiences of children who participated in the intervention, their caregivers, and community professionals who implemented the intervention. Our primary purpose for mixing quantitative and qualitative approaches in this strand primarily was initiation. By investigating our mental health intervention for children from rural methamphetamine-involved families using both quantitative and qualitative methods we aimed to uncover any contradictions, dissonance, or paradox and in so doing to strengthen our understanding and the intervention. Secondly, we intended qualitative and quantitative components to be complementary, providing a broader understanding of the impact of the intervention on the mental health of rural children from methamphetamine-involved families.

Life Story Intervention

We designed Life Story Intervention specifically for rural children from families involved with methamphetamine. Life Story Intervention is narrative based, drawing on local story telling traditions. Narratives of personal experience have composed a central component of a wide range of therapies. Therapists working within a narrative framework emphasize the importance of creating stories as a way to help children interpret and gain a feeling of control and continuity in their lives, rethink views of themselves and others, and begin to alter problematic beliefs. In the context of children's own stories, clinicians also educate and correct misinformation about substance abuse.

Life Story Intervention also is a relationship-based intervention. Many children in our study suffered from clinically significant levels of trauma. There are a range of approaches to intervention with traumatized children from psychodynamic to cognitive behavioral. A common characteristic of these diverse approaches is the importance of establishing a trusting relationship with a reliable, supportive adult (*see* Haight, Ostler, et al., 2009, for literature review).

We recruited rural, community-based, master's degree level professionals experienced in working with children to administer the intervention. They were retired teachers, child welfare professionals, and master's level social workers and counselors. We asked each one to work with one or two children. They brought to our project much experience and wisdom in working with children. They also understood local narrative practices. Narrative seems to be a universal human practice, but the conventions for story telling are culturally specific. These *community grandparents* received weekly training and supportive supervision from a PhD level clinical psychologist or psychiatrist experienced in working with traumatized children and drug-involved families.

Life Story Intervention was administered while children and community grandparents were engaged in culturally normative activities in and around the children's homes. By bringing the intervention to the children, we sidestepped a perennial obstacle in rural areas: access to mental health care. Providing care in and around children's own homes and communities also gave us insights into children's functioning as we observed their interactions with family and community members. Children's natural environments also provided many cues that supported them in telling their life stories. For example, after she saw a truck similar to the one her father had driven, one girl began to talk for the first time of her father, then imprisoned for methamphetamine production.

Life Story Intervention was administered over approximately a seven-month period during which time children met individually with their local community grandparents for weekly sessions lasting one hour. In the first phase of the intervention, lasting approximately two months, community grandparents focused on establishing an emotionally supportive relationship with the children. They engaged in activities such as walking in the woods, eating at fast food restaurants, and playing with pets. The focus of the next approximately four months was the co-construction of personal narratives. Children were invited, but never pressured, to talk about their lives in familiar surroundings in and around the home while engaged in familiar activities they enjoyed such as fishing, mushroom hunting, or visiting a fast food restaurant. Termination issues were the focus of the final month of Life Story Intervention. During this time, the end of the intervention was discussed with children, and mementos of the time spent together (e.g., stories, pictures, and other artwork) were created. The children knew that they would not be seeing their community grandparents weekly, but that like former teachers they would be present in the community and would remain interested in their lives. Several dyads developed ongoing rituals such as meeting for birthdays or other important occasions including graduations and adoptions. In addition, children were helped to identify a trustworthy supportive adult in their existing social network, for example, a grandparent or teacher, who could provide ongoing emotional support.

Pilot Evaluation of Life Story Intervention. The second strand of our research was designed to evaluate the effectiveness of Life Story Intervention (LSI). In this case, we used a QUANT → qual research design, where the quantitative component was implemented first and was dominant in answering the primary cause-probing research questions:

- Do children who receive Life Story Intervention show significantly less externalizing behaviors following the intervention than those in a wait-list control group?
- Are any treatment gains maintained over a six-month follow-up interval?
- In this design, the qualitative component was implemented second and was intended to answer the question: How do children, their caregivers, and professionals experience the intervention? (Haight, Black, et al., 2010).

We invited twenty-five children to participate, selecting from all children involved with a rural field office due to parental methamphetamine misuse during the previous three-month period. A risk of using a relatively small sample size was that our study would be inadequately powered to detect effects of the intervention that were modest, that is, that we would make a Type II error (fail to reject a false null hypothesis that the intervention is ineffective). The issue of low power was somewhat lessened by our longitudinal design in which each participant provides data at multiple time points. Even after we identified children to participate, it was very difficult to retain them, because their family lives were chaotic, for the entire intervention. The advantage of our relatively small sample was our ability to invest significant resources to address issues of retention and to provide an intervention that was intensive and sustained, realistically the most likely to affect children with multiple needs.

Twenty children agreed to participate. They were randomly assigned to an intervention group or wait list comparison group, balancing for gender and age. All children received the standard child welfare intervention (typically, placement in foster care). In addition, the children in the intervention group received Life Story Intervention. During this time, the children on the wait list served as a comparison group. Fifteen children completed the study: eight from the intervention and seven from the wait list group. These fifteen children were followed for a total of thirteen months. At the completion of the study, children in the wait list group received Life Story Intervention. Although they had to wait longer to receive the intervention, these children likely benefited from the feedback and experience we gained from having administered it with the initial group of children.

Children were administered a battery of standardized assessments including the CBCL at pretest, posttest, and follow-up. These assessments corresponded to months 1, 7, and 13 for the children in the intervention group. Children in the intervention group, their caregivers, and community grandparents also participated in qualitative interviews. They were asked to "tell . . . about your experiences with Life Story Intervention. In what ways was Life Story Intervention helpful? How was it challenging? How would you recommend that we improve Life Story Intervention?"

Table 8.6 summarizes the mixed methods analysis of Life Story Intervention. It is an integrated data display that shows the back and forth conversation between qualitative and quantitative components of our cause-probing design. A repeated measures analysis of variance (ANOVA) revealed a statistically significant group (intervention or wait list) by time (pretest or posttest) interaction for children's externalizing behavior. As shown in the figure within Table 8.6, externalizing scores for the intervention group children decreased modestly whereas those for the wait list children increased modestly from times 1 to 2. Intervention group gains remained stable over the seven-month follow-up period.

The interviews provided some clues as to how the intervention may have been helpful and how it needed to be improved. Children and their

TABLE 8.6
Mixed Methods Analysis of Life Story Intervention

Integrated display of quantitative and qualitative data

Quantitative Analyses	Qualitative Analyses
Mean externalizing over time for control and intervention groups	Interview Responses

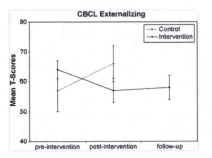

Children & Caregivers:
Enjoy relationship
Helpful: share, solve problems
Problem: Too focused on unpleasant memories

Community Grandparents:
Enjoy relationship
Emotionally & clinically difficult
Boundaries difficult

caregivers said that they enjoyed the relationship with their community grandparents and found it helpful to share and solve problems with them. For fourteen-year-old Brad, it was important that Lynn (a community grandmother) was "a local person." As he elaborated, "It helped that I already knew Lynn from before. She lived around here so I'd seen her around the area and one of my brother's best friend's mother is Lynn's daughter" (Haight, Black, et al., 2010, p. 1451).

When asked about the intervention, several children discussed the importance of having someone to talk to about problems and share memories about their families. Brad, whose foster mother maltreated him, emphasized Lynn's role:

> most of the time we just talked about things. Usually it was problems I was having with B (foster mother) or something like that. . . . it's just having somebody to talk to. Somebody I know that I can talk to that understands . . . it's like kinda relieving to know that somebody else listens to you and understands you and cares about what's happening to you. . . . She (Lynn) understood everything I was going through and kinda helped me with it. (Haight, Black, et al., 2010, p. 1451)

Of course, not all children responded so positively. Some participants critiqued Life Story Intervention as too focused on unpleasant memories. Eleven-year-old Miranda noted:

I really didn't like it. . . . I don't know why . . . I just didn't like it at all. . . . But then, after a while it was kind of fun . . . and then I didn't like it and we had to talk about my past tense and I just got out of that and I was feeling like I was being pulled back in . . . and she asked me, "Do you want to talk about your family?" and I said, "No . . . Because I'm trying to get over what's happened in the past and I'm trying to start a new one . . . what I'm trying to say is that I really didn't like talking about my past." (Haight, Black, et al., 2010, pp. 1451–1452)

Community grandparents said that they enjoyed the relationships with the children, but noted that these children represented some of the most emotionally and clinically challenging cases of their careers, and that boundaries were difficult to establish in the informal home- and community-based contexts of the intervention. Lynn (a community grandparent) said:

Meeting with Jason has been a wonderful experience for me as far as getting to know a delightful young man. I have also been touched emotionally by Jason: the thought of all of the loss he has suffered, his desire to "be normal," and the struggle as he lets go of his family of origin while attempting to connect with his foster/adoptive family has been heart wrenching for me. . . . I am not sure how well I have been able to keep a "professional distance" due to the informality of our meetings and the needs that Jason brings to this relationship. . . . As [supervisor] reminded me often, these kids truly do "hook us" emotionally, and it is definitely a challenge to maintain the role of professional in such an informal atmosphere. (Haight, Black, et al., 2010, p. 1452)

Opportunities and Challenges to Research Quality

An advantage to flexible emergent mixed methods designs is that we have the opportunity to discover new knowledge. In this case, we did not anticipate girls' narratives of their own physical aggression or the potential protective role of children's relationships with their grandparents, many of whom had misused substances when their own children were growing up. All research designs are subject to particular challenges and limitations. In this case, more research needs to be done to replicate any gender differences in externalizing behaviors in children from rural drug-involved families and to understand their origins, and more research is needed to explore systematically potential protective factors such as positive relationships with grandparents. In addition, the pilot intervention, Life Story Intervention, needs to be scaled up and evaluated. Further, our qualitative analyses suggest a number of ways in which Life Story Intervention needs to be strengthened—for example, by increasing supportive supervision of community grandparents and focusing more on children's present circumstances and more hopeful future.

This research program also reflects challenges more broadly characteristic of mixed methods research. In particular, the quantitative component of the evaluation of Life Story Intervention was weakened by a relatively small sample size. Because resources were diverted into the qualitative component of the evaluation of Life Story Intervention, fewer resources were available to search out, recruit, and retain a larger sample of children for the quantitative analysis. Similarly, more in-depth qualitative analysis of the intervention could have been accomplished, such as changes in perspectives over time from the beginning of the intervention through the six-month follow-up, if resources were not expended on the quantitative component. The goal of mixed methods research is to balance these inevitable trade-offs with the advantages gained through the integration of qualitative and quantitative approaches. In our research, we attempted to balance the limitations of somewhat less elaborate qualitative and quantitative components with the gains in understanding emerging from the conversation between qualitative and quantitative components.

The Experiences of Our Community-Based Social Work Coinvestigator

An important component of our mixed methods research program with rural polysubstance-involved families was the involvement of community professionals as partners. Linda Kingery was one of the MSW level social workers who first approached Wendy Haight about children from methamphetamine-involved families. She participated actively as a coinvestigator and coauthor of research publications over approximately a six- year period. She also served as a community grandparent for two children in Life Story Intervention. At the time we started the research, Linda was a child protection worker and had been working with rural substance-involved families for more than twenty years. Our ability to engage rural professionals and methamphetamine-involved families was possible only because of our community-based social work partners. Linda, in particular, was well respected by law enforcement and other professionals in her community and had unusually positive relationships with families. It is unlikely that we university-based social workers would have been able to even talk with methamphetamine-involved families were we not introduced as friends of Linda. Furthermore, our community partners coached us university-based social workers in our interactions with rural drug-involved families and helped us to interpret their responses. They were critical to the design, implementation, and evaluation of Life Story Intervention.

CONCLUSION

The promise of mixed methods research is to provide a deep and broad understanding of pressing social issues such as substance misuse that face social workers on a daily basis. Mixed methods research draws on the range of social science research tools and tailors them to address particular observational and cause-probing research questions. These designs are flexible and emergent. Sometimes the final design emerges only as data from one method or strand of research informs the other. Many mixed methods studies will not fit perfectly in any one design. Nonetheless, a number of eminent scholars in mixed methods research have presented useful typologies of mixed methods designs. These typologies are not necessarily intended to be comprehensive, nor are they intended to be followed in a script-like fashion. Rather, they can be useful models for thinking about the potential scope, diversity, and flexibility of complex mixed methods designs including that of our study of the impact of parental methamphetamine misuse on rural children.

We encourage you to integrate the concepts we've introduced in this book to design a study in your area of interest. The outline presented in Box 8.2 can be used to generate a generic mixed methods grant proposal or begin a mixed methods capstone project, master's thesis, or dissertation proposal. To achieve the full potential of mixed methods designs it is necessary to carefully plan the integration of qualitative and quantitative components. It is equally necessary to remain flexible and be open to modifying this plan as the study progresses and the qualitative and quantitative components interact in mutually informative and even unexpected ways. In other words, plan carefully *and* be open to surprises! In Appendix A, we include Johanna Creswell Báez's mixed methods dissertation proposal described in chapter 9. In Appendix B, we include the research plan of the grant proposal, funded by the National Institute of Drug Abuse (NIDA), for the first strand of the parental methamphetamine study described in this chapter.

••

BOX 8.2
Building a Mixed Methods Social Work Research Project: Putting All the Pieces Together— Mixed Methods Research Proposal Outline

Introduction *(Refer especially to chapter 4)*
1. State the problem to be addressed.
2. Discuss the problem and motivation of the study in relation to the existing literature.
   A. Consider interdisciplinary literature as appropriate for your particular problem.
   B. Consider academic research as well as practice and policy literature as appropriate.
3. State your specific research questions or hypotheses.
   A. Consider questions and hypotheses generated from quant and qual perspectives.

4. Briefly describe your approach and rationale.
   A. Describe why you have chosen a mixed methods approach. In particular, specify the relative advantages of mixed over mono method approaches for addressing this particular problem.

Method *(Refer especially to chapters 5–8)*

1. Design
   A. Is your design observational, cause probing, or some combination?
   B. Describe the mixed methods design features (i.e., purpose, priority of methods, sequence, integration, number of strands/phases of the research or signature mixed method design (i.e., as described by John Creswell, 2015).
   C. Describe any design features you are employing to enhance rigor (reduce validity threats), such as random assignment to intervention and comparison groups or multiple coders for qualitative analyses.
2. Site
   A. Describe where the research will be conducted.
   B. Describe how qual and quant priorities for site selection will be balanced/integrated.
3. Participants
   A. Include sampling and recruitment strategies, desired participant characteristics, and any assignment to group.
   B. Describe how qual and quant priorities for sampling will be balanced/integrated.
4. Measures/instruments
   A. Indicate all measures used and connect them to your research questions/ hypotheses.
   B. Include psychometric properties of any quantitative measures.
   C. Include any interview and document review guides and plans for participant observation for qualitative components.
5. Procedures
   A. Describe how the data will be collected, or in the case of secondary analyses, how data were collected. What will/did participants experience?
6. Analysis plan
   A. Outline a plan for quant and qual data and any interaction between them.
7. Human subjects protections
   A. Describe risks to participants. Do not forget to include psychological risks such as distress upon revisiting difficult experiences.
   B. Describe how you are minimizing risks to participants.

    C. Do a risk/benefit assessment. Do benefits to individuals and/or to the field in general outweigh the risks to participants?
8. Engaging community partners
    A. Describe how you will engage community partners in your research as appropriate.

Discussion

1. Summary (focus on connection and contribution to existing research).
2. Strengths (focus on method).
3. Limitations (focus on method).
4. Implications (hypothetical: consider possible contributions to research, practice, and policy).

• •

SUGGESTIONS FOR ADDITIONAL READING

Creswell, J. (2014). *Research Design: Qualitative, quantitative, and mixed methods approaches* (4th ed.). Los Angeles: SAGE.

    Chapter 10 of this textbook contains some excellent graphic illustrations of mixed methods designs. It is appropriate for MSW or PhD students.

Creswell, J. (2015). *A concise introduction to mixed methods research.* Los Angeles, CA: SAGE.

    This textbook includes Creswell's more recent conceptualization of mixed methods research designs. It is appropriate for MSW or PhD students.

Creswell Báez, J. (2014). *Testing and explaining a social emotional learning program and the intersection of trauma in urban, low-income students: A mixed methods study*. Dissertation proposal submitting in partial fulfillment of the PhD requirements, Smith College.

    This mixed methods dissertation proposal can provide a model for PhD students planning their own mixed methods dissertation.

Part 3

Building a Twenty-First-Century Mixed Methods Social Work Research Career

---

In the coming years it is expected that there will be more mixed-methods research. Moreover, it appears there will be fewer debates about quantitative or qualitative methods; instead, it is likely there will be more attempts at including multiple methods within the same studies. New debates might deal with best practices for combining research methods, and to what extent diverse methods stemming from different epistemological points of view can be combined (Tripodi and LaLayants, 2008, p. 515).

In Part 3, we will conclude with some reflections on building a mixed methods social work research career as well as on challenges and opportunities for mixed methods social work researchers as we progress through the twenty-first century:

- Chapter 9. Finding Mentors, Working in Teams, Writing, and Publishing
- Chapter 10. Opportunities and Challenges

9

Finding Mentors, Working in Teams, Writing, and Publishing

There's success and there's success. There's external success and those standards are clear, but then there's internal success. Whose definition of success are you interested in? A lot of young professionals coming into academia have that desire to understand. If they don't nurture that, they're taking a big risk in terms of what life is gonna mean to them down the road. But they have to figure out "How do I negotiate the requirements of academia with what I'm really interested in?" And I think that's the big question for younger people. The overall point is that, yes, do what you have to do to have the external success, but at the same time don't let that flame go out. So take two hours every week at the same time doing what really turns you on. And that could be writing a theoretical paper. That could be doing focus groups or interviews or doing extra reading or whatever it is, but you surely have two hours a week to keep that flame going. And then once young people are more used to being professors, there are ways that they can leverage that. But you don't wanna risk that flame going out. It will compromise your physical and mental health. This work has been very challenging to me, but wonderfully so. And I've worked very closely with practitioners and talk about "flow" there. That was just marvelous. When I'm sitting in my rocking chair at the nursing home, I can reminisce about the incredible experiences I had with practitioners working on [research] projects they wanted done. (J. Gilgun, personal communication, April 30, 2014)

In the above interview excerpt, Jane Gilgun provides some important advice to early career social work researchers as she reflects on her decades-long career in social work research: maintain a strong connection to work that is meaningful despite external pressures and the fads of the day. A fact of life for contemporary social work graduate students, professors, and professionals is that we all must balance many competing demands. There is no doubt that conducting mixed methods research is challenging. Yet looking back on her own career, Gilgun emphasizes the profound and sustaining joy she has experienced from pursuing pioneering research on meaningful topics, the depth and breadth of which would not have been possible without the integration of qualitative and quantitative traditions. In this chapter we will discuss issues new social work researchers may confront as they build their mixed methods research careers. We will begin with the reflections of two early career researchers on finding mentors. We will conclude with brief discussions of working in research teams and writing and publishing mixed methods social work research based on our own experiences.

FINDING MENTORS

In this chapter, we will highlight the reflections of two early career social work researchers who are poised to take leading roles in the twenty-first century. Daphne Watkins, assistant professor at the University of Michigan, has already established herself as a mixed methods social work researcher. Johanna Creswell Báez, PhD candidate at Smith College School of Social Work and director of a nonprofit in New York City, is engaged in mixed methods research for her dissertation. One common theme across these two interviews is the challenges individuals beginning their research careers face due to inadequate educational opportunities in graduate schools of social work. Mixed methods courses typically are not offered in schools of social work and, if they are available to social work students, they are taught in other professional schools such as education, nursing, or public health. Social work students are typically presented with separate courses in qualitative methods and quantitative methods and then expected to pursue one of these two methodological areas in their own research. Watkins and Báez instead actively sought the mentors and education they needed to conduct mixed methods research outside of their schools of social work.

Conducting a Mixed Methods Social Work Dissertation

When we interviewed Johanna Creswell Báez, she was a PhD candidate at the Smith College School of Social Work. She graciously shared with us her dissertation proposal (see appendix A) and participated in an interview that focused on her experience as a graduate student involved with mixed methods research. She represents a new generation of social work researchers who will bring attention to the importance of mixed methods research to the social work profession. In our interview, Báez described the path that led her to mixed methods research, some of the challenges that she encountered along the way as a social work doctoral student, and how she addressed them.

As is the case with many social work graduate students around the country, Báez brings to her dissertation rich practice experience. She is the cofounder and director of Wediko Children's Services New York, a nonprofit offering school-based mental health services for youth and families within seventeen public schools in low-income minority communities in New York City. Using a trauma-informed clinical lens, Wediko aims to build social and emotional skills with youths and families who are struggling. The program includes a comprehensive system of school-based educator workshops, parent outreach, and individual and group counseling for youth. Báez's work in Wediko became her inspiration for her mixed methods dissertation. She wanted to understand and evaluate the multifaceted work of Wediko. She chose a mixed methods design in order to: (1) assess the impact of Wediko on youths' socioemotional skills and problem behaviors, (2) explore the moderating effects of trauma, and (3) use qualitative data to better understand and interpret quasi-experimental outcomes pertaining to social and emotional skill building and trauma. Quantitative components of her study include a pre-post measurement of youths' social and emotional skills and a measure of trauma exposure. Qualitative components include youths' lived experiences of the program, including the types of social and emotional skills they felt they had learned in the program and how trauma affects their learning.

In our interview, Báez spoke about some of the challenges that she has encountered in using mixed methods as a new researcher. Similar to many PhD programs that focus on particular qualitative or quantitative approaches, the doctoral program at Smith College as described by Báez is primarily mono method in focus. In this case, she found her program to be focused more on qualitative methods with a curriculum designed to support qualitative dissertations. However, she had encountered some articles on mixed methods research in her doctoral social work research methods class and felt that this approach might be a better fit for her specific research interests:

> I was reading an article and learning about these [paradigm] wars going on and they talk about what mixed methods is in this article and that there's a journal for it. It was just an "ah-ha" moment. Like *this makes sense*. I'm a director of a nonprofit in New York City and we often need numbers, numbers, numbers! But what I find is when I sit and tell the stories of a student it illuminates what I know. (J. Báez, personal communication, June 13, 2013)

Báez realized that she would need to take the initiative in finding resources for learning to conduct mixed methods research and discovered a resource in her own family. Her father, John Creswell, is a leading educational psychologist and mixed methodologist. Up until that point, Báez had not made a conscious connection between her father's scholarship and her own research interests. She thought that it would be beneficial for her and her peers to learn more about mixed methods and invited her father to present at Smith College. She describes this visit:

> Smith is very clinical. We've got a really rigorous clinical, psychodynamic training in addition to research. [My dad started] out his talk, talking about the bombings that happened at the 2013 Boston marathon. He had sent me

the slides beforehand and said: "I'll start out my talk talking about all the numbers, the temperature that was there, how many runners, and then I'm going to talk about the stories and my own story (he was watching close to the finish line)." I think he was teaching at Harvard [at that time] so he had a qualitative story that went behind [all the numbers]. It was a great opening and he opened [our eyes to] how important it is to merge these two different stories (qualitative and quantitative). What if he would have just stuck with the numbers rather than sharing his personal story? And then another cool thing he did is he walked us through different social work articles and how they were using mixed methods. (J. Báez, personal communication, June 13, 2014)

Báez used her father's visit as a jumping-off point. The framework he provided for the deliberate integration of qualitative and quantitative traditions allowed her to make connections to her previous education in mono method qualitative and quantitative research. In her work as a social work doctoral student, she had been educated primarily in qualitative research, and as an undergraduate and postbaccalaureate researcher at the National Institutes of Health (NIH) in the field of neuroscience, she had been educated within a quantitative tradition. Based on her own experiences in both traditions, she saw the utility of mixing methods in a way that would capture the complex nature of human experience using both numbers and stories.

To gain a better understanding of mixed methodology, Báez read textbooks by John Creswell and other authors that provided a framework to support her work and give her a vocabulary and set of tools as she began her research. She also sought out more formal training including a two-day workshop on Mixed Methods in Mental Health Services Research offered in the summer institute at Johns Hopkins Bloomberg School of Public Health.

Báez explained that she began her mixed methods journey understanding that she didn't have mentors who were well versed in mixed methods, but was confident that she could put together a strong group of faculty members from both qualitative and quantitative traditions who were respectful of diverse social science research traditions and open to mixed methods approaches. She also stated that, without consultation with John Creswell, it would have been much more difficult for her to engage in mixed methods research for her dissertation. When asked to reflect on the challenges facing many social work doctoral students interested in mixed methods research, Báez said that, for students especially, venturing outside of more familiar approaches can be intimidating: "You just want to be safe. You want to do qualitative or quantitative. I don't think I'd be doing the mixed methods dissertation if my dad hadn't [introduced me to it]." She argued, "We need the curriculum to be there. We need more social work scholars who are trained in it, who are at least doing research with mixed methodology, and who can turn that information back to their students."

Launching a Mixed Methods Social Work Research Career

Daphne Watkins is an early career researcher who studies black men's mental health (*see* Watkins, 2012; Watkins & Neighbor, 2012). At the time of our interview with her, she was assistant professor of Social Work and Psychiatry at the University of Michigan and a faculty associate at the Research Center for Group Dynamics, Institute for Social Research. Realizing the need for resources within social work, she developed one of the first mixed methods online certificate programs for social work graduate students and professionals.

Watkins' research on the mental health of black men began in the early 2000s when she was a graduate student. Her interests grew out of personal experiences growing up with black men in her family and in her local community. As a doctoral student, she engaged in both qualitative and quantitative research, not anticipating that this path would lead to a very fulfilling mixed methods program of research. At that time, there was little research on black men's mental health, and she focused primarily on qualitative approaches. Measures or tools had not yet been developed that contained the right questions for this group of men. Watkins wanted to begin by asking questions and getting a handle on mental health issues from the perspectives of the black men themselves to better understand their experiences and to build a language to probe these issues further.

Watkins felt that as a PhD student she had built a strong base in qualitative research and was interested in building an equally strong base in quantitative methods. As a postdoctoral researcher at the University of Michigan, she engaged in quantitative survey research that complemented the stories she had compiled through her qualitative investigations. She took a number of quantitative courses and workshops in order to strengthen her skills and knowledge base. In our interview with her, Watkins described how she began using mixed methods, and how she overcame challenges in integrating qualitative and quantitative traditions as a new researcher:

> So, I kind of fell into it [mixed methods research]. And at the time I started doing mixed methods, I didn't know it was called mixed methods. I just knew that I had a topic for which I had incredible interest and I really wanted to dive deeper into the topic and become an expert in that topic. And I have problems that I need to solve, and I don't care how I do that. I don't care what methods I use, who I talk to. For me it was about the research question more than the method. And then one morning I woke up and all of a sudden people started calling me a mixed methods researcher. That's sort of how it happened for me. But I consider myself an interdisciplinary researher—as sort of the poster child for interdisciplinary work. I have training in anthropology and public health. My first postdoc involved working alongside social psychologists and then I did another postdoc in the department of ob-gyn at the medical school. And so I'd come at my problem with very different

perspectives and angles and lenses. And along the way I just learned research methods in each of these different disciplines. And I think at some point I realized if I can just take a little bit from all of these different disciplines, I can solve my problems. I can solve the community-based problems that I see. I think I was fortunate to have doctoral mentors and advisors who said, "Ok Daphne, you're the only one focusing on this topic at our school, we don't know how to advise you, but we'll help you get whatever you need." And so I was very much in tune with what I needed to get my questions answered. There was no formal mixed methods class. There were formal qualitative classes and quantitative classes but they were across campus. For example, the majority of my statistics classes were in educational psychology. And then later on in my career, I put it all together and said, "Oh my goodness, this has been around for a while and it's called mixed methods." (D. Watkins, personal communication, June 27, 2014)

Watkins' story reflects the stories of many mixed methods social work researchers. They are passionate about their research questions and are likely to have engaged in interdisciplinary work. Many embrace the need for a holistic approach to very practical questions. In our interview with Watkins, she described what keeps her research moving forward and why she finds mixed methods research so compelling including from an ethical standpoint:

I always kept the question at the forefront. And for me I always told myself that I owe it to my participants to have the best methods, the most rigorous approach to addressing this problem. The communities I want to help deserve the best quality research I can provide. I should know this topic so well that I am fine with being considered the mixed methods police. So it's exciting and I find that at the end of the day I really want to do something to improve mental health outcomes for black men. I like knowing that my work is rigorous and it takes into account various methods to help really unpack and uncover what it is that makes men feel like they can't be open and free with how they express their masculinities. Because there's a lot of work out there that talks about how men who tend to adhere to traditional masculine ideologies have poor mental health. And I think that's *definitely* the case in the black community. These guys are putting on masks and they're saying, "I have to look like this and act like this and be this way." And they are suffering on the inside. And that gets me going. And I find that more than anything else is why I wake up every morning. I see my role in that. I have a voice. (D. Watkins, personal communication, June 27, 2014)

A key feature of Watkins' story is that she used her passion for a particular issue to guide the questions that she asked. Then, she allowed these questions to guide her choice of research methodology. Similar to Báez's experiences, Watkins' PhD program favored mono method research with little guidance for mixed methods dissertations. Watkins' questions, like so many issues in social work, are complex and multifaceted. She needed methods that were equally complex. We asked her to share her advice to social work students interested in mixed methods research:

> I remind my students almost on a daily basis that you cannot compare your journey to anyone else's because that will be the kiss of death. The day that you begin to compare yourself to other people is really the day that you don't let your own light shine. Because when we begin to use other people as our measuring sticks, a lot of times we can restrict our own growth, because we feel like, "Hey, compared to this person, I've done better or worse." And we don't really see our own journey as *our* journey. It's almost like we have blinders on and we don't open ourselves up to all these different experiences that may have *nothing* to do with your work but somehow inform your work. I really don't feel like I blossomed as a researcher until I stopped comparing myself to other people, and I stopped apologizing for my differences. So I encourage my students to not apologize for how you feel, for what you do, and for not having the same journey as someone else.
>
> My advice would be to find mentors who, if they don't know mixed methods, appreciate it enough to make sure you get what you need to be successful. I think I was fortunate in that my mentors—I always encourage students to have multiple mentors—I don't think any of them did mixed methods, but they appreciated it. And they made sure I got what I needed. And I think a lot of times as doctoral students it's almost as if we feel like we have to do what our major professor does whether we like it or not, but that wasn't my story at all. My story was like this: I sort of came to my mentors and I said, "Okay, you are my dream team of mentors, this is what I want to do." And they were on board with that. And they said, "You need to talk to this person and you need to read this book." And I loved that instead of them saying, "Oh well, you don't do what I do so you need to go work with someone else." So my advice to doctoral students is certainly read everything, learn everything, but particularly for doctoral students, they need someone to take them under their wing, or several people to take them under their wings, who if they're not experts in mixed methods—because we're few and far between—appreciate it enough to make sure that they get what they need. (D. Watkins, personal communication, June 27, 2014)

WORKING ON RESEARCH TEAMS

As mixed methods researchers move through their careers, they likely will work within research teams. Given the complexity of issues addressed by many mixed methods programs of research, it often is desirable to collaborate with colleagues from allied professions, those with diverse life experiences and those with different types of technical expertise necessary to conduct the qualitative and quantitative components with rigor. For example, the research on families involved with child protection and methamphetamine abuse described in chapter 8 included social workers in child protection, a children's clinical psychologist, a psychiatrist with a subspecialty in addiction medicine, and a developmental psychologist. The team also included a social worker raised near the rural community under study by a mother with an addiction. She provided invaluable perspectives on family loyalty and children's experiences as well as engaging stigmatized, substance-involved families. In addition, team members included those with expertise in qualitative, quantitative, and mixed methods.

Even single studies employing mixed methods designs can benefit from diverse research teams. The study of parents with low incomes accused of maltreatment described in chapter 6, for instance, included an expert on propensity score matching and an expert on ethnography. This project also included individuals with varying areas of professional expertise: a lawyer and an expert in child welfare. In addition, the team included two parents and an individual raised in a lower income family.

To be successful, most members of the team should have a basic familiarity with the underlying logic of the mixed methodology as well as quantitative and qualitative components or be motivated to learn. A team leader who has expertise in multiple social science research traditions can focus on integration of qualitative and quantitative components.

Working with others on research teams has many advantages. Clearly, it expands the mental models, the expertise, and the personal and professional perspectives we can draw upon in addressing complex social problems. In addition, such research teams can be very stimulating because members have the opportunity to learn about others' areas of expertise and experiences. Also, research teams can be very social. Planning, conducting, and especially writing about research can be a solitary process. Interacting with others around areas of mutual fascination can be personally enriching and motivating.

Working in mixed methods research teams, however, is not without its challenges, particularly navigating issues of status. Some researchers view other traditions (quantitative or qualitative) as inferior. As we have emphasized throughout the book, both qualitative and quantitative traditions have invaluable contributions to make in understanding and addressing complex social issues. Some researchers view research methods as a hierarchy with randomized controlled trials (that is, experiments using quantitative methods) as the gold standard and other designs viewed as providing inferior information. As we have emphasized throughout this book, research questions determine our design choices and research designs do not ensure valid inferences (see especially chapter 5). Social workers, however, are well versed in navigating the politics of professional teams. School social workers, hospital social workers, and others work successfully within host settings in which the primary service is not social work, and social workers are not necessarily of high social status. These social workers have much to teach those of us working in mixed methods research teams about when and how to assert our own expertise.

WRITING AND PUBLISHING A MIXED METHODS MANUSCRIPT

The first step in planning to write a mixed methods manuscript is to identify an appropriate journal and investigate its requirements for manuscript preparation. Fortunately, more and more journals, including *Journal of Mixed Methods Research, International Journal of Social Research Methodology, Quality and Quantity, International Journal of Multiple Research Approaches*, and *Evaluation*, are publishing mixed methods research. There also are a number of mainstream social work journals including *Social Work* and *Children and Youth Services Review* that publish mixed methods research.

In many respects, writing a strong mixed methods manuscript is no different from writing a strong mono method manuscript. Compelling, well-organized, and well-argued content, as well as clarity, economy, and accuracy of expression, are critical. Given our discussion in part 2 of this book, however, the mixed methods manuscript will have some additional components. In particular, the design section will need to describe the mixed methods design, for example, using Creswell's (2015) typology described in chapter 8, including the rationale for using mixed methods. In various subsections of the methods, separate qualitative and quantitative methods will need to be described as discussed in chapter 6. In addition to qualitative and quantitative results, integrated analyses may be presented in the results as discussed in chapter 7. Thus, the final manuscript likely will be longer than most mono methods manuscripts, sometimes longer than what is allowed by various journals including those that publish mixed methods research. Mixed methods social work researchers have dealt with this challenge in a variety of ways:

First, the mixed methods researcher can seek journals open to mixed methods research that accept longer manuscripts. Finding a high-quality peer-reviewed journal that accepts longer manuscripts has the advantage of allowing the strengths of mixed methods research to be fully communicated. In social work, for instance, *Children and Youth Services Review* not only publishes mixed methods research, but it also does not have strict page limitations. We have published a number of our own mixed methods manuscripts, some more than forty pages long, in this journal. However, not all areas of specialization in social work have journals with such generous page allocations.

The mixed methods social work researcher also may choose to divide parts of the study into separate journal articles. This strategy has the advantage of allowing various members of the research team to take turns as lead author and various components of the study to be more fully elaborated. Mixed methods studies may be divided up in a number of ways. Different mixed methods research questions from a larger study may be published as separate articles. We used this strategy in the larger study of families involved with methamphetamine described in chapter 8. For example, we published as separate journal articles a mixed methods study of physically aggressive girls (Haight, Marshall, et al., 2010) and a mixed methods study of the role of grandparents in preventing children's externalizing behavior problems (Sheridan et al., 2011).

The content of mixed methods studies also may be divided according to professional audiences. We published mixed methods research from the rural methamphetamine study, for instance, in psychiatry (Black et al., 2006), child clinical (Ostler et al., 2007), and social work venues (e.g., Haight, Black, et al., 2010). The articles are from a larger study, but each contains original data, and they are geared toward the concerns of various professional audiences involved in responding to the impact of rural substance abuse on children.

In other cases, mixed methods researchers may publish quantitative and qualitative study components in separate journal articles. This strategy is particularly appropriate for sequential designs in which the qualitative component informs the quantitative component, or vice versa. Jane Gilgun's research on violence described in chapter 4 and Patricia Shannon's research on refugees experiencing war trauma described in chapter 5 are excellent examples of this publication strategy.

If the mixed methods study or program of research is divided into separate journal articles, the researcher may then combine and expand them to tell the whole story in a book chapter or full length book. As long as the research results are first published in a journal, and permission from that journal to reproduce some of the content of the article is granted, authors are free to elaborate and integrate multiple journal articles. We have successfully used this strategy to publish a number of our own programs of research, including the study of rural families involved with methamphetamine (Haight, Ostler, et al. (2009), as peer-reviewed books through university presses.

Finally, it is important to remember that most research manuscripts are not accepted after the first round of reviews. Typically, editors will ask the authors to respond to concerns raised by reviewers. It is critical to address carefully each point in a dispassionate response letter indicating where you have made changes to the manuscript in response to reviewer comments and clearly describing why you chose not to make any other recommended changes. Responding to reviews nearly always strengthens the manuscript. Sometimes, however, reviewers may not respond favorably to mixed methodologies, or the editor may deem the content area of insufficient interest to readers of that journal. In these cases, you may need to submit to a different journal. In any case, it is important to cultivate resilience when embarking on the publication of your research.

Box 9.1 summarizes some strategies for publishing mixed methods manuscripts *after* you have identified relevant journals that publish mixed methods studies.

●●

BOX 9.1

Some Strategies for Publishing Mixed Methods Manuscripts

Strategy	*Advantage*
1. Seek journals with longer page limits.	Allows the strengths of the integrated design to be fully communicated.
2. Divide the larger study into separate journal articles by (a) research question, (b) professional audience, or (c) QUANT and QUAL components.	Allows team members to share lead authorship; allows various study components to be fully elaborated.
3. Reintegrate components of the research published as separate journal articles into a book chapter or full-length academic book.	Allows the full story to be told.
4. Cultivate resilience.	Allows researchers to persevere through the review process.

CONCLUSION

In order to build a mixed methods research career, the next generation of social workers needs texts, courses, and mentors. Yet our graduate curricula by and large remain stuck in the qualitative/quantitative dichotomy of the late twentieth century. Relatively few social work programs offer specific courses in mixed methods research, and mentors for the next generation of mixed methods researchers may be hard to find. Early career researchers also may benefit from guidance in writing up and publishing mixed methods research as well as working on mixed methods research teams comprised of allied professionals and researchers with different commitments to qualitative and quantitative traditions.

10

Opportunities and Challenges

Although social work has a long history of integrating diverse social science methodologies, there has been relatively little mutual exchange between mixed methodologists in other disciplines and social work researchers. Yet such exchanges promise mutual benefits. For mixed methods researchers generally, social work research provides important opportunities for putting theory into action and, in the tradition of American Pragmatism, strengthening theory in response to those transactions. To borrow a metaphor from Dewey, social work research allows us to keep the "vine of pendant theory" firmly attached at both ends to direct experience. Likewise, as we have described throughout this text, mixed methods research offers important opportunities for social work.

OPPORTUNITIES AFFORDED BY MIXED METHODOLOGY TO SOCIAL WORK RESEARCHERS

First, mixed methods inquiry allows social workers to achieve a comprehensive holistic understanding of multifaceted social issues addressed in practice and policy. Mixed methods research draws upon our rich history of social science research, strategically integrating qualitative and quantitative traditions to address particular questions. It does not privilege a priori particular traditions, designs, or methods. Rather, mixed methods researchers choose the perspectives, designs, and methods appropriate for fully and rigorously addressing the social issue under study. Surely an adequate understanding of complex social issues is prerequisite to designing useful interventions and policies, and for effectively evaluating them.

Next, mixed methods approaches can strengthen evidence-based practice. Evidence-based practice depends on integrated (mixed) thinking as qualitative and quantitative research is combined with practitioner (qualitative) knowledge of context and diverse client preferences. Mixed methods research is a model of the deliberate integration of diverse perspectives and methodological traditions. It offers an alternative to a design hierarchy recognizing both the primacy of the research question in design decisions, and validity as a quality of inference and not design.

In addition, mixed methods research can facilitate the engagement of multiple and diverse scholarly, practice, administrative, and policy audiences. Social workers often practice in interdisciplinary contexts that include colleagues who vary in their familiarity and preferences for using qualitative or quantitative methods and reasoning. Mixed methods social work researchers can engage a diverse audience and also address barriers to communication across disciplines.

Further, mixed methods approaches can facilitate the translation of research into practice. Mixed methodology is congruent with social work's commitment to study complex social issues holistically and in context and with its emphasis on diversity. This congruence can enhance communication between social work researchers and practitioners, including about how research can contribute to understanding and address actual problems in practice and policy.

INTERNATIONAL MIXED METHODS SOCIAL WORK RESEARCH

Given the opportunities afforded by mixed methodology, it is not surprising to find many contemporary social workers engaged in mixed methods research. In this book we have highlighted a few mixed methods social work research projects published in English. It is important to underscore, however, that mixed methods social work research is occurring throughout the world, not just in North American and Europe. For instance, May Lee Ku, professor at Fu-Jen Catholic University in Taipei, Taiwan, is conducting a mixed methods evaluation of an intervention for at-risk youth in juvenile corrections facilities and other institutions including those for juvenile prostitutes (M. Ku, personal communication, May 20, 2014). Consistent with the openness of mixed methodologists such as Jennifer Greene to integration at all levels including mental models (see especially chapter 1), the intervention is based on a blend of Confucian philosophy and Catholicism. For the past ten years, Taiwanese Catholic nuns and social workers have begun developing relationships with youths aged twelve to twenty-four, when they are institutionalized, and then have continued to provide support, guidance, and opportunities to them after they are released. The expectation is not that the complex long-term problems in these young peoples' lives are going to be solved by teaching a set of discrete skills or other short-term interventions, but that they will be ameliorated by providing meaningful models of healthy caring relationships over an extended period of five to ten years.

The Catholic perspective is reflected in a variety of ways including the nuns' commitment to doing good works as part of their Christian responsibility. The Confucian assumption underlying the intervention is that everyone is born with a good heart. Through abuse, neglect, or other hardships, youths lose touch with their inherent goodness. Delinquent or other antisocial behavior is a reflection of this loss. The intervention goals are to give youth the opportunity to learn about their good hearts—to get back what they have lost. This is accomplished by patiently showing them kindness and support (including supporting their educations, helping them to get needed medical or mental health care, and giving them opportunities for healthy leisure activities). The youths then gain the self-confidence necessary to become functioning members of a harmonious society.

The qualitative component of Ku's evaluation includes in-depth interviews with youths to explore their relationships with the nuns and social workers. As one youth described, "They are always nagging me [because they have confidence in me], but I like it." The nuns and social workers also discussed with Ku their relationships with the youth. They characterized their relationships with youths as like family, but not family. They have closer relationships than other professionals but are clear that they are not their mothers.

The quantitative component of the evaluation involved a systematic review of case records to describe the referrals, opportunities, and services the nuns provided to the youths. A longitudinal quantitative extension could compare public health records (for example, regarding pregnancies, marriages, divorces, substance abuse, and mental health problems) for youths in the national population and the youths in the intervention. If the nuns and social workers have successfully altered the problematic developmental trajectories of youths in their program, then outcome data from these youths should look very similar to national statistics.

In describing the challenges she has encountered in this evaluation research, Ku indicated that the "poor quality of the case records made it a painstaking process to code." In addition, "the hesitation of the juveniles or their poor education level" sometimes made in-depth discussion of their experiences difficult. In reflecting on advice for new mixed methods researchers, Ku suggests that "you have to expect the unexpected" and she underscores the importance of conducting mixed methods research to understand innovative areas of practice that potentially can "serve as a new frame of reference for the field."

CHALLENGES FACING TWENTY-FIRST CENTURY MIXED METHODS SOCIAL WORK RESEARCHERS

Despite social workers' engagement in mixed methods research, the opportunities it affords, and the alignment of mixed methods research with social work goals, very few social workers have contributed to the lively interdisciplinary discussions of mixed methodology. Given the complex issues social workers address on a daily basis as well as social work's deep roots in American Pragmatism, social workers clearly have much to contribute to interdisciplinary discussions. We also have much to learn from these discussions. There are a number of challenges remaining for social workers engaging with mixed methods research that may compromise their ability to realize the potential of mixed methodology, as well as to participate fully in multi-disciplinary dialogues.

Some widespread challenges confront mixed methods social work researchers as we move into the twenty-first century. First, mixed methods researchers have consistently identified the need for development of integrated data analyses to fully realize the potential for integrated data analysis. As described in chapter 8, some progress also has been made in integrating data analyses (e.g., quantitizing qualitative data, qualitizing quantitative data, and integrating data displays). The development of such strategies, in which mixed methodologists are currently actively engaged, is critical to realize the full potential of mixed methods social work designs.

In addition, chapter 4 indicated that social work scholars have identified purposes for mixing methods including enhanced understanding, rigor, and development. Less attention, however, has been paid to the purpose of mixing for gaining new insights, that is, deliberately juxtaposing diverse perspectives and traditions in the service of provoking fresh insights, new perspectives, and original understandings (Greene, 2007). Engaging with interdisciplinary discussions of mixed methodology may initiate new understanding of the full potential of mixed methods social work research. The purpose of gaining new insights may be particularly significant as social work researchers increasingly engage in research with international communities. Misa Kayama and colleagues, for instance, are using qualitative and quantitative methods to deliberately contrast educators' views of disability in the United States and several East Asian contexts (in Japan, South Korea, and Taiwan) to generate new insights and creative solutions to an intransigent and widespread social problem: the stigmatization of children with disabilities in school.

Next, as with all research, mono or mixed method, compromises are made in the planning and execution of the research design. In a mono method quantitative study employing an experimental design, for instance, adding design features to strengthen internal validity can compromise external validity. In mixed methods research, resources (money, time, investigator and participant energy, etc.) are spread over quantitative and qualitative components and their integration. Often separate quantitative and qualitative components are not as fully developed as they would be if all resources were devoted to a mono method study. The question for social work researchers therefore becomes whether or not the benefits of the integration outweigh the costs for their particular studies.

Further, methodologists have been actively and explicitly working on the development of mixed methods research at least since the 1980s, but many professionals in administrative positions, funders, and other community partners are most knowledgeable about quantitative approaches and may have limited understanding of qualitative or mixed method approaches.

Many will need thorough explanations and demonstrations of the relative strengths and limitations of integrated approaches.

Finally, there are some distinct norms in quantitative and qualitative research that may well conflict, even in the absence of more basic paradigm issues. Amy Krentzman's ongoing research on the role of a positive psychology intervention in recovery from addiction described in chapter 7 provides an excellent example. In her mixed methods evaluation, Krentzman found substantial individual variation among individuals in recovery from alcohol addiction (for example, in how difficult participants found the Three Good Things exercise). Within the qualitative tradition, researchers would draw upon their knowledge of context and individual cases to interpret these outcomes. Failing to do so would be seen by many mono method qualitative researchers as an incomplete and therefore problematic analysis. Yet such interpretive practices certainly would not be acceptable to many mono method quantitative researchers. For them the appropriate course of action might be to set these outcomes aside for examination in future research. Krentzman's gratitude study provides just one small example of the challenges mixed methods researchers may face not only in integrating paradigms, but also in balancing norms across research traditions.

SOME FINAL THOUGHTS

Relative to quantitative and qualitative traditions, mixed methodology clearly is in its adolescence. Yet the time has never been more favorable for social work researchers to actively engage with multidisciplinary efforts to strengthen mixed methods approaches to research. As noted in chapter 9, the number of journals publishing mixed methods research is increasing. In addition, in 2014 the Mixed Methods International Research Association held its first annual international mixed methods conference where scholars from multiple disciplines and countries gathered to discuss mixed methodology. In the United States, the Office of Behavioral and Social Science Research recently issued a resource titled "Best Practices for Mixed Methods Research in the Health Sciences" (Creswell, Klassen, Plano Clark, & Smith, 2011). Although not specific to social work, this resource addresses many relevant topics such as the challenges and opportunities for teamwork in mixed methods research.

Thus, the time is ripe for an explosion of mixed methods social work research. We have an opportunity to reach a wide range of social workers who may have historically found themselves on one side or the other of the paradigm wars. We also have much to gain and much to contribute by engaging with our social science and professional counterparts in areas such as psychology, sociology, public health, education, evaluation, and nursing to further develop mixed methods research.

Appendix A

Dissertation Proposal (Without Appendices)
Testing and Explaining a Social Emotional Learning Program and the Intersection of Trauma in Urban, Low-Income Students: A Mixed Methods Study

JOHANNA CRESWELL BÁEZ, LCSW

Submitted in partial fulfillment of the Degree of Doctor of Philosophy

Smith College School for Social Work, Northampton, MA 01063

INTRODUCTION

Statement of Study Issue

The purpose of this study is to examine the intersection of social and emotional learning (SEL) and the known effects of trauma in urban, low-income students participating in Wediko Children's Services school-based programming. Social and emotional learning programs have been found to be highly effective in teaching social and emotional skills to students, reducing problem behaviors, and promoting mental health (Durlak, Weissberg, Dymnicki, Taylor, & Schellinger, 2011; Payton, 2000). Despite the overwhelming evidence of cumulative trauma present in urban low-income students (McKay, Lynn, & Bannon, 2005) and a burgeoning movement to provide trauma-informed care (TIC) in schools (National Child Traumatic Stress Network Schools Committee, 2008), including recent 2014 trauma-informed legislation in Massachusetts for Safe and Supportive Schools (MA-HR 4376, 2014), social and emotional school programming has yet to take into consideration other environmental factors (Durlak & Dupre, 2008) such as trauma. There is currently no empirical research that has specifically evaluated SEL programming for urban low-income students who have been exposed to trauma or to the combination of providing SEL and TIC in schools.

This dissertation will seek to evaluate Wediko's school-based programming with urban low-income students that includes teaching social and emotional learning and trauma-informed approaches to students and staff. This study will evaluate a comprehensive social and emotional learning program, Side by Side, developed by clinical social workers over the past decade at Wediko Children's Services. Wediko's school-based programming is an innovative model that brings together whole-school culture change, professional development for staff, and direct clinical support in the context of the classroom through weekly social and emotional skill building workshops (Side by Side), parent outreach (workshops, home visits, and community referrals), and individual and small group counseling.

Wediko Children's Services, Inc. is a nonprofit organization committed to improving children's lives since 1934. Using a strength-based approach, Wediko responds to the needs of children who face repeated obstacles to development due to emotional, behavioral, environmental, and learning issues (Wediko Children's Services, 2014). Wediko's school-based services provide support to seventeen public schools in New York City (co-founded by the primary researcher, J. C. Báez [JCB], in 2011), thirty public school in Boston, and at Wediko's residential school and summer program in New Hampshire. All of Wediko's New York City school-based services are provided in high-needs districts where students are primarily from low-income minority communities. Many families are single-parent households, 100 percent receive Title 1 funds, and approximately 28 percent live below the poverty line.

To address the mental health needs of students in inner-city urban schools, a comprehensive preventative school-wide approach needs to include social and emotional skill building and trauma-informed approaches. Currently, SEL (Collaborative for Academic, Social, and Emotional Learning [CASEL], 2003, 2013; Elias et al., 1997; Zins & Elias, 2007; Zins, Weissberg, Wang, & Walberg, 2004) and trauma-informed care (Cole et al., 2005; Jennings, 2008; National Child Traumatic Stress Network Schools Committee, 2008) are often practiced and researched as separate fields. Trauma-informed care takes into consideration the need to address the complex social and emotional health needs of urban low-income students (Oehlberg, 2008). A merger between SEL and trauma-informed approaches is necessary in working with the cumulative trauma that is overwhelmingly present in urban low-income students in inner-city schools (McKay et al., 2005).

This mixed methods quasi-experimental study will examine the pre-test and post-test social and emotional skill development and level of problem behaviors using the Social Skills Improvement System rating scales (SSIS–RS; Gresham & Elliott, 2008) for students who have participated in Wediko's school-based programming. The known effects of trauma will be controlled using a trauma assessment scale, the Adverse Childhood Experiences Study (ACE) Questionnaire (Felitti et al., 1998) of the Centers for Disease Control and Prevention (CDC). The trauma questionnaire will be given to students during the intervention to obtain an assessment of previous childhood trauma. The trauma assessment scale will be used based upon a theoretical model of the impact of trauma on students and the benefits of providing trauma informed care in schools (Cole et al., 2005; National Child Traumatic Stress Network Schools Committee, 2008). In addition, after the experiment has been completed, follow-up one-on-one qualitative interviews will be conducted with students depending on level of SEL skill building and trauma to help explain the experimental results. Lastly, a small focus group with students will be held to validate the overall results.

Rationale

There is a timely need to identify intervention models that support social and emotional learning for urban low-income students who often lack access to universal preventive mental health services. Most students in stressed urban school systems are not able to take advantage of school mental health services, and there is a lack of service providers for the high needs of students who would benefit from social and emotional skill building (Cooper, 2008). Further, social and emotional programming in urban low-income schools needs to take into account the students' level of trauma because of the direct link between trauma and impairment in school functioning, including social and emotional competency (Nadeem et al., 2014). Social and emotional programs and trauma-informed practices need to be viewed as *complimentary* programs and approaches that together provide robust mental health services for students. Social and Emotional Learning programs with a trauma-sensitive approach are tailored to the needs of urban low-income students who have a higher percentage of adverse childhood trauma experiences as compared to the general population (Institute for Safe Families, 2013).

This study will make a significant contribution to (a) the scholarly literature, (b) Wediko's evaluation efforts, (c) school-based programming, and (d) the field of clinical social work. To date, there are no empirical studies looking at the intersection of social and emotional skill building and the mediating effects of trauma. Further, a comprehensive evaluation of Wediko's school-based program has yet to be undertaken, although the program has been operating since 1980 in inner-city Boston schools and for the past three years in New York City. To benefit school-based mental health programming, this study will provide the first framework for providing SEL programming combined with TIC for urban low-income students.

Lastly, this study will show that clinical social workers are in a unique position to provide multitiered SEL programming (McKay, 2010) and TIC (Walkley & Cox, 2013) with clinical social workers taking on a training role in a school *and* being trauma-informed practitioners who can provide individualized counseling. According to the Code of Ethics of the National Association of Social Workers (NASW, 2008), social workers strive to enhance the well-being of individuals, families, social groups, organizations, and communities within a social context. School social workers are well suited to becoming SEL leaders in their school communities because of the emphasis they place on the person-in-environment framework, their use of practice approaches from an ecological framework (intervening at micro, meso, and macro system levels), and their role of often serving the students with the most SEL-related needs (Kelly, 2008). From the 2008 National School Social Work Survey, with over 1,600 surveyed, school social workers were found to be the primary and often the only mental health professionals with whom students are engaged in their communities. The survey also found that social workers are practicing primarily with a clinical casework orientation, and recommendations were made for school social workers to become more involved in collaborating with teachers, increasing their roles in prevention activities, and improving overall school culture (Kelly et al., 2010).

Specific Aims

The three specific aims of this study include: (1) to assess the impact of the SEL programming on socio-emotional skill building and problem behaviors in urban low-income students participating in Wediko's school-based program, (2) to understand the moderating effects of trauma in urban low-income students participating in Wediko's school-based program, and (3) to explain the experimental outcomes with qualitative data in terms of level of social and emotional skill building, trauma, and number of Wediko services provided. This leads to several quantitative, qualitative, and mixed methods research questions:

- *Quantitative Research Questions*: Are there pre and post changes in the students' level of social and emotional skills and problem behaviors? Did childhood trauma moderate pre-post intervention changes on overall social skills and problem behaviors? Did the level of Wediko services utilized by students correlate with their SEL change scores?
- *Qualitative Research Question*: What were the primary themes identified by students in terms of social and emotional skills learned in Wediko's school-based programming and during the Side by Side intervention? From students who have different change levels of SEL and different levels of trauma (low, medium, high), what themes emerged in terms of social and emotional skills learned (see Table 1 in Methods section for the purposeful interview sampling)?
- *Mixed Methods Research Questions*: How do the qualitative interview questions explain the experimental outcomes on level of SEL and trauma? Do students who have differing levels of SEL change scores and different levels of trauma differ in their experiences of SEL?

The overall research objective will be to assess the impact of Wediko's school-based programming, including the Side by Side SEL program, with the moderating factor being the level of trauma.

LITERATURE REVIEW

This literature review will address the following three areas: SEL and social skill building, TIC, and the intersection of SEL and TIC.

Social and Emotional Learning (SEL)

There has been a growing body of research over the past two decades on social and emotional skill building and how it relates to improved student outcomes (Durlak et al., 2011; Elias et al., 1997; Zins, Weissberg, Wang & Walberg, 2004). According to CASEL (*see* http://www.CASEL.org), an organization that works to advance the practice of SEL, "schools that encourage social and emotional development reap important rewards for their students, including greater academic success, fewer problem behaviors, and improved relationships between students and significant people in their lives" (CASEL, 2003, p. 6).

Although there is no one definition of SEL programs, social and emotional learning programs seek to provide a process to learn and manage emotions, care for others, make responsible decisions, choose ethical behaviors, and develop supportive relationships (Zins et al., 2004, p. 4). The social piece of SEL focuses on fostering positive relationships with others and the emotional piece focuses on promoting self-awareness of emotions or feelings and the corresponding thoughts. The learning aspect implies a natural link to schools and the concept that emotional growth can be taught and learned (Merrell & Gueldner, 2010, p. 6).

Durlak and colleagues (2011) studied the impact of enhancing students' social and emotional learning through a meta-analysis of 213 school-based SEL programs. The meta-analysis examined only experimental studies with SEL programs that were published by 2007. All of the studies emphasized the development of one or more SEL skills with students ages five to eighteen. The major independent variables were intervention format (class by teacher, class by non-school personnel, or multicomponent programs), the use of recommended practices related to skill development, and reported implementation problems. The dependent variables were in line with previous studies that looked at students' outcomes including social and emotional skills, attitudes toward self and others, positive social behaviors, conduct problems, emotional distress, and academic performance. From the analysis, just under half (47%) of the studies were conducted in urban schools.

The meta-analysis found that SEL programs increased SEL competencies and positive views about self, others, and school. Further, the analysis found

TABLE 1
Mean Effect Sizes of Dependent Variables

Group	SEL skills	Attitudes	Positive social behavior	Conduct problems	Emotional distress	Academic performance
No problems	.86*	.29*	.31*	.27*	.35*	.33*
Implementation problems	.35	.19*	.01	.15*	.15	.14

that classroom teachers effectively conducted SEL programs and that implementation problems moderated positive student outcomes. The study concluded by noting that more attention is needed to attend to systemic factors, environmental factors, and other potential moderators of program outcomes (Durlak et al., 2011). Reported implementation problems were also noted to moderate outcomes. Mean effect sizes (Table 1) were calculated for moderators by outcome categories and it was found that interventions without any implementation problems yielded significant mean effects in all six categories ($^*p \leq .05$).

Although SEL programs have been shown to be highly effective, research has only begun to consider the possible benefits that school-based clinical social workers can provide in SEL program implementation. Overall, school-based social workers are in the unique role of being able to support in-school programming and out-of-school time, including promoting family and community supports (McKay, 2010).

Trauma-Informed Care (TIC)

Trauma-informed care is the missing piece in school reform and is part of a new movement in education that blends education and mental health systems to provide prevention and intervention in a multitiered framework. This movement is designated by several different terms including trauma-sensitive schools (Cole et al., 2005; Cole, Eisner, Gregory, & Ristuccia, 2013), trauma-informed care (Jennings, 2008), compassionate schools (Wolpow, Johnson, Hertel, & Kincaid, 2009), safe and supportive schools (Learning First Alliance, 2001), and safe and successful schools (Cowan, Vaillancourt, Rossen, & Pollitt, 2013). All of these different movements and frameworks have provided the necessary momentum to help schools understand that trauma is playing a key role in many of the problems they are seeing in students, especially in urban low-income students (Kauffman, 2014).

Mental health providers in schools need to incorporate a trauma-informed perspective to enhance the quality of care for all children. The trauma-informed care framework includes such functions as ensuring that children and adolescents are screened for trauma exposure, that service providers use evidence-informed practices, that resources on trauma are available and taught to all in a school, and that there is a continuity of care across all service systems (Ko et al., 2008). Specifically, school-based social workers are in a unique role to be trauma-informed practitioners and trainers, to support the collaboration between all who are involved in a student's life, and to take a leadership role in moving their schools toward whole-school trauma responsive practices (Walkley & Cox, 2013).

Burke, Hellman, Scott, Weems, and Carrion (2011) were the first to investigate the level of adverse childhood experiences in children living in urban neighborhoods and the impact of these experiences on learning and behavior problems. The authors conducted a retrospective review of medical charts from pediatric patients at the Bayview Child Health Center in San Francisco, California. The study looked at nine categories of adverse childhood experiences (ACEs), corresponding to previous ACE studies (Felitti & Anda, 2010; Felitti et al., 1998) including (1) physical abuse; (2) emotional abuse; (3) sexual abuse; (4) an alcohol and/or drug abuser in the household; (5) an incarcerated household member; (6) someone who is chronically depressed, mentally ill, institutionalized, or suicidal; (7) mother treated violently; (8) one or no parents; and (9) emotional or physical neglect. It was found that 67.2 percent ($n = 471$) of the children had experienced at least one or more of the nine ACE categories. Further, an ACE score of 4 or more was associated with significantly increased rates of learning and behavior problems as compared with an ACE score of 0 ($OR = 32.60$, $p < 0.001$), with 51.2 percent of participants with an ACE score equal to or greater than 4 displaying learning/behavior problems. Overall, children were found to be 32 times more likely to be categorized as having a learning problem (i.e., low academic achievement) or behavior problem (i.e., history of violent behavior) than a child with no adverse childhood experiences.

In terms of screening for trauma, the National Survey of Children's Health (NSCH, 2012) found that almost 44 percent of New York City children have experienced at least one or more types of serious childhood trauma. And around 17 percent have experienced two or more adverse trauma experiences. An urban study by the Institute for Safe Families (2013) surveyed a total of 1,784 Philadelphia adults and found a high level of adverse childhood experiences (ACEs) of trauma with over 37 percent reporting four or more ACEs. Further, The National Survey of Child and Adolescent Well-Being (NSCAW, 2013), studied 5,873 children in the child welfare system (ages 2 months to 17.5 years) from 2008 to 2009, and found that 73 percent reported three or more ACEs. And, for surveyed students between the ages of 11 and 17, 68 percent reported four or more ACEs—more than four times the rate of the general population (Stambaugh et al., 2013). Currently, more than twenty states are collecting ACE data and a number of human service agencies in New York City are beginning to routinely assess ACE scores (Scaglione, 2014).

Intersection of SEL and TIC

The culture and politics of school reform has resisted integrating preventative mental health and SEL strategies because of a focus on academic achievement (Aber, Brown, Jones, Berg, & Torrente, 2011). However, efforts should be undertaken to evaluate the multiple environmental factors that hinder or promote effective implementation of SEL programs (Durlak & Dupre, 2008). More attention is needed in SEL research to systemic factors, environmental factors, and other potential moderators of program outcomes (Durlak et al., 2011), including trauma and trauma-informed care.

Despite the high evidence of trauma in urban low-income students (McKay et al., 2005) and state-wide standards for social and emotional learning (New York State Board of Regents, 2011), there is currently no empirical research that has specifically evaluated SEL programming for students who have been exposed to trauma or SEL and trauma-informed practices. A pilot program in California, Unconditional Teaching, with SEL and trauma-informed care, is currently being evaluated (Adams, 2014), but no data exist other than anecdotal evidence that this merger is important for urban low-income students. Further, positive behavioral interventions and supports (PBIS), a research-based framework to provide behavioral and mental health interventions, is beginning to include treatment of traumatized students with social and emotional learning through an Interconnected Systems Framework (ISF) that links school mental health and positive behavioral supports (Barrett, Eber, & Weist, 2013).

One empirical study looked at the effectiveness of a school-based group psychotherapy program with war-exposed Bosnian secondary students with trauma ($N = 159$). The program consisted of a classroom-based psychoeducational and skill intervention program (similar to an SEL program) alone or a treatment group of the classroom intervention and a trauma and grief group therapy intervention. The skill intervention program included teaching common distress reactions, coping skills, relaxation training, skills to self-regulate emotions and behavior, social support skills, and problem-solving skills. The randomized control trial study found significant pretreatment and posttreatment reductions in posttraumatic stress disorder and depression symptoms (both p values $<.01$). Further, the marginal mean (i.e., mean posttraumatic stress score averaged across both groups) decreased significantly between pretreatment ($M = 33.99$, $SD = 13.13$) and posttreatment ($M = 25.60$, $SD = 13.05$). Although this study points to the importance of providing a multitiered intervention (tier 1: school-wide psycho-education and SEL skills; tier 2: trauma and grief groups) for students who have trauma, the study did not specifically evaluate social and emotional learning (Layne et al., 2008).

Lastly, one framework by the New York State Technical and Education Assistance Center for Homeless Students (NYS-TEACHS; 2012) has been

TABLE 2
A Framework for the Intersection of SEL and TIC in Homeless Students

Known effect of trauma	Behavioral manifestation	Relation to social-emotional skills	Consequences or outcome
Social, emotional, and/or cognitive impairment	Overreacting; becoming easily agitated; lashing out	Inability to *self-manage* and/or regulate	Sent out of the classroom (further isolation)
Decreased ability to trust or attach to others	Acting unusually withdrawn or aggressive; lacking appropriate boundaries	Poor or immature *relationship skills*	Social isolation from peers; not asking for help; school detention or suspension (further traumatization)

advanced for homeless students—joining social and emotional learning and trauma-informed care to promote positive educational outcomes. This framework outlines trauma's impact on students, the behavioral manifestations, the relation to social-emotional skills and the consequences or outcomes. The example in Table 2 illustrates the NYS-TEACHS framework for two social and emotional skills.

As is outlined in the above NYS-TEACHS framework, there is a direct link between trauma, social and emotional skill building, and consequences at school. The framework illustrates how students affected by trauma need continual support around social and emotional skills with a trauma-sensitive approach. Overall, the framework outlines that trauma-informed practice fosters social and emotional development.

METHOD

Research Design

A mixed methods intervention explanatory-sequential design will be used (Creswell, 2014). This design uses a single group pre- and post-test quantitative assessment (quasi-experimental design) with qualitative data collection at the end of the intervention. Figure 1 is a diagram of the procedures of this design. The Wediko school-based services will be the intervention, including clinical social workers overseeing the SEL program Side by Side.

Diversity in terms of the methods is important because of the practical demands of assessing real-world social service programming, as well as understanding the contextual stories of the real-life students in urban low-income communities (Greene, 2008). Using mixed methods is recommended when it can offset the weaknesses of both quantitative and qualitative research by explaining and providing more comprehensive evidence and answering questions that cannot be answered by one approach alone, among many other premises (Creswell & Plano Clark, 2011). In the current study, quantitative data will provide a comparison of social and emotional skill level and problem behaviors that will be augmented by qualitative data that can expand or clarify the results, in the words of the students themselves.

Mixed methods designs are also highly applicable to evaluating school-based mental health services with students living in poverty (Cappella, Frazier, Atkins, Schoenwald, & Glisson, 2008), trauma research (Creswell & Zhang, 2009), and social work research, where Padgett (2009) stated, "mixed-methods studies present unique possibilities for synergy and knowledge growth that mono-method studies cannot match." Further, qualitative research is used widely in the field of mental health and social services and is a respected research approach across a variety of disciplines and contexts (Gibbs, 2007). Overall, qualitative research seeks to listen to participants and draw on their experience to better understand their viewpoint through identified themes (Crabtree & Miller, 1999).

Data Source

Data will be collected in one case study school (a middle school in the South Bronx) with urban low-income students. Students will be recruited at the school by Wediko staff. Quantitative data will be collected from students ($N = 100$) completing the standardized measurement. The Social Skills Improvement System (SSIS) rating scales (SSIS–RS; Gresham & Elliott, 2008) will be used to evaluate social skills and problem behaviors pre- and post-intervention. The CDC's ACE Questionnaire modified for adolescents (Felitti et al., 1998) will be used during the intervention to evaluate the level of previous childhood trauma for the students ($N = 100$). Qualitative data will then be collected after the intervention with students in the school ($N = \leq 20$), depending upon level of saturation (Guest, Bunce, & Johnson, 2006), to help explain why the experimental results occurred with SEL programming, the known effects of trauma, and the level of Wediko services provided. The estimated time required for each interview will be thirty minutes and interviews will be completed outside of academic instruction time. Further, other demographic factors such as age, grade, GPA, office disciplinary referrals, and attendance will be collected for all participating students.

Intervention

Wediko's school-based programs, led by clinical social workers, provides whole-school culture change programs (PBIS), professional development for staff (including workshops on PBIS, SEL, and TIC), direct clinical support in the context of the classroom, weekly SEL skill building workshops (Side by Side), parent outreach (workshops, home visits, and community referrals), and individual and small group counseling with a trauma-informed lens. Side by Side is a manual-based weekly SEL program in which Wediko clinicians and teachers work together in the classroom to teach specific social skills to students using experiential games and activities (Wediko Children's Services, 2010). At the case study school, the Wediko team will be overseen by a director (.5 days per week, LCSW) and the team will consist of a program manager (2 days per week, LMSW), site director (5 days per week, LMSW), and five bachelor's level staff as advocate counselors (5 days per week, with at least one summer at the Wediko residential program). The number of services provided will be tracked and presented in a table that includes the number of PBIS programs, professional development workshops, Side by Side workshops, parent outreach services, and individual and small group counseling sessions.

Wediko's school-based programs take a three-tiered approach (multi-tiered framework) in providing clinical services to students and staff at all levels of support: primary, tier 1 (e.g., entire school receives the support); secondary, tier 2 (e.g., specified groups of students/staff receive support); and tertiary support, tier 3 (e.g., individual student/staff receives support) (Barrett et al., 2013; Walker et al., 1996). Examples of tier 1 interventions include weekly Side by Side classes (all students receive one SEL class per week for one class period), PBIS campaigns, universal screening for trauma, and attendance monitoring. Tier 2 interventions include group advisory sessions on topics of need (social skills, dropout prevention, etc.), small group counseling (grief support, stress/anger management, etc.), and staff coaching on PBIS, SEL, and TIC. Tier 3 interventions include many individualized services such as ongoing weekly counseling for identified high-risk students, crisis counseling, individual SEL coaching for Side by Side teachers, and referral to outside community services.

Standardized Measures

The SSIS rating scales are norm-referenced measures for screening and classifying student social behaviors that are important for school success (communication, cooperation, assertion, responsibility, empathy, engagement, and self-control) and problem behaviors that impede academic success (externalizing, bullying, hyperactivity/inattention, and internalizing). The SSIS-RS is a seventy-five-item questionnaire that can be completed by students in fifteen to twenty minutes with seven subdomains in social skills and four subdomains in problem behaviors (see appendix, SSIS-RS scale, sample first page). Items are completed using both frequency ratings and importance ratings, with Likert-like items based on a scale from *not true* to *very true* and *not important* to *critical*. The SSIS-RS has updated norms based on the 2006 U.S. Census Bureau demographic data with 4,700 students in 36 states at 115 sites participating in the standardization (Doll & Jones, 2010). For reliability, coefficient alphas for the social skills scale ranged from .72 to .95 on the student form. The authors also report extensive construct validity for the measure with consistent moderate to high intercorrelations among scales and subscales (Gresham, Elliott, Cook, Vance, and Kettler, 2010). There are also parent and teacher versions of the SSIS rating scales, but for purposes of the research focus, only the student version will be used in English and Spanish (as needed).

The SSIS-RS was pilot tested at the proposed study school during the 2013–14 school year, in April for time one and in June for time two. The pilot test was given to thirty-three students. A paired-samples *t*-test was conducted to compare the level of overall social skills and problem behaviors before and after the Wediko intervention. There was not a statistically significant difference in the social skills scores pretest ($M = 2.79, SD = .61$) and posttest ($M = 2.62, SD = .51$), $t(33) = 1.73, p = .094$. There was a statistically significant difference in the problem behavior scores for pretest ($M = 2.17, SD = .71$) and posttest ($M = 1.91, SD = .50$), $t(33) = 2.32$, $p = .026$. These results suggest that students reduced their overall level of problem behaviors after the Wediko intervention and that the level of social skills did not change over the intervention. The level of social skills might not have changed because of the short time frame between administrations (two months; the current proposed study will be five months). With reference to the subscales for the problem behaviors, NDSS students also showed a statistically significant difference between pretest and posttest on externalizing behaviors (e.g., I talk back to adults; I fight with others) and bullying behaviors (e.g., I say things to hurt people's feelings; I try to make others afraid of me). Overall, the NDSS students reduced problem behaviors, specifically externalizing behaviors and bullying behaviors

The ACE Questionnaire came out of one of the largest research studies to assess connections between chronic stress caused by early adversity and later-life health outcomes, as undertaken by Kaiser Permanente and the CDC (Centers for Disease Control and Prevention, 2014). The ten-item questionnaire measures adverse childhood experiences (abuse, neglect, and household dysfunction) on a simple yes/no scale with exposure to any one of the following adverse experiences being scored as one point: psychological, physical, or sexual abuse; violence against mother; or living with household members who were substance abusers, mentally ill or suicidal, or ever imprisoned (Felitti et al., 1998).

Felitti found that more than half of respondents reported at least one adverse childhood experience, one-fourth reported at least two categories of childhood exposures; individuals with multiple exposures were more likely to have multiple health risk factors later in life, including alcoholism,

TABLE 2
Purposeful Sampling for the Qualitative Interviews of Students

Change/trauma	Low trauma score 0–1	Medium trauma score 2–3	High trauma score ≤ 4
Low change	$N = 2$	$N = 2$	$N = 2$
Medium change	$N = 2$	$N = 2$	$N = 2$
High change	$N = 2$	$N = 2$	$N = 2$

*Maximum variation sampling, $N \leq 20$ students

depression, heart disease, and obesity. This study was based on 17,377 respondents primarily from middle to upper class backgrounds who were Health Maintenance Organization (HMO) members undergoing a comprehensive physical examination. The test-retest reliability for each ACE and the ACE score were in the good to excellent range (range of Cohen's kappa: 0.46–0.86; Dube, Williamson, Thompson, Felitti, & Anda, 2004).

In line with the National Survey of Children's Health (2012) and the Child Trends Research Brief on Adverse Childhood Experiences (Sacks, Murphey, & Moore, 2014), a modified version of nine adverse childhood experiences will be used for this research (omitting sensitive questions around neglect and abuse): (1) socioeconomic hardship, (2) divorce/separation of parent, (3) death of parent, (4) parent served time in jail, (5) witness to domestic violence, (6) victim of neighborhood violence, (7) lived with someone who was mentally ill or suicidal, (8) lived with someone with alcohol/drug problem, (9) treated or judged unfairly due to race/ethnicity (see appendix B, ACE Questionnaire in English and Spanish).

Study Participants

Wediko's school-based programming will be studied in one case study school in the South Bronx, New Directions Secondary School (NDSS), for over-age and under-credited middle school students from ages twelve to eighteen. The sampling for the quantitative measures will be a convenience sample ($N = 100$), based on the convenience of students at NDSS and their availability (Creswell, 2013). Purposive sampling (see Table 3) will be used for the qualitative interviews to create new understanding of the role of trauma in SEL programming. The sampling strategy involves selecting individuals and sites for study because they can purposefully inform the research and the central phenomenon (Creswell, 2013). This sampling strategy will focus on maximizing differences—looking at different levels of SEL or problem behavior change scores during the experiment and level of childhood trauma to provide variation and obtain diverse perspectives in up to twenty students (Crabtree & Miller, 1999). The levels of trauma scores (low, medium, and high) were determined based upon previous ACE study results and percentage of reported ACEs (Felitti et al., 1998; Stambaugh et al., 2013).

New Directions Secondary School was selected because of an existing partnership with Wediko and previous Wediko school-based services. It was also chosen because of the high numbers of low-income students and a supportive principal with a commitment to data-informed practices and weekly SEL programming. Further, Wediko ran a pilot study at NDSS during the 2013–4 school year collecting data on social and emotional skill building using the SSIS-RS measure.

New Directions Secondary School is a school focused on supporting over-age and under-credited middle school and high school students, located in New York City Community School District 9. District 9 is a high-needs school district where students are primarily from a low-income minority community. Many families are single parent households and approximately 28 percent live below the poverty line with 100 percent of the students qualifying for free and reduced lunch. New Directions is a new New York City Department of Education (DOE) school open for school year 2013–14 with an enrollment of approximately one hundred middle school students (growing in size each year by one grade, about fifty students). New Directions offers a full learning experience that incorporates rigorous but engaging competency-based academic curricula with credit recovery, physical and mental health services, college and career preparation, youth development, multitiered systems of support, and extended day and extended year opportunities for students and their families. Currently, New Directions and Wediko Children's Services are partners in providing daily social and emotional support services.

Collecting Data

Data will be collected through two phases. The first is the quantitative phase in which the following two standardized measures will be used: the SSIS-RS (pre- and post-intervention) and the ACE questionnaire (during intervention). The second qualitative phase will consist of interviewing purposefully selected students from the study population to further elucidate the intersection of SEL, trauma, and level of change scores and a focus group to validate the results. Further, the number of Wediko services that students use will also be analyzed. The timeline, as outlined in Figure 1, includes administering the pre-SSIS-RS in October 2014, running the intervention with Wediko's school-based programming including the SEL program Side by Side and administering the ACE questionnaire from October through March 2015, administering the post SSIS-RS in March 2015, and then conducting the semi-structured interviews in April of 2015 and a follow-up focus group in May/ June of 2015.

Face-to-face interviews will be conducted with the purposefully selected and recruited students in April 2015 by audio recording. Interviews will be semi-structured interviews that are "guided, concentrated, focused, and open-ended communication events that are co-created by the investigator and interviewee" (Crabtree & Miller, 1999). Interview questions are listed in appendix C including ten open-ended questions on social and emotional learning, school services, and academic goals. Questions were selected based on their ability to elucidate the level of social and emotional learning, including improving academics, in context. The questions work toward face validity in that they are focused on social and emotional learning, goal setting, and ecological validity and that they fit the sample of NDSS students (Creswell, 2011). Depending on the quantitative results, further qualitative questions may be added to elucidate the research questions (Creswell, 2013).

These interview questions were pilot tested with two student interviews during the 2013–14 school year and the following themes were found: (1) social and emotional skills included being real and honest about one's feelings; (2) social skills and how to communicate with others were taught during the school day; (3) Wediko counselors provided help through talking, solving problems, and facilitating meetings; and (4) NDSS provided more opportunities for success and students improved their grades.

Analyzing the Data

The quantitative data analysis will be completed using SPSS for Windows 22.0. The quantitative data will first be analyzed in terms of descriptive information on age, grade level, and gender, as well as the means, modes, range, and standard deviations for the SSIS-RS scores and ACE trauma score. Then inferential statistical analyses (paired-samples t-tests, repeated measures ANOVA, and multiple regression) will be conducted to test the primary study predictions. All results will be reported as significant using an alpha $= .05$ significance threshold, along with their corresponding effect size and 95-percent confidence interval. The data analysis for each quantitative research question is described below:

1. It is hypothesized that there will be significant increases in the social skills subscales and decreases in the problem behavior subscales of the SSIS-RS measure.
   a. It is hypothesized that the social skills subscales will significantly increase.
   b. It is hypothesized that the problem behavior subscales will significantly decrease.
   These hypotheses were developed from previous existing SEL research on improvements in SEL skills and decreases in problem behaviors after an SEL intervention (Durlak et al., 2011; Payton, 2000). To compare pre and post levels of social and emotional skills

and problem behaviors, a paired-samples *t*-test will be used to determine if there is a significant increase or decrease, including analyzing all subscale scores. Only the How True scale will be used and the Importance scale will be omitted because of a focus in the current study on how true the social skill or the problem behavior is for the student.

2. Did childhood trauma moderate pre-post intervention changes on overall social skills and problem behaviors?

   a. It is hypothesized that higher trauma scores will be associated with decreased social skills scores.

   b. It is hypothesized that higher trauma scores will be associated with decreased problem scale scores.

   A repeated measures Analysis of Variance (ANOVA) will be used to test the predicted childhood trauma interaction at posttest, namely that trauma will decrease the overall social skills score and that the Problem scale scores will still decrease, based on previous literature that has found a direct link between trauma and impairment in school functioning, including social and emotional competency (Nadeem et al., 2014). Specifically, this repeated measures ANOVA will include time (within-subjects variable with two levels: pre- and post-intervention) and childhood trauma (between-subjects variable with three levels: low, moderate, and high childhood trauma).

3. Did the level of Wediko services utilized by students correlate with their SEL and problem behavior improvements at post-treatment?

   a. It is hypothesized that students who have a higher utilization of services will show a greater improvement in SEL at post-treatment.

   b. It is hypothesized that students who have a higher utilization of services will show a greater reduction in problem behaviors at post-treatment.

   A multiple regression analysis will be used to estimate the relationship between the level of Wediko services used by the students and the improvements in SEL score at posttreatment. To test this, a multiple regression analysis will test whether there is a significant predictive effect of the level of Wediko service utilization during the intervention period (in minutes) on posttreatment SEL score, controlling for pre-SEL score. It is predicted that the students who utilize a higher level of services will reduce their problem behavior scores and have higher SEL scores based on previous SEL interventions and dosage research (Greenberg, Domitrovich, & Bumbarger, 1999).

The qualitative data will be analyzed in six steps: (1) preparing and organizing the data, (2) exploring the data through coding, (3) using codes to develop descriptions and themes, (4) presenting the findings through narratives, (5) interpreting the meaning of the results by reflexively looking at the findings and literature, and (6) validating the findings (Creswell, 2011). The qualitative findings will be developed through direct narratives in a case study format that provides a detailed description of the setting and individuals, followed by the themes found in the analysis (Yin, 2009).

Exploring coding steps 2 and 3 in more detail, the analysis will start by going back to the qualitative research questions and identifying the evidence that addresses the questions to create codes. Tentative conclusions will then be drawn from meaningful patterns that emerge with specific examples of evidence (Yin, 2009). The process will be iterative between data collection and analysis in order to get a broader understanding of social and emotional learning. Audio data from interviews will be transcribed and organized into computer files. The qualitative data analysis computer program MAXQDA10 (VERBI, 2010) will be used to organize and code all data.

A reflexivity process will be used whereby, through self-reflection and the literature (Crabtree & Miller, 1999), the primary researcher (JCB) will share her own experiences in providing school-based SEL programs and TIC with Wediko and also talk about her potential bias in the interpretation. If funding permits or a colleague researcher is available, another coder will analyze the data to support reliability through inter-coder agreement (Creswell, 2013). Lastly, the findings will be validated by the trustworthiness of the data (Padgett, 1998) according to a focus group made up of invested students for member checking (Crabtree & Miller, 1999).

The mixed methods data will be analyzed to determine how students at different SEL and trauma levels experience the Wediko program and SEL skill building. To integrate the data, the differences will be presented in a joint display (Creswell, 2014) that shows the quantitative categories (low, medium, and high for SEL change and trauma) against the themes that emerge from the qualitative interviews. Further, a discussion of how the qualitative findings help interpret the meaning of the experimental results will be included.

ADDRESSING ETHICAL ISSUES

Informed consent will be obtained from all student participants and their parents/caregivers through a letter home to parents stating that the research is voluntary or during intake interviews during the summer of 2014. (Appendix D includes the letter, approved by the New York City Department of Education Institutional Review Board and Wediko Children's Services Institutional Review Board, to solicit subjects, the informed consent letter for the SSIS-RS administration (English and Spanish) and ACE Questionnaire, the student assent forms for the SSIS-RS and ACE Questionnaire administration, the informed consent for the interviews, and the assent for the interviews. The primary researcher (JCB) submitted an amendment to the New York City

Department of Education Institutional Review Board to be the co-principal investigator, after the Smith IRB letter of approval, and the approval letter is included in the dissertation appendices.

Potential institutional review board concerns include the need to get informed consent from a high-risk student population, the sensitivity of the questions in the ACE Questionnaire pertaining to past adverse trauma experiences, and confidentiality because research and input will be assessed and shared with Wediko staff and key NDSS staff. The high-risk population and the sensitivity of the ACE questions will be addressed by having individual Wediko counselors help students complete the ACE questionnaire and follow up with needed counseling and referrals, as part of Wediko's assessment for each student. Confidentiality will be addressed by requiring informed consent before the research is begun and making it clear that research will be used in real time to benefit the school. Another concern is that the primary researcher (JCB) will be conducting the semi-structured interviews and will need to make boundaries explicitly clear regarding the lack of follow-up counseling and referrals provided by JCB. This will be addressed by the primary researcher providing referral sources to the Wediko clinical social workers, as needed.

FEASIBILITY

Approval has been obtained from the New York City Department of Education Institutional Review Board (see appendix E, including an amendment to administer the ACE Questionnaire and run a small focus group at the end and an amendment to include the primary researcher, JCB, as a co-principal investigator), Smith Institutional Review Board (see appendix F), and the Wediko Children's Services Institutional Review Board (see appendix G, including an amendment approval to administer the ACE Questionnaire). Further, the principal at NDSS, James Waslawski, has provided verbal and written approval to conduct research at his school (see appendix H). There is also full support from the executive director of Wediko Children's Services, who is a part of the Wediko Institutional Review Board team. In the New York City Department of Education Institutional Review Board, Wediko included the primary researcher (JCB) to have full access to the shared data. Last year, Wediko New York piloted an individual case study at NDSS and collected pre and post data using the SSIS-RS and post qualitative interviews. The current proposed study will build on our pilot study to further look at the intersection of SEL and TIC.

REFERENCES

Aber, L., Brown, J. L., Jones, S. M., Berg, J., & Torrente, C. (2011). School-based strategies to prevent violence, trauma, and psychopathology: The challenges of going to scale. *Development and Psychopathology, 23*(02), 411–421.

Adams, J. M. (2014, February 3). *New 'trauma-informed' approach to behavioral disorders in special education* [EdSource online article]. Retrieved from http://edsource.org/2014/new-trauma-informed-approach-to-behavioral-disorders-in-special-education/56753#.U9gLe_ldVdc

Barrett, S., Eber, L., & Weist, M. (2013). *Advancing education effectiveness: Interconnecting school mental health and school-wide positive behavior support* [Brief]. Retrieved from http://www.pbis.org/school/school-mental-health/interconnected-systems

Cappella, E., Frazier, S. L., Atkins, M. S., Schoenwald, S. K., & Glisson, C. (2008). Enhancing schools' capacity to support children in poverty: An ecological model of school-based mental health services. *Administration and Policy in Mental Health and Mental Health Services Research, 35*(5), 395–409.

Centers for Disease Control and Prevention. (2014). *Injury prevention & control: Adverse childhood experiences (ACE) study* [Brief]. Retrieved from http://www.cdc.gov/violenceprevention/acestudy/index.html

Cole, S. F., Eisner, A., Gregory, M., & Ristuccia, J. (2013). *Helping traumatized children learn: Safe, supportive learning environments that benefit all children, creating and advocating for trauma-sensitive schools.* Boston, MA: Massachusetts Advocates for Children.

Cole, S. F., O'Brien, J. G., Gadd, M. G., Ristuccia, J., Wallace, D. L., & Gregory, M. (2005). *Helping traumatized children learn: Supportive school environments for children traumatized by family violence, a report and policy agenda.* Boston, MA: Massachusetts Advocates for Children.

Collaborative for Academic, Social, and Emotional Learning. (2003). *Safe and sound: An educational leader's guide to evidenced-based social and emotional learning programs* [Guide]. Retrieved from http://casel.org/publications/safe-and-sound-an-educational-leaders-guide-to-evidence-based-sel-programs/

Collaborative for Academic, Social, and Emotional Learning. (2013). *Effective social and emotional learning programs* [Guide]. Retrieved from http://www.casel.org/guide

Cooper, J. L. (2008). The federal case for school-based mental health services and supports. *Journal of the American Academy of Child & Adolescent Psychiatry, 47,* 4–8. doi:10.1097/chi.0b013e31815aac71.

Cowan, K. C., Vaillancourt, K., Rossen, E., & Pollitt, K. (2013). *A framework for safe and successful schools* [Brief]. Bethesda, MD: National Association of School Psychologists.

Crabtree, B. F. & Miller, W. L. (Eds.). (1999). *Doing qualitative research* (2nd ed.). Thousand Oaks, CA: SAGE.

Creswell, J. W. (2007). *Qualitative inquiry & research design: Choosing among five approaches.* Thousand Oaks, CA: SAGE.

Creswell, J.W. (2011). *Educational research: Planning, conducting, and evaluating quantitative and qualitative research* (4th ed.). Upper Saddle River, NJ: Pearson Education.

Creswell, J. W. (2013). *Research design: Qualitative, quantitative, and mixed methods approaches.* Thousand Oaks, CA: SAGE.

Creswell, J. W. (2014). *A concise introduction to mixed methods research.* Thousand Oaks, CA: SAGE.

Creswell, J. W., & Plano Clark, V. L. (2011). *Designing and conducting mixed methods research*. Thousand Oaks, CA: SAGE.

Creswell, J. W., & Zhang, W. (2009). The application of mixed methods designs to trauma research. *Journal of Traumatic Stress, 22*(6), 612–621.

Doll, B. & Jones, K. (2010). Test review of the social skills improvement systems rating scales. In R. A. Spies, J. F. Carlson, & K. F. Geisinger (Eds.), *The eighteenth mental measurements yearbook*. Retrieved from http://www.buros.org/

Dube, S. R., Williamson, D. F., Thompson, T., Felitti, V. J., & Anda, R. F. (2004). Assessing the reliability of retrospective reports of adverse childhood experiences among adult HMO members attending a primary care clinic. *Child Abuse & Neglect, 28*(7), 729–737. doi:10.1016/j.chiabu.2004.08.009

Durlak, J. A., & Dupre, E. P. (2008). Implementation matters: A review of research on the influence of implementation on program outcomes and the factors affecting implementation. *American Journal of Community Psychology, 41*, 327–350

Durlak, J. A., Weissberg, R. P., Dymnicki, A. B., Taylor, R. D., & Schellinger, K. B. (2011). The impact of enhancing students' social and emotional learning: A meta-analysis of school-based universal interventions. *Child Development, 82*(1), 405–432. doi:10.1111/j.1467-8624.2010.01564.x

Elias, M. J., Zins, J. E., Weissberg, R. P., Frey, K. S., Greenberg, M. T., Haynes, N. M., . . . Shriver, T. P. (1997). *Promoting social and emotional learning: Guidelines for educators*. Alexandria, VA: Association for Supervision and Curriculum Development.

Felitti, M. D., Vincent, J., Anda, M. D., Robert, F., Nordenberg, M. D., Williamson, M. S., . . . Marks, J. S. (1998). Relationship of childhood abuse and household dysfunction to many of the leading causes of death in adults: The adverse childhood experiences (ACE) study. *American Journal of Preventive Medicine, 14*(4), 245–258.

Felitti, V. J., & Anda, R. F. (2010). The relationship of adverse childhood experiences to adult health, well-being, social function and healthcare. In R. Lanius, E. Vermetten, & C. Pain (Eds.), *The hidden epidemic: The impact of early life trauma on health and disease*. MA: Cambridge University Press.

Gibbs, G. R. (2007). *Analyzing qualitative data*. Thousand Oaks, CA: SAGE.

Greenberg, M. T., Domitrovich, C., & Bumbarger, B. (1999). *Preventing mental disorder in school-aged children: A review of the effectiveness of prevention programs*. Report submitted to the Center for Mental Health Services (SAMHSA) by the Prevention Research Center, Pennsylvania State University [Online]. Retrieved from http://www.psu.edu/dept/prevention

Greene, J. C. (2008). Is mixed methods social inquiry a distinctive methodology? *Journal of Mixed Methods Research, 2*, 7–22.

Gresham, F., & Elliott, S. N. (2008). *Social skills improvement system (SSIS) rating scales*. Bloomington, MN: Pearson Assessments.

Gresham, F. M., Elliott, S. N., Cook, C. R., Vance, M. J., & Kettler, R. (2010). Cross-informant agreement for ratings for social skill and problem behavior ratings: An investigation of the social skills improvement system—Rating scales. *Psychological Assessment, 22*, 157.

Guest, G., Bunce, A., & Johnson, L. (2006). How many interviews are enough? An experiment with data saturation and variability. *Field Methods, 18*, 59–82.

Institute for Safe Families (2013). Findings from the Philadelphia urban ACE study [Brief]. Retrieved from http://www.instituteforsafefamilies.org/philadelphia -urban-ace-study

Jennings, A. (2008). *Models for developing trauma-informed behavioral health systems and trauma-specific services.* Alexandria, VA: National Association of State Mental Health Program Directors, National Technical Assistance Center for State Mental Health Planning.

Kauffman, D. (2014, July 16). Failing schools or failing paradigm? [Blog post]. Retrieved from http://acestoohigh.com/2014/07/16/failing-schools-or-failing -paradigm/#more-3294

Kelly, M. S. (2008). *The domains and demands of school social work practice: A guide to working effectively with students, families and schools.* New York, NY: Oxford University Press.

Kelly, M. S., Berzin, S. C., Frey, A., Alvarez, M., Shaffer, G., & O'Brien, K. (2010). The state of school social work: Findings from the national school social work survey. *School Mental Health, 2*(3), 132–141.

Ko, S. J., Ford, J. D., Kassam-Adams, N., Berkowitz, S. J., Wilson, C., Wong, M., . . . Layne, C. M. (2008). Creating trauma-informed systems: child welfare, education, first responders, health care, juvenile justice. *Professional Psychology: Research and Practice, 39,* 396–404.

Layne, C. M., Saltzman, W. R., Poppleton, L., Burlingame, G. M., Pašalić, A., Duraković, E., . . . Pynoos, R. S. (2008). Effectiveness of a school-based group psychotherapy program for war-exposed adolescents: A randomized controlled trial. *Journal of the American Academy of Child & Adolescent Psychiatry, 47*(9), 1048–1062.

Learning First Alliance. (2001). *Every child learning: Safe and supportive schools* [Report]. Retrieved from http://www.learningfirst.org/sites/default/files/assets/ LFASafeSupportiveSchoolsReport.pdf

VERBI. (2010). MAXQDA (Version 10). [Computer software for qualitative data analysis]. Berlin-Marburg-Amöneburg, Germany: Author.

McKay, C. (2010). Critical service learning: A school social work intervention. *Children & Schools, 32,* 5–13.

McKay, M. M., Lynn, C. J., & Bannon, W. M. (2005). Understanding inner city child mental health need and trauma exposure: Implications for preparing urban service providers. *American Journal of Orthopsychiatry, 75*(2), 201.

Merrell, K. W., & Gueldner, B. A. (2010). *Social and emotional learning in the classroom: Promoting mental health and academic success.* New York: Guilford Press.

Nadeem, E., Jaycox, L. H., Langley, A. K., Wong, M., Kataoka, S. H., & Stein, B. D. (2014). Effects of trauma on students: Early intervention through the cognitive behavioral intervention for trauma in schools. In M. D. Weist, N. A. Lever, C. P. Bradshaw, & J. S. Owens (Eds.), *Handbook of school mental health: Research, training, practice, and policy: Issues in clinical child psychology* (vol. 145, pp. 145-157). NY: Springer Science + Business Media.

National Association of Social Workers. (2008). *Code of ethics of the National Association of Social Workers.* Washington, DC: Author.

National Child Traumatic Stress Network Schools Committee. (2008). *Child trauma toolkit for educators.* Los Angeles, CA: Author.

Data Resource Center for Child & Adolescent Health. (2012). Data query from the child and adolescent health measurement initiative, data resource center for child and adolescent health website [Online query]. Retrieved from http://www.childhealthdata.org/learn/NSCH

New York State Board of Regents (2011). Educating the whole child, engaging the whole school: Guidelines and resources for social and emotional development and learning (SEDL) in New York State [Online state guidelines]. Retrieved from http://www.p12.nysed.gov/sss/sedl/SEDLguidelines.pdf

New York State Technical and Education Assistance Center for Homeless Students. (2012). *The intersection of social-emotional learning and trauma-informed care in relation to students in temporary housing* [Brief]. Retrieved from http://nysteachs.org/media/InfoBrief.SEL.TIC_final.pdf

Oehlberg, B. (2008). *Why schools need to be trauma informed* [Online article]. Retrieved from https://www.starr.org/research/why-schools-need-be-trauma-informed

Padgett, D. K. (1998) *Qualitative methods in social work research: Challenges and rewards*. Thousand Oaks, CA: Sage.

Padgett, D. K. (2009). Qualitative and mixed methods in social work knowledge development. *Social Work*, 54(2), 101–105.

Payton, J. W., Wardlaw, D. M., Graczyk, P. A., Bloodworth, M. R., Tompsett, C. J., & Weissberg, R. P. (2000). Social and emotional learning: A framework for promoting mental health and reducing risk behavior in children and youth. *Journal of school health*, 70(5), 179-185.

Sacks, V., Murphey, D., & Moore, K. (2014). *Adverse childhood experiences: National and state level prevalence* [Research brief]. Retrieved from http://www.childtrends.org/wp-content/uploads/2014/07/Brief-adverse-childhood-experiences_FINAL.pdf

Scaglione, F. (2014, April). ACES recovering from a bad hand. *The New York Nonprofit Press*, pp. 1, 8, 9, & 16.

Stambaugh, L. F., Ringeisen, H., Casanueva, C. C., Tueller, S., Smith, K. E., & Dolan, M. (2013). *Adverse childhood experiences in NSCAW* (OPRE Report 2013-26), Washington, DC: Office of Planning, Research and Evaluation, Administration for Children and Families, U.S. Department of Health and Human Services.

Walker, H. M., Horner, R. H., Sugai, G., Bullis, M., Sprague, J. R., Bricker, D., & Kaufman, M. (1996). Integrated approaches to preventing antisocial behavior patterns among school-age children and youth. *Journal of Emotional and Behavioral Disorders*, 4, 193–256.

Walkley, M., & Cox, T. L. (2013). Building trauma-informed schools and communities. *Children & Schools*, 35(2), 123–126.

Wediko Children's Services (2010). *Side by Side: A collaborative model for building resilient school communities* [Unpublished manual]. Boston: Wediko Children's Services.

Wediko Children's Services (2014). *About us*. Retrieved from http://www.wediko.org/about-us.html

Wolpow, R., Johnson, M. M., Hertel, R., & Kindcaid, S. O. (2009). The heart of learning and teaching: Compassion, resiliency, and academic success. Retrieved from http://www.k12.wa.us/CompassionateSchools/pubdocs/TheHeartofLearningandTeaching.pdf

Yin, R. K. (Eds.). (2009). *Case study research: design and methods* (4th ed.). Thousand Oaks, CA: SAGE.

Zins, J. E., & Elias, M. J. (2007). Social and emotional learning: Promoting the development of all students. *Journal of Educational and Psychological Consultation*, *17*(2-3), 233–255.

Zins, J. E., Weissberg, R. P., Wang, M. C., & Walberg, H .J. (Eds.). (2004). *Building academic success on social and emotional learning: What does the research say?* New York: Teachers College Press.

Appendix B

Excerpt from Funded National Institute on Drug Abuse Mixed Methods Grant Proposal
Rural Methamphetamine-Abusing Parents and Their Children

SENIOR/KEY PERSONNEL

Wendy Haight, PhD, University of Illinois at Urbana-Champaign, PD/PI
James Black, MD, Southern Illinois University, Co-PD/PI
Jennifer Greene, PhD, The University of Illinois at
Urbana-Champaign, Co-PD/PI
Sydney Hans, PhD, The University of Chicago, Co-PD/PI
Teresa Ostler, PhD, The University of Illinois at
Urbana-Champaign, Co-PD/PI
Patrick Tolan, PhD, The University of Illinois at Chicago Consultant

NOTE: Text in italics is material added or changed in response to issues and questions raised in the first round of peer review.

To protect confidentiality, the name of the county in which this research was conducted has been changed to the pseudonym "RURAL."

A. SPECIFIC AIMS

The abuse of methamphetamine, a powerful central nervous system stimulant and neurotoxin, is a growing and urgent problem across the United States including the rural Midwest. Methamphetamine use is a problem that affects not just individuals, but whole families. Rural law enforcement officers and health, mental health, and child welfare professionals increasingly encounter children living in homes where methamphetamine is produced and abused. These children often are exposed to toxic chemicals, violence, criminal behavior and neglect as well as physical, sexual and emotional abuse (Anglin, Burke, Perrochet, Stamper, & Dawad-Noursi, 2000; Cretzmeyer, Sarrazin, Huber, Block, & Hall, 2003; Haight et al., 2005; Haight, Ostler, Black, Sheridan, & Kingery, 2006). As a result, they are at high risk for developing mental health and substance abuse disorders. With rural methamphetamine use often occurring in home environments, it is critical to increase our understanding of family ecologies, socialization practices and parent and child belief systems related to methamphetamine abuse. Such knowledge will constitute a crucial first step towards elaborating generic prevention and intervention services to culturally-sensitive interventions aimed at improving the psychological development and well-being of rural children whose parents abuse methamphetamine.

The proposed, exploratory-developmental research will study rural, Mid-western, methamphetamine-abusing parents and their 7- to 10-year-old children who are involved in the public child welfare system. The goal of the study is to obtain rich, contextualized descriptions of parent and child behavior and belief systems related to parent methamphetamine abuse and its effects on children. Young school-aged children are the focus on the study because many children of methamphetamine using parents begin using substances in late childhood or early adolescence, and hence younger children are the most likely targets of future preventive intervention services.

The four specific aims of this study are as follows:

1. *To describe rural families involved with methamphetamine abuse: their physical and social ecologies.*
2. *To describe the parents: their socialization practices and beliefs about their methamphetamine abuse and its effects on their 7- to 10-year-old children, and their functioning (social and medical histories, mental health, substance use).*
3. *To describe the children: their experiences and beliefs about their parents' methamphetamine abuse and its effects on their own lives, and their functioning (medical and developmental histories, mental health, substance use).*
4. *To explore, using case cluster analysis, any patterns emerging across families especially pertaining to possible risk and protective factors for children's substance use and mental health problems.*

We approach the study of rural, school-aged children and their parents who abuse methamphetamine from an ecological perspective. We use a mixed methods design which is primarily qualitative but includes some quantitative components. In-depth, semi-structured interviews will provide rich descriptions of the beliefs and experiences of parents and their children. Information on family ecology will be obtained through examination of child welfare investigative reports and home visits. Information on child and parent functioning will be obtained from structured, clinical instruments. This pluralistic strategy will allow us to examine patterns of child functioning in relation to parent and child beliefs and experiences, and parent functioning. Such contextualized descriptions will suggest risk and protective factors to be examined in future research, and to inform the elaboration of prevention and intervention services to rural, methamphetamine-abusing families.

B. BACKGROUND AND SIGNIFICANCE

B.1. Introduction: The Problem of Methamphetamine Abuse in the Rural Midwest

Since the mid 1990s, methamphetamine production and abuse has become a major public health and criminal justice problem. Methamphetamine is a form of amphetamine with strong central nervous system effects (Wermuth, 2000). It is highly addictive, both physically and psychologically (Rawson, Gonzales, & Brethen, 2002; SAMHSA, 2002). The initial effect of methamphetamine is a ''rush'' from the release of high levels of dopamine (Rawson et al., 2002). The user experiences euphoria, decreased fatigue and appetite, and increased energy and alertness (Anglin et al., 2000). Unfortunately, methamphetamine is neurotoxic. High resolution magnetic resonance imaging reveals significant structural abnormalities in the brains of methamphetamine users, and these abnormalities may account for some of the symptoms of methamphetamine abuse. Abusers may experience psychiatric disorders such as psychosis, depression, paranoia, rapid mood changes; and violent behavior (Anglin et al., 2000; Cretzmeyer et al., 2003; Substance Abuse and Mental Health Services Administration [SAMHSA], 2002). Methamphetamine's ability to disrupt normal brain functioning can be long lasting (Copeland & Sorensen, 2001; Rawson et al., 2002; SAMHSA, 2002) and psychotic symptoms may persist for months or years after use of methamphetamine has ceased.

Methamphetamine production and abuse has become a serious problem in many rural U.S. communities. Initially limited to the western states and Hawaii, methamphetamine has spread throughout the nation (Cretzmeyer et al, 2003; Hohman, Oliver & Wright, 2004; Rawson et al., 2002). Methamphetamine production laboratories often are located in rural areas to avoid detection from the powerful fumes emitted during the manufacturing process, and because rural areas offer access to precursors used in the production of methamphetamine. Methamphetamine is relatively easy to produce, and instructions can be downloaded from the internet. Many rural methamphetamine abusers manufacture methamphetamine for their own use. These ''mom and pop cooks'' produce methamphetamine in and around their homes where children are living. Methamphetamine production and abuse has increased dramatically in Illinois. In 1997, police seized 24 labs statewide. In 2001, they seized 666 methamphetamine labs (ICJIA, 2004). In Illinois, methamphetamine abuse and production is largely a rural problem. One of the counties included in the proposed research had 220 drug crime arrests in 2001, more than a 100% increase over the previous year's 101 arrests for crimes associated with drugs (Illinois State Police, 2003). This county "boasts" the largest number of methamphetamine labs seized in the state of Illinois in 2001 (97 labs) (Adrian, 2003; Illinois Criminal Justice Information Authority [ICJIA], 2004).

The rise of methamphetamine production and abuse in rural Illinois has taken a serious toll on children. The RURAL Field Office of the Illinois Department of Children and Family Services, the site of the proposed research, handles between 95 and 100 child abuse hotline reports of child maltreatment per month. Approximately 25% of these cases involve parent methamphetamine abuse. Indeed, the most frequently cited reason for opening a case at the RURAL Field Office is parent substance abuse (27%) (U.S. Department of Health and Human Services, 2004). Little empirical research is available to guide elaboration of preventive and intervention services to rural families involved with methamphetamine. Understanding the context of methamphetamine abuse in predominantly white, rural communities is necessary to the elaboration of any effective preventive and intervention services within this distinct cultural context. The proposed research will provide such information.

B.2 Parent Methamphetamine Abuse and Children

Methamphetamine use is reported at highest rates among 20- to 29-year-olds who often have children (West & Stuntz, 2000). A growing literature addressing parent abuse of illicit drugs suggests a variety of risks for children (Etz et al., 1998; Merikangas, Dierker, & Fenton, 1996) including genetic risks and the adverse effects of prenatal exposure to drugs on the developing brain (Merikangas et al., 1996). Environmental risks derive from the family contexts in which children are reared (e.g., Johnson, Dunlap, & Maher, 1998). These contexts may include exposure to criminal behavior including the use of illicit drugs, family attitudes accepting of substance use (Hawkins et al.,1992; Kumpfer, Olds, Alexander, Zucker, & Gary, 1996), and the availability of drugs (Merikangas et al., 1996). In addition, parenting may be compromised by substance abuse (Kandel, 1990). For example, parental discipline may be inconsistent and monitoring inadequate (Dishion & McMahon, 1996; Hawkins et al, 1992).

Further, children whose parents abuse drugs are much more likely to be maltreated than children whose parents do not abuse drugs (National Center on Addiction and Substance Abuse at Columbia University, 1999). These children also face stigma from a public (e.g., Klee, 1998) that views substance abuse not as a mental illness, but as a voluntary activity and moral failure (Hans, 2004). These multiple stressors place the children of substance-abusing parents at high risk for the development of substance abuse and mental health disorders (Cretzmeyer et al., 2003; National Center on Addiction and Substance Abuse, Columbia University,1999) as well as early pregnancy, dropping out of school, and involvement in criminal and other antisocial behavior (Millar & Stermac, 2000).

There is some evidence that exposure to parent methamphetamine abuse compromises children's physical development, health and safety. Prenatal exposure to methamphetamine is associated with spontaneous abortion, premature births, low birth weights, small head circumference, cerebral infarctions, and congenital abnormalities (*see* Hohman, Oliver, & Wright., 2004; Stewart & Meeker, 1997). After birth, children may be exposed to toxic chemicals from methamphetamine labs. More than one-third of the children found in homes during methamphetamine laboratory seizures tested positive for illicit drugs because of environmental exposure (*see* Hohman et al., 2004). In addition, such children may be living in homes with no running water, limited and unsafe electrical power, extremely poor sanitation, and little food (see Haight et al., 2005; Hohman et al., 2004). Such children also may be exposed to hazardous conditions such as explosions and fire from the dangerous process of producing methamphetamine (Cretzmeyer et al., 2003; Hohman et al., 2004; West & Stuntz, 2000; Manning, 1999).

Little research has considered the impact of parent methamphetamine abuse on children's psychological development, mental health and substance use. Yet, clinical reports and pilot data suggest that parent methamphetamine abuse is associated with children's stress and trauma. Such children may be exposed to violence associated with methamphetamine abuse including severe domestic violence; criminal behavior related to the production and purchase of methamphetamine; neglect from parents who are preoccupied with obtaining the drug and who may sleep for as long as 3 days after binging; as well as physical, sexual, and emotional abuse from substance-abusing parents and other users who frequent the home (Cretzmeyer et al., 2003; Haight et al., 2005, 2006; Hohman et al., 2004; Manning, 1999; West & Stuntz, 2000). Parent methamphetamine abuse and associated stressful and traumatic experiences place children at high risk for mental health and substance abuse disorders. Prospective studies show that child maltreatment is associated with conduct problems, disruptive behavior disorders, attention problems, anxiety disorders (including PTSD) and mood disorders (Cicchetti, Toth, & Maughan, 2000). Egeland (1997) found that 90% of maltreated children showed at least one diagnosable disorder at age 17-1/2 years, compared to 30% of children who were impoverished but not maltreated. In comparison with other maltreated children, sexually abused children show more forms of pathology and more extreme forms. Sexual abuse is strongly associated with PTSD and depression (Sroufe, Dougal, Weinfeld, & Carlson, 2000).

Domestic violence, also common in homes where methamphetamine is abused, is consistently associated with child behavioral and emotional problems (Sroufe et al., 2000). Evidence from the trauma and substance abuse literatures, however, suggests that not all children exposed to parent methamphetamine abuse will develop mental health and substance abuse disorders. For example, some school-aged children raised by methamphetamine abusing parents develop positive relationships with peers and community members, and perform well in school (Ostler et al., 2006). In addition, a small but growing body of qualitative research (e.g., Kearney, Murphy, & Rosenbaum, 1994; Rosenbaum & Murphy, 1987) suggests that many chemically dependent parents feel love toward their children (Hans, 2004), are concerned about their children's exposure to adult substance abuse (Woodhouse, 1992), and attempt to protect their children from exposure to adult substance abuse (Kearney et al., 1994). Some chemically dependent mothers do provide environments that meet children's basic needs (Hans, 2004).

Understanding the sources of such diversity in parent socialization beliefs and practices, and children's psychological development is important information for effective preventive and intervention services. One protective factor underlying such diversity may be beliefs about parent methamphetamine use and its effects on children. For example, children may develop beliefs about their parents' methamphetamine use that facilitate more positive developmental outcomes, for example, that their parents' addiction is not the children's fault, that their parents are ill, and that a better future is possible. One important source of such protective interpretations is adults.

Indeed, a stable, caring relationship with a supportive adult is a social protective factor for substance abuse disorders (e.g., National Institute on Drug Abuse [NIDA], 2003) and mental health disorders in traumatized children (e.g., Lynsky & Fergusson, 1997; Pynoos, Steinberg, & Goenjian, 1996). Consistent with research on children of substance abusers (e.g., Kroll, 2004), knowledgeable adults with regular contact with children of methamphetamine addicts (e.g., educators, mental health and substance abuse counselors, child welfare workers, and foster parents) stress the importance of helping children to understand their experiences in ways that facilitate more positive developmental outcomes (Haight et al.,2005). How adults help children to understand and respond to their experiences including parent methamphetamine abuse is likely to reflect their culturally-constituted socialization beliefs. Evidence from North American families suggests that normative socialization strategies for helping children through adverse life events vary across communities in relation to culturally-specific belief systems (Burger & Miller, 1999; Cho & Miller, in press). At present, relatively little is known about the belief systems of rural Midwesterners regarding parent methamphetamine abuse. Understanding the beliefs of rural Midwestern parents who abuse methamphetamine and their children is a necessary first step in the development of any effective prevention intervention within this cultural community.

B.3 A Focus on School-Aged Children Involved in the Public Child Welfare System and Their Parents

Not surprisingly, methamphetamine abuse increasingly affects child welfare systems in the United States (Shillington, Hohman, & Jones, 2002). Preliminary data from rural Illinois suggest that approximately 25% of child abuse hotline calls in this area involve parent methamphetamine abuse (Haight et al., 2005). The proposed study will focus on children and parents who are involved with the Illinois Department of Children and Family Services (DCFS). There are several important reasons for focusing on children involved with the public child welfare system. First, from a scientific perspective, sampling children from DCFS may limit variability of parent substance abuse. Parent methamphetamine abuse ranges in intensity and duration, and such variation likely affects children's responses. By sampling children involved with DCFS, we limit our sample to children who have experienced parent methamphetamine abuse of sufficient intensity and duration to draw outside intervention. Second, from a pragmatic perspective, by sampling children and families involved with DCFS we increase our opportunities of recruiting methamphetamine-involved families. These high-risk families are unlikely to come forward prior to their involvement with law enforcement and child welfare systems. Third, from an ethical perspective, the more than one-half million children involved with public child welfare systems (U.S. National Center for Resource Family Support, 2003) are arguably our most vulnerable. They experience high rates of mental and physical health problems and educational underachievement (Blatt & Simms, 1997; Cicchetti & Toth, 1995). They are an appropriate place to begin our studies of children exposed to parent methamphetamine abuse because developing effective interventions with this group is vital to the alleviation of long-term suffering. Fourth, from a public policy point of view, methamphetamine abuse is placing high demands on publicly supported institutions such as child welfare systems (Haight et al., 2005). Although state child welfare systems have long struggled with this issue, recently a variety of federal agencies including the Substance Abuse and Mental Health Services Administration's Center for Substance Abuse Treatment (CSAT) and the Administration on Children, Youth and Families (ACYF), Children's Bureau's Office of Child Abuse and Neglect (OCAN), have acknowledged the urgent public need for more information on the interrelated problem of substance abuse and child maltreatment.

There are several important reasons for focusing on younger, school-aged children (aged 7-10 years). Most children within this age range will be capable and motivated to explore their experiences with parent methamphetamine abuse with an adult when explicitly invited to do so within a supportive context (Ostler et al., 2006). In addition, our goal is to develop a prevention intervention. Pilot data indicate that by early adolescence many children of methamphetamine abusing parents are abusing illegal drugs (Ostler et al., 2006). Therefore, an effective prevention intervention needs to target young, school-aged children. We recognize that parents involved with DCFS may not be representative of all methamphetamine abusing parents. They are individuals who are sufficiently impaired to draw outside intervention, and who have agreed to undergo intensive outpatient substance abuse treatment in order to maintain custody of their children. They may, however, represent the parents most likely to present with their children for intervention.

B.4 Conceptual Framework and Specific Research Questions

Recent studies report variability in the mental health and substance abuse attitudes of school-aged children of methamphetamine abusers (Ostler et al., 2006), as well as in the parenting of substance abusers (e.g., Hans, 2004; Kearney et al., 1994). A sociocultural perspective (e.g., Gaskins, 1994; Goncu, 1999; Greenfield & Suzuki,1998; Miller et al., 2003; Rogoff, 2003; Shweder et al.,1998; Vygotsky, 1962; Wertsch, 1985), a variant of ecological theory, suggests that such diversity results from the complex interaction of biological, psychological, and social factors operating within particular cultural-historical contexts. The proposed study focuses on social and psychological factors, a significant gap in the current literature. More specifically we focus on the dialectical processes of socialization and acquisition within the rural Midwest. Socialization is the process by which adults within particular cultural contexts structure the social environment and display patterned meanings for children; for example, a parent instructs his school-aged child in stealing anhydrous ammonia, or a child observes her parents use methamphetamine. Acquisition is the process through which children interpret, respond to, and ultimately embrace, reject, or elaborate upon the social patterns to which they are exposed (e.g., Miller & Sperry, 1988; Wentworth, 1980).

A socioocultural perspective directs our attention to the meanings participants ascribe to socialization experiences. Parent and child belief systems about methamphetamine are an important place to begin the study of socialization and acquisition within methamphetamine-involved families. These belief systems form a frame of reference for daily life and problem solving, including parents' socialization strategies for supporting children's well-being in the context of parent methamphetamine abuse (for example, sending their children to stay with grandparents during methamphetamine production) and children's acquisition strategies for functioning within a home where parents are abusing methamphetamine (for example, resistance to using substances). Understanding, elaborating, and sometimes changing belief systems is a central component of effective, empirically supported mental health and substance abuse interventions (e.g., Kazdin & Weisz, 1998). Parent beliefs about drug use appear to play a key role in children's drug use (Merikangas et al., 1996). Interventions for adults, children, and adolescents with substance abuse disorders include a focus on recurring or intrusive thoughts and feelings about a substance that predict relapse (Bukstein, 1997). Cognitive therapies for traumatized (Cohen, 1998; Cohen, Deblinger, Mannarino, & Steer, 2004) and depressed children and adults (Reinecke, 2002) emphasize examination and modification of negative or maladaptive belief systems.

Building on existing, evidence-based models is critical to addressing substance abuse prevention within the context of rural, methamphetamine-abusing families. Ecological systems theory, of which our sociocultural perspective is a variant, has provided a framework for the development of a number of empirically-validated, family-based prevention interventions (e.g., see Etz et al., 1998). Family strengthening interventions are a critical component of any effective approach to the prevention of youth substance abuse (e.g., Dishion, 1996; Kumpfer et al., 2002). For example, the NIDA-funded Strengthening Families Program was developed as a selective prevention program for children of substance abusers (e.g., Kumpfer & Alvarado, 2003; Kumpfer et al., 2002). The proposed research will build on and further the knowledge base in substance abuse prevention research concerned with elaborating generic, family-centered prevention interventions to culturally sensitive prevention interventions for distinct high risk groups. Although much progress has been made in family-centered prevention research over the past two decades, challenges remain regarding the implementation of effective interventions for culturally diverse families (see Spoth et al., 2002; Turner, 2000). The limited research with culturally adapted prevention programs suggests that these adaptations can enhance effectiveness with non mainstream families (Kumpfer et al., 2002). Existing cultural adaptations, however, have been criticized as superficial, e.g., changing photos to depict the targeted group. Researchers have argued that a deeper understanding of cultural context will lead to even stronger outcomes (e.g., Kumpfer et al., 2002; Spoth, et al., 2002). For example, family-focused prevention intervention models seek to reduce risk factors and enhance protective factors. What constitutes a risk and protective factor can vary across cultural contexts (e.g., Haight, 2002). Our descriptive, pilot research (Haight et al., 2005) suggests several risk factors that may be relatively unique to methamphetamine-abusing families: (1) the rate at which parents become disabled may be rapid relative to other substances, (2) parental judgment may be especially impaired given the psychiatric effects of regular methamphetamine use, (3) the stigma experienced by methamphetamine-involved families in rural communities may be greater than that experienced by rural families involved with alcohol or marijuana, (4) reunification of children in foster care and their parents may be less likely given extended prison sentences and other harsh legal responses to this illness, and (5) children may enter into care with mental health needs, particularly related to trauma, that are urgent relative to children of other substance abusers. Possible protective factors include rural educators committed to supporting children's physical, social and emotional well-being, as well as academic achievement and rural churches, which provide informal social services and counseling.

We know of no previous substance abuse prevention research targeted to children of parents who abuse methamphetamine. The present study builds the necessary foundation for systematically extending existing family based substance abuse prevention interventions to the cultural context of the impoverished, rural, white Midwest. For example, education and skill-oriented family-based prevention interventions may require elaboration of clinical components addressing high levels of trauma symptoms experienced by both children and parents in methamphetamine-abusing families. Previous prevention intervention research has elaborated a variety of important behavioral and cognitive behavioral skills for both parents and children. Somewhat less attention has been paid to clinical issues (although see Luthar and Suchman, 2000). The vast majority of children in our pilot studies demonstrated clinically significant symptoms of trauma including anxiety disorders, dissociation, and rage responses that also are risk factors for substance abuse (Ostler et al., 2006). Recent research also indicates extremely high levels of interpersonal violence and PTSD symptoms among adult methamphetamine users (e.g., Cohen et al., 2005).

Research questions:
The specific research questions addressed by the proposed exploratory study are:

1. *What are the characteristics of families involved with parent methamphetamine abuse; particularly, their physical (e.g., condition of the dwelling) and social ecologies (e.g., residents of the home, presence of domestic violence)? (Aim 1)*
2. *What are parents' socialization practices and beliefs about their methamphetamine abuse and its effects on their children; and their functioning (social and medical history, mental health and substance use? (Aim 2).*
3. *What are the experiences and beliefs of rural, school-aged children about their parents'methamphetamine use and its effects on their own lives and their functioning (medical and developmental history, mental health, substance use)? (Aim 3)*
4. *What patterns emerge across families in regard to family ecology, and parent and child characteristics, especially those pertaining to possible risk and protective factors for children's substance use and mental health problems? (Aim 4).*

B.5 Significance

The abuse and production of methamphetamine is a growing and urgent problem in the rural Midwest. Available research on the effects of parent methamphetamine abuse on children focuses on biological and health factors that are critical to intervention. Yet, children of methamphetamine abusers typically experience significant psychological trauma and exposure to antisocial behavior. Little research has addressed mental health implications that also are critical to successful intervention efforts. Descriptive information on rural Midwestern parents' and children's belief systems about parent methamphetamine abuse contextualized by information on family characteristics; and parent and child development, mental health and substance use is urgently needed to elaborate effective, culturally sensitive prevention and intervention services. The goal of the proposed research is to contribute to the development of effective services by providing such a description. Future, longitudinal research may then explore hypotheses regarding possible causal mechanisms in the development of mental health and substance abuse problems in children of methamphetamine-abusing parents.

C. PRELIMINARY STUDIES

We (Haight, Ostler and Black) have been involved in several collaborative pilot studies with families involved with the Illinois public child welfare system (DCFS) including rural children and their methamphetamine-abusing parents. Our pilot studies have allowed us to (1) successfully address complex ethical issues with the University of Illinois and DCFS institutional review boards; (2) develop, pilot test, and revise methodological and analytic tools appropriate to rural children and their parents who are experiencing significant stress and trauma; (3) develop cooperative relationships with public child welfare professionals who facilitate our access to these vulnerable families; (4) collect ethnographic data describing socialization contexts experienced by children of methamphetamine abusers in rural Illinois; as well as the perspectives of substance abuse and mental health counselors, law enforcement, educators, and child welfare professionals; and (5) collect pilot data from methamphetamine-abusing parents and their children.

The proposed research systematically builds on this pilot work by focusing on the perspectives of methamphetamine abusing parents and their children, and by including systematic contextual information on family, mental health and substance abuse. Our pilot work was funded, in part, by the Children and Family Research Center (CFRC). The CFRC is an ongoing collaboration between the University of Illinois School of Social Work and Department of Children and Family Services (DCFS). This ongoing collaboration provides unique research opportunities for involvement with extremely vulnerable families including those experiencing methamphetamine abuse.

C.1 Studies with Vulnerable Families and Traumatized Children Involved with DCFS

Our (Haight & Black) prior, collaborative research has included a total of 45 families of preschool-aged children in foster care because of maltreatment. These pilot studies were designed to describe the interactions of biological mothers with their young children during parent-child visits; to explore the beliefs of mothers, foster parents and child welfare workers about parent-child visits; and to develop and assess an intervention designed to support the relationships of mothers and their young children in foster care. (Haight, Black, Workman, & Tata, 2001; Haight et al., 2002; Haight et al., 2006; Haight, Mangelsdorf, Black, et al., 2006).

C.2 Ethnographic Study of Parent Methamphetamine Abuse in the Rural Midwest

This pilot study described parent methamphetamine abuse in the rural Midwest and its possible effects on the development and well-being of school-aged children. Methods included record reviews, participant observation (shadowing a DCFS professional investigating families with suspected methamphetamine abuse), and 35 interviews with knowledgeable adults. Adult informants (child welfare workers, educators, counselors, law enforcement personnel, substance abuse treatment providers, and foster caregivers) described their experiences with parent methamphetamine abuse and associated behaviors. Overall, informants described that children are brought by their addicted parents into a rural drug culture with distinct antisocial beliefs and practices. Children's experience of this culture includes environmental danger, chaos, neglect, abuse, loss, and isolation. Informants believed that children develop antisocial beliefs and practices such as lying, stealing, drug use, and violence through direct teaching by their parents and, indirectly, through observing parents' own antisocial behavior. Informants described children as displaying psychological, social, and educational disturbances. They attributed individual variation in children's functioning to a variety of protective factors including a caring relationship with a stable adult (see Haight et al., 2005 in PHS398 Research Plan: Appendix)

C.3 The Perspectives and Mental Health Status of Children Whose Parents Abuse Methamphetamine

Pilot research, completed subsequent to the *second* submission of our grant, and using the instruments described in section D.8, addresses the beliefs and experiences of 18 children (aged 6-14) in foster care because of parent methamphetamine abuse *(Haight et al., 2006; Ostler et al., 2006)*. It also describes their development, mental health status, and substance abuse attitudes. These preliminary data indicate that most children (16) are functioning in the average to above average range on a measure of vocabulary, the

Peabody Picture Vocabulary Test (PPVT), suggesting adequate understanding of interview questions. As indicated by the Childhood Behavior Checklist (CBCL), half of the children (9) experience internalizing, externalizing or trauma symptoms in the clinical or sub-clinical range. In semi-structured interviews, most children (13) did report traumatic experiences associated with observing parents' active substance abuse (11), observing violence between adults at home (9), and observing parents' criminal behavior and its consequences (e.g., drug busts) (9). Some children (6) also expressed distress at participation in antisocial activities associated with parents' methamphetamine abuse, e.g., stealing precursors and lying to teachers. These reports are consistent with adult reports from the first pilot study. Unlike adult reports, however, children did not report neglect as an issue. Many (9) did, however, spontaneously report traumatic separation from and loss of parents, an issue not emphasized by knowledgeable adults. Most children (10) spontaneously described their parents' methamphetamine abuse as a taboo topic. Very few children (3) reported discussing their experiences within their families with an adult outside of the family. Not surprisingly, then, many children expressed beliefs about themselves and their families that may inhibit positive development, for example, that they and their families are "bad," that it is their fault that their parents use methamphetamine, and that other families do not experience similar struggles.

C.4 The Perspectives of Mothers Who Abuse Methamphetamine

Pilot data also suggest that the proposed research will provide critical information for effectively implementing interventions. We have pilot tested the interview for our proposed study with 3 mothers who abuse methamphetamine. Many of their responses were consistent with those of other knowledgeable adults. Their responses also suggest how interventions may be implemented. For example, mothers discussed difficulties with access to services. They also perceived school to be a safe context where children could receive services.

C.5 Studies of Parent-Child Relationships in Addicted Families

In addition to the pilot work being conducted in rural Illinois, our collaborator, Sydney Hans, has over twenty years of experience working with families affected by substance abuse. She has written extensively about issues of prenatal exposure to drugs of abuse (Hans, 1998), but in particular has focused on issues of how postnatal rearing conditions affect the development of children in families where the mother uses drugs (Hans, 2002, 2004) and how women's comorbid mental health problems and exposure to family violence affect parenting and parent-child attachment (Hans, 1999; Hans et al, 1999).

C.6 Summary

Our collaborative pilot research establishes the importance and feasibility of our conducting research on parents who abuse methamphetamine and their children using families involved in the public child welfare system. Our pilot research also begins to describe the range of child and adult beliefs and socialization practices relevant to parent methamphetamine abuse. The proposed research will build substantially upon this base to (1) provide a fuller description of parent and child beliefs about methamphetamine abuse and its effects on children; (2) provide a fuller description of children's experiences and parents' socialization practices; (3) contextualize parent and child belief systems through the use of home visits and structured assessments of child and parent development, mental health, and substance use; and (4) focus efforts on an age group (7 to 10 years) important to the development of future preventive interventions.

D. RESEARCH DESIGN AND METHODS

D.1 Introduction

We will address our aims by integrating methods from developmental and clinical psychology, and ethnography (see Jessor, Colby, & Shweder, 1996). We will study parents who abuse methamphetamine and their 7-10 year-old children beginning approximately one month following DCFS involvement (the time frame needed to substantiate allegations and put services in place). We will focus on qualitative descriptions of parents' and children's beliefs about parent methamphetamine abuse based on in-depth, semi-structured interviews, as well as descriptions of family ecology from home visits, and children's and parents' development, mental health and substance use based on structured, clinical and developmental instruments. This methodology allows (1) a combination of research strategies designed to tap different aspects of socialization and acquisition related to parent methamphetamine abuse; (2) culturally relevant descriptions of beliefs about parent methamphetamine abuse, a topic on which relatively little is known, contextualized by descriptions of family context, development, mental health, and substance abuse from existing, structured, clinical instruments; and (3) a description of the perspectives and experiences of members of a typically hidden population. This information will generate questions regarding the bases of individual variation in children's mental health and substance abuse to be explored in future research. For example, is children's belief that talking about methamphetamine is taboo related to their mental health?

This research program will contribute to the development of preventive and intervention services. The implementation of these methods is enabled by our strong, interdisciplinary research team with expertise in child welfare (Haight, Ostler, Black); ethnography (Haight, Ostler, Black); developmental and child clinical psychology (Haight, Ostler, Hans); parent substance abuse (Hans, Ostler); parenting (Haight, Ostler, Hans) and adult and child psychiatry (Black); *the design and analysis of mixed methods research (Jennifer Greene); and interventions for antisocial youth (Patrick Tolan)*. In addition, our long-standing collaboration with DCFS allows us unique access to vulnerable families struggling with methamphetamine abuse.

D.2 Timeline

The proposed research will be carried out over a two-year period.
Year 1
Start-up (Months 1-3)
Begin recruitment (Month 4)
Collect data for 15 families (Months 5-12)
Begin coding and analysis (Months 9-12)
Year 2
Continue recruitment and data collection for another 15 families. (Months 1-6)
Continue coding and analysis. (Months 1-9)
Writing (Months 8-12).

D.3 Design

The proposed research is descriptive and primarily case-based (Stake, 2000). The purpose is to understand, in depth, the coherence and diversity of parent and child beliefs about parent methamphetamine abuse, child experiences and parents' socialization practices within the cultural context of rural Illinois. The goals are to provide a meaningful basis of comparison with other cultural contexts studied in future research, and to provide useful information for the development of preventive intervention services within this area of rural Illinois.

D.4 Research Site

The research site is the seven county area served by the RURAL Field Office of the Illinois Department of Children and Family Services (see PHS 398 Research Plan: Letters of Support). The region served by the RURAL Field Office is predominantly rural, white, and working-class. It covers a total of 3,492 square miles with a population of 160,284. In all seven counties more than 95% of the population is white. The median annual family income in the counties ranges from $37,313 to $40,084. The percentage of the population with at least a high school education ranges from 79%-84% with 10% to 21% having graduated from college (www.ePODUNK.com).

The service area of the RURAL Field Office of DCFS is an excellent site to conduct the proposed research. Professionals from the RURAL Field

Office and their colleagues (educators, law enforcement personnel, and sub-stance abuse counselors) are very concerned about the significant and grow-ing problem of methamphetamine in their communities and how it impacts the children and families they serve (Haight et al., 2005). Child protection workers from the RURAL Field Office have requested our help as they urgently need information to inform the development of intervention efforts. In addition, the RURAL Field Office is an effective service provider and DCFS professionals in this office typically enjoy good relationships with clients. Indeed, a recent, in-depth federal review specifically cited the RURAL Field Office, in contrast with other Illinois field offices, as excellent on achieving a variety of safety, permanency, and well-being goals for children. In addi-tion, the success of DCFS professionals from RURAL in building relationships with clients and other community members is apparent from findings that community stakeholders consistently reported examples of their positive interaction with them (U.S. Department of Health and Human Services, 2004). This competence will continue to be invaluable to us in accessing and establishing rapport with study participants.

D.5 Participants

Participants will be 30 mothers, 5 fathers, and 30 of their 7- to 10-year-old children involved with DCFS because of parental methamphetamine abuse and *referred by DCFS family preservation caseworkers. All families whose records indicate substantiated findings of child maltreatment related to parent methamphetamine abuse who are participating in the "Family Preservation Program" will be invited to participate until 30 families are recruited. Eligibility of referred families will be confirmed via case record review by researchers. The DCFS has already given us permission to review confidential records for eligibility and UIUC and DCFS IRB boards also have approved.*

Families participating in the Family Preservation Program remain intact while parents receive intensive outpatient drug rehabilitation, and the chil-dren's safety is monitored daily by DCFS for a period of 3 to 6 months. During this time, parents and children typically do not receive other services or mental health counseling. *Note that parents who have been involved in methamphetamine production are not eligible for this program.* The fam-ily preservation program is a highly stable program that has functioned in the RURAL Field Office for 14 years. It provides unique access to metham-phetamine-abusing parents.

We anticipate based on pilot data and agency information that most par-ticipating parents will be single mothers, but any fathers who have contact with children will be invited to participate. We focus on 7- to 10-year-olds because pilot research indicates that by early adolescence many of these children have become regular substance users (Haight et al., 2006; Ostler et al., 2006). All children and parents meeting selection criteria will be invited to participate as soon as they enter the system. One child per family will be the designated target child. If more than one child within the family meets the selection criteria, the target child will be randomly selected or selected to ensure a gender balance. Data from the RURAL Field Office of the DCFS indicate that the recruitment of 30 children and parents is a realistic goal within the time frame of the proposed study (see PHS 398 Research Plan: Letters of Support). Pilot research suggests that saturation will be reached by 30 children and 30 mothers. Participants also will include approximately 10 caseworkers who will be providing intensive services to families during the study. All caseworkers are female and have a minimum of 3 years experience working at the RURAL Field Office. *Parents will be paid $25.00 in grocery scripts for the first interview and $25.00 in grocery scripts for the HOME visit. They will be paid $25.00 in cash for the final interview.* All target children will choose a present for themselves and siblings from an assortment of new, attractive, developmentally appropriate toys. Given our previous research, we expect that approximately 95% of DCFS professionals and 75% of eligible parents will agree to participate. Parents are likely to be European American, and from working-class backgrounds (Haight et al., 2005).

D.6. Entry into the Field and Relationships with Participants

Prolonged, sustained community engagement and our prior studies have facilitated strong, trusting collaborative relationships between the researchers, DCFS professionals, and other community members. From April 2004 to September 2004, Haight and Ostler have conducted more than 100 hours of participant observation. Participant observation consisted largely of shadowing DCFS professionals investigating families because of suspected parent methamphetamine abuse. It also included observations of a staffing of investigators, supervision of an investigation, court appearance of methamphetamine involved parents, Illinois state legislative methamphetamine task force meetings, visits to rural schools, and multiple visits to the RURAL Field Office. Haight, Ostler, and Black interviewed 35 community members (police officers, educators, substance abuse counselors, DCFS professionals) regarding methamphetamine abuse in their communities and its impact on children. Findings from this pilot ethnographic research were presented to DCFS practitioners and administrators, as well as the Illinois legislative task force on methamphetamine. Ostler and Black also collected pilot interview data from three mothers struggling with methamphetamine abuse, and interviewed 18 children whose parents abuse methamphetamine, to obtain information about their experiences, mental health, and substance use. Ostler and Black will be introduced to each child and parent at their home by a DCFS professional known to the family. On the days of the testing and interviews, time will be spent with parents and children in casual conversation, i.e., "visiting." Relationships with children are promoted through multiple contacts, by spending time with the child in positive activities such as play and by pacing interviews and testing at a rate comfortable to the child. Relationships with the parents will be promoted through respect, a nonjudgmental attitude towards their substance abuse, and interest in their families.

D.7 Setting

Interviews and testing will be conducted primarily at rural outpost offices of the RURAL Field Office of the DCFS. These small rural field offices are distributed across the area served by the RURAL Field Office. They provide quiet private areas within reasonable driving distance of DCFS clients. Participants will be reminded that researchers are not employed by DCFS and will not report to DCFS professionals regarding any individual's participation (or lack thereof). Transportation will be provided to parents and children.

D.8 Instruments

In the proposed project, we will rely on qualitative interviews with children and parents as our primary source of information about socialization practices, as well as beliefs about methamphetamine and other substances. Family visits, structured questionnaires, and interviews also will be utilized to supplement this information and to provide contextual information on family ecology and parents' and children's development, mental health, and substance use. The supplemental instruments will be used to interpret children's and parents' answers to the qualitative interviews. For instance, in understanding children's and parents' answers to the qualitative interviews, it will be useful to know if the child or parent has experienced mental health problems. Our assessments of "development" will focus on verbal ability because of their centrality in our measure of beliefs about methamphetamine. The qualitative interviews and all supplementary measures are included in PHS 398 Research Plan: Appendix.

Family Ecology (Aim 1)

1. Record reviews. We have been granted permission to review case records for study participants (See PHS 398 Research Plan: Letters of Support). These records contain the investigative report which includes evidence of child maltreatment; caseworker's court report which summarizes the case and parents' criminal histories; all notes on the caseworker's contact with the family; and service plan. These notes also include a basic description of who was living with the child and the condition of the home at the initiation of child welfare services.

2. HOME. The HOME (see "Socialization practices" below) includes a "physical environment" subscale.
3. Domestic violence assessment. Current and past domestic violence will be assessed with the Revised Conflict Tactics Scales (CTS2; Strauss, Hamby, Boney-McCoy, & Sugarman, 1996) completed by the parents. The CTS consists of a list of actions that a family member might take in a conflict with another member. The items start with those low in coerciveness and gradually become more coercive and aggressive towards the end of the list. The measure takes about 15 minutes to complete. CTS has been widely used in studies of domestic violence. They have good reliability (Wilson et al, 1996).
4. Field notes. By design, field notes will be less structured and more narrative-like than other instruments. Given how little evidence is available about the rearing environments of children from methamphetamine abusing families, it is likely that we have not anticipated all relevant characteristics. Less structured, more narrative-like accounts can raise important questions, allow correction of methods, and contribute to the rich contextualization of instruments such as the HOME. Examples of field notes from home visits during the pilot ethnographic research include descriptions of the type and condition of home and property (e.g., hot, one bedroom trailer with holes in wall, located 5 miles from town, dirt yard with outbuilding, unleashed dogs, guns in the home, target child sleeps with younger sibling on couch in main room, unwashed dishes).
5. Nonparticipating fathers. Note that for women whose partners are not participating in the study, brief questions will be asked of her regarding his substance abuse and history of antisocial behavior. There is evidence that mothers can provide such information about their children's fathers reliably (Caspi, et al., 2001).

Parents

Beliefs about Methamphetamine (Aim 2)

1. Socialization practices and beliefs about methamphetamine interview. The semi-structured, individual interview focuses on parents' beliefs about methamphetamine abuse, its effects on children, and appropriate parenting strategies. It also probes related beliefs, for example, about alcohol and marijuana, to place beliefs about methamphetamine within a broader system of beliefs. It takes approximately 1-1/2 to 2 hours to complete and is audiotaped. Questions include: Tell me about your family. Tell me about your family when you were using methamphetamine. What do you see as the effects of parent methamphetamine abuse on your child? How can adults support the well-being and development of children whose parents

abuse methamphetamine? Interviews will be conducted by a PhD-level psychologist or MSW-level social workers closely supervised by Ostler and Black. This interview was successfully employed in our pilot research.

Socialization Practices (Aim 2)

1. Socialization practices and beliefs about methamphetamine interview. Includes discussion of parenting practices.
2. HOME. The Home Observation for Measurement of the Environment (HOME) Inventory (Caldwell, & Bradley, 1984) will be used to measure the quality and quantity of stimulation and support available to a child in the home environment. The focus is on the child in the environment, and on events and transactions observed by the visitor. In this study we will use the Middle Childhood HOME version (MC) for children between the ages of 7 and 10 years. The MC version contains 59 items clustered into eight subscales: (1) Parental Responsivity, (2) Physical Environment, (3) Learning Materials,(4) Active Stimulation, (5) Encouraging Maturity, (6) Emotional Climate, (7) Parental Involvement, and (8) Family Participation. The information is obtained during a home visit and involves a low-key semi-structured observation and interview done so as to minimize intrusiveness and allow family members to act normally (Caldwell & Bradley, 1984). The measure has been used in a wide variety of clinical and research settings and has good reliability. Systematic training on the HOME Inventory has been developed and training tapes will be used. *To protect the safety of our staff, DCFS workers who monitor the families for relapse and child endangerment on a daily basis will be contacted before staff members are sent to the home. Staff members will communicate with other project staff via phone before and after each visit.*

Parent Functioning (Aim 2)

1. Parent background information. The Addiction Severity Index-Background (ASI-B; *see* below) also provides parent background information including demographic characteristics, medical history, areas of stress, employment history, legal history, family and other social relationships, and psychiatric history (McLellan et al., 1992). Additional questions will be added focused on the specific needs of the population being studied, including childbearing history, child school and day care arrangements, and history of involvement with the child welfare system.

2. Verbal and intellectual functioning. The Beliefs about Methamphetamine Interview described above is dependent on verbal ability.
Therefore, we will screen for any significant language deficits using
the Shipley Institute of Living Scale-Revised (Zachary,1991), a measure designed to assess verbal and intellectual functioning in adults.
Using a 40-item vocabulary test, individuals are asked to choose
which of four possible words is equivalent to a specified target word.
The Shipley takes about 10 minutes to complete. It correlates highly
with the Wechsler scales and has been widely used as a research
instrument and for verbal screening of psychiatric patients. It has
demonstrated good reliability and validity (Zachary,1991).

3. Parent substance abuse. The Addiction Severity Index (5th ed.)-
Baseline (ASI-B), a semi-structured interview, will provide information on parents' substance abuse histories, current substance use patterns, and addiction severity. This instrument assesses potential
problem areas relating to the parent's addiction: medical status,
employment and support, drug use, alcohol use, legal status, family/
social status, and psychiatric status. The measure has been widely
used in substance-using populations and provides reliable and valid
information on substance use and addiction severity (McLellan et al.,
1992). The measure takes about 1 hour to complete and will be done
using the interview format.

4. Parent psychopathology. The Symptom Checklist 90-Revised (SCL-
90R, Derogatis, 1993) is a brief, multidimensional self-report inventory that assesses a broad range of psychological problems and
symptoms of psychopathology. This measure provides information
on the following nine symptom scales: Somatization, Obsession-
Compulsive, Interpersonal Sensitivity, Depression, Anxiety, Hostility,
Phobic Anxiety, Paranoid Ideation, and Psychoticism. In addition,
information can be gathered on three global indices: a global severity
index, a positive symptom distress index, and a positive symptom
total. The measure takes about 15 minutes to complete. The SCL-90
R has demonstrated reliability and validity. It has been used extensively with adult psychiatric and substance using populations and has
been used to measure patient progress in treatment.

5. Trauma symptoms. As a second index of parent psychopathology, we
will administer the Trauma Symptom Checklist-40 (TSC-40). The TSC-
40 is a standardized assessment used in the evaluation of acute and
chronic posttraumatic symptomatology, including the lasting se-
quelae of childhood abuse and other early traumatic events. The various scales of the TSC-40 assess symptoms typically associated with
posttraumatic stress disorder (PTSD) or acute stress disorder (ASD),
but also intrapersonal and interpersonal difficulties often associated
with more chronic psychological trauma. The TSC-40 takes about

15 minutes to complete. It has been widely used and scales have moderate to high reliabilities, and concurrent and construct validity (Elliot & Briere, 1992).

Children

Experiences and Beliefs about Methamphetamine (Aim 3)

1. Experiences and beliefs about methamphetamine interview. Children will participate in semi-structured, individual interviews that are approximately 60 minutes long and are audiotaped. Given the nature of the subject matter and children's possible trauma histories, the interviews will be conducted by an experienced psychiatrist or child clinical psychologist. They will employ a flexible strategy for supporting children's responses. Children will be given the opportunity to choose among a variety of expressive toys (puppets, dollhouse and props) and art supplies (clay, drawing). As the interviewer and the child engage in this activity of the child's choosing, the interviewer will invite the child to respond to interview questions. This interview strategy was successfully employed in our pilot research (Ostler et al.,2006). Because not all children may be fully aware of their parents' methamphetamine abuse, the interview will begin with some fairly open-ended questions: "Tell me about your family," and "Tell me about a time in your family that was happy." Children also will be asked to "Tell me about a time in your family that was sad or scary." It is in this context that several probes for beliefs about methamphetamine will be included: What is methamphetamine (or crystal, meth, ice, or speed)? Sometimes adults use methamphetamine. How does that make them act? How about your (mom/dad)? Tell me about when they used methamphetamine. What did you do? How did you feel? What advice can you give to other kids whose parents use methamphetamine? To place children's beliefs about methamphetamine within a larger system of beliefs, this portion of the interview also will probe related beliefs, for example, about alcohol and marijuana abuse. The interview will conclude with an invitation for children to "Tell me about a time in your family that was fun," and then choose a game to play with the interviewer. This interview was successfully employed in our pilot research.

Child Functioning (Aim 3)

1. Medical and developmental history. The Developmental History Questionnaire (DHQ) (Garber, 1990) will provide information on the child's developmental, school, and medical history, starting in

infancy up to their current age. Completed by the mother, the DHQ asks about the child's delivery and birth, whether the mother smoked tobacco or drank when pregnant, when the child reached important developmental milestones, his or her relationships with siblings and other family members, his or her school experiences, friends, and medical history. The measure has been widely used in research and clinical studies (Garber, 1993). It takes approximately 25 minutes to complete.

2. The Peabody Picture Vocabulary Test. The Beliefs about Methamphetamine Interview is dependent on verbal ability. Therefore, we will screen for children's significant language delays using the PPVT-3 a norm-referenced, individually administered measure of receptive vocabulary for individuals from age 2-1/2 to adult (Dunn & Dunn, 1997). The PPVT-3 takes approximately 11-12 minutes to administer and requires that children point to pictures. It has excellent reliability and validity. It is related to measures of general intellectual functioning such as the WISC. During our pilot studies with school-aged children of parents who abuse methamphetamine, children appeared to enjoy the PPVT and the vast majority scored within the average range.

3. Children's attitudes about drugs and alcohol. The American Drug and Alcohol Survey- Children's Form (ADAS) and the Prevention Planning Survey (PPS) will provide supplementary information on children's beliefs and attitudes about methamphetamine, alcohol, and other substances. Administered together, these two paper and pencil measures ask questions about children's attitudes about substance use, including their perception of the harmfulness of drugs, their intention to use in the future, and any current use. The PPS provides contextual information about risk and protective factors related to substance use. It focuses on risk and protective factors in the social environments that make up most children's daily lives: peer groups, family, and school. The ADAS and PPS Children's versions were designed for elementary school students. As in our pilot research, we will read the forms to all children, as it provides an opportunity to clarify responses and understanding. The forms are generally completed in about 45 minutes. These instruments are reliable when used in the general population and with rural children (Edwards, 1992; Oetting, Edwards, & Beauvais, 1985; Oetting, Edwards, Kelly, & Beauvais, 1997).

4. Child behavior and mental health. Parents and caseworkers will complete the Child Behavior Checklist (CBCL, parent report form). Developed for children between the ages of 6-18, this measure is a checklist of children's internalizing, externalizing and trauma symptoms. The Social Competence section includes items addressing the

child's activities, peer relationships, and academic performance. The Behavior Problem section consists of 118 specific problem items concerning the child's behavior within the past 6 months. The checklist takes 15 minutes to complete. The CBCL is well standardized and has adequate reliability and validity (Achenbach, 1991).

5. Trauma symptoms. The Trauma Symptom Checklist for Children (TSCC) is a standardized assessment used in the evaluation of children's acute and chronic posttraumatic symptomatology. The TSCC consists of 44 items that yield two validity scales (Under-response and Hyper-response) and six clinical scales (Anxiety, Depression, Anger, Posttraumatic Stress, Dissociation, and Sexual Concerns). The child is asked to mark in a test booklet how often different thoughts, feelings and behaviors happen to him or her. The questionnaire checklist will be read to all children to clarify responses and ensure understanding of all questions. The TSCC has been widely used and scales have moderate to high reliabilities, and concurrent and construct validity (see Briere, 1997; Ebert & Fairbank; 1996). It takes approximately 15 minutes to complete.

D.9 Procedures

Record Review

Upon referral, researchers will review the family's DCFS file. Home visit researchers will conduct an initial home visit during which they will be introduced to family members by a DCFS professional. The purpose of this visit is to establish rapport with parents and children, and to make informal observations of the home. Informal observations and impressions of the home will be described in field notes. Immediately subsequent to the home visit, the researcher will complete the HOME. The home visit will last approximately 45-60 minutes.

Testing

Within two weeks of the home visit, standardized assessments will be administered to parents and children in a counterbalanced order. The first session will be approximately two hours for parents and one hour for children (child care will be provided during the second hour). In the event that any child or parent scores in the clinical range on any instrument or expresses a desire or plan to hurt him/herself or others, an appropriate individual (e.g., caseworker or local crisis worker) will be notified immediately and referrals provided. Children and their parents will be individually tested, at the same time, in separate, private rooms at the RURAL Field Office or its rural outposts. Children will be tested by a licensed child clinical psychologist experienced in working with children in foster care (Ostler) or a board certified psychiatrist experienced in working with traumatized children (Black). Parents will be tested and interviewed by experienced MSW-level social work research assistants closely supervised by Ostler and Black. They will be tested by the same individual who conducted the home visit.

Interviewing

Within two weeks of testing, children and parents will complete the beliefs about methamphetamine interview, again in separate rooms. This session will be approximately 1-1/2 hours for parents and one hour for children (child care will be provided during the final 30 minutes). They will be interviewed by the same individual who conducted their home visit and testing.

D.10 Analytic Strategy

Analysis of the multiple data sets in this study will be organized in three phases: (1) a descriptive variable-oriented analysis, (2) a descriptive case-oriented analysis, and (3) a case cluster analysis. In this analysis, the case is the family, as contextual factors and patterns of interaction among family members are assumed to importantly influence individual parent and child beliefs, characteristics, and behaviors. Overall, this analysis plan is designed to generate a rich descriptive portrait of this sample of rural Midwestern families involved with methamphetamine abuse. In addition to descriptive understanding, this portrait is intended to represent a first step towards a conceptual model of behavior and belief systems in methamphetamine-using families and, in turn, intervention services targeted at improving the well being of children whose parents abuse methamphetamine.

Phase one of the data analysis addresses aims 1–3. It is a "variable-oriented" descriptive analysis (Ragin, 1987), organized by variable (or construct) and method. It is intended to provide descriptive information about the parents and children in the study, including indicators of central tendency and dispersion as appropriate, as well as information about where these samples are located in the broader populations of adults and children on these variables, again as appropriate. As an example of descriptive analyses for quantitative data, parents' scores on the nine symptom scales on the Symptom Checklist 90-Revised will be analyzed, and the resulting statistics will contribute to the descriptive portrait of the psychological health status of the parents in the sample, including comparative information on this sample in relation to the population of adults. Similarly, data from other instruments, record reviews, and home observations will be descriptively analyzed and compared to norms.

The qualitative data from the child and parent interviews regarding beliefs about methamphetamine will first be coded as follows. Two types of descriptive codes based on parent and child interviews will comprise the center of our qualitative data analysis. First, content codes will be induced from the transcribed text to describe cognitive components of participants' beliefs. For example, what are the beliefs of methamphetamine-abusing parents concerning the effects of parent methamphetamine abuse on children? How do children interpret their parents' drug seeking behavior? Building on our pilot research (Haight et al., 2005), descriptive codes will be developed through repeated readings of the interview transcripts using analytic induction techniques (Denzin, 1989). All interviews will be read by Haight and Ostler, both of whom have extensive experience in coding qualitative or clinical interview data, and who independently, and through discussion, will generate a list of descriptive codes characterizing participant responses. Peer debriefing will be utilized as we seek feedback regarding coding from knowledgeable colleagues (see Denzin & Lincoln, 2000; Lincoln & Guba, 1985; Miles & Huberman, 1984.) Examples of codes of participants' beliefs that emerged from pilot work (Haight et al., 2005, Ostler et al., 2006) pertain to the presence and effects of (1) children's exposure to environmental danger and chaos; (2) child abuse; (3) children's neglect and isolation; (4) children's loss of home, family, and community; (5) children's exposure to criminal and other antisocial adult behavior including substance abuse and domestic violence; (6) children's disturbed psychological, social, and educational development; and (7) individual-, family-, and community-level risk and protective factors.

We are concerned with affective and motivational as well as cognitive components of belief systems. In a second set of analyses, the affective and motivational quality of parents' and children's interview responses will be coded building on clinical scales derived from our previous work on mothers involved with the public child welfare system (Shoppe-Sullivan et al., 2006), and from the adult attachment literature (e.g., Fiese, et al, 1999; George, Kaplan, & Main, 1984). These rating scales may include (1) the degree of match between the content of the participants' responses and expressed affect; (2) the frequency and intensity of expressions of anger or hostility; (3) the frequency and intensity of expressions of sadness or distress; (4) the frequency and intensity of positive statements parents make about the target child, and the target child makes towards the parent; (5) the extent to which the participant volunteered complete elaborated responses to interview questions; and (6) the quality of the interviewer's rapport with the participant. (We will use NVivo to facilitate data management.)

Then, as part of phase 1 of the analysis, a description of each of the codes emerging from the interview analysis, with connections to larger populations of children and adults as possible, will be added to the descriptive variable oriented portrait of this sample of rural children and adults.. For example, the description of the "child abuse" code or category—for both the parent and child samples—will comprise the multiple meanings and enactments of abuse for this sample, perhaps with an illustrative example or two. The final task in phase one of the analysis will be to begin to assess patterns of correlation and relationship among the variables in the study. This will include simple bivariate correlations among quantitative variables, NVIVO analyses assessing co-occurrence of codes for the qualitative data, and possible cross-method matrices or displays (Miles and Huberman, 1984) assessing simple patterns of relationship between selected quantitative variables and qualitative codes. At this time, these analyses will be conducted within the parent and child samples but not across them.

Phase 2 of the analysis will concentrate on developing a case-oriented descriptive portrait of the sample (Ragin, 1987). This analysis will be organized—not by variable (or construct or qualitative code/theme) as in phase one analysis—but by the family as the case. Phase 2 will also contribute to research aims 1 and 2, but from the holistic perspective of the family unit. This phase of the analysis will thus reorganize and integrate the descriptive data from phase 1 into comprehensive case narratives for each of the 30 families in the study. These case narratives will include the following sections: (1) context and history, comprising data from record reviews, domestic violence assessments, HOME observations, and field notes; (2) parent mental and behavioral health profile, comprising data from the parent mental health and substance abuse assessments, parent background information, and verbal development assessment; (3) child mental and behavioral health profile, comprising data from the child mental health and substance abuse assessments, development history, and verbal development assessment; (4) parent beliefs about methamphetamine use, from the parent interviews; and (5) child beliefs about methamphetamine use, from the child interviews. For each of these subsections, data from diverse sources will be integrated to develop a coherent narrative, following the integrative strategies recommended by Caracelli and Greene (1993) and Li, Marquart, and Zercher (2000), among others. In this integrative process, convergence across different data sources will be documented, and divergence will be examined further for possibly deeper understandings (Greene, 2005; Trend, 1979).

In phase 3 of the analysis, the cases presented in phase two will be analyzed for common patterns and connections. This will contribute primarily to aim 4. Based on the work of Caracelli & Greene (1993), the analytic strategy in phase 3 will focus on the development of clusters of cases, such that each cluster shares critical common features, for example, parental history of substance abuse or profile of child mental health. The preliminary relational analyses conducted in phase 1 will be a starting point for this clustering analysis. In addition, various analytic strategies, including typology development and analysis of extreme cases (Cara-celli & Greene, 1993) will be used in this analysis. The intent is to identify possibly relevant patterns of characteristics, beliefs, and behaviors that distinctively portray various types of rural families in which parents abuse methamphetamine. For example, the bivariate analyses conducted in phase 1 may reveal a negative relationship between two parental background factors—longevity of residence in a particular rural community and extent of methamphetamine use. The longer parents have lived in a particular community, the less severe their long-term methamphetamine use. Further analyses of this relationship may reveal further associations with parent mental health and with parent beliefs about methamphetamine use. Three clusters of families could emerge from such an analysis: (1) long-term residents with relatively less severe histories of methamphetamine use and relative stronger health profiles, (2) short-term residents with more extensive histories of methamphetamine use and relatively more impaired mental health profiles, and (3) parents with mixed residential and use histories. Then, child variables could also be clustered into these same three groups and analyzed for both common and divergent patterns. This kind of analysis could well generate preliminary hypotheses and linkages relevant to the development of a conceptual model of possible risk and protective factors for child substance abuse and mental health problems.

D.11 Transcription, Coding and Reliability

Interviews will be transcribed verbatim by trained research assistants. Two PhD student research assistants will be trained by Haight and Ostler to code the beliefs about methamphetamine interviews for children and parents. They will use the coding and clinical rating schemes to independently code 20% of interviews. Disagreements will be resolved through discussion. Our previous research has yielded good reliability for content codes (see Haight et al., 2001, 2005; Ostler et al., 2006) and affective quality scales (Shoppe-Sullivan et al., 2006). Interrater agreement for the content codes will be computed using Cohen's Kappa. Interrater reliability for each clinical rating scale will be conducted using two techniques: gamma coefficients and within one scale point percent agreement. Gamma will be used as a measure of interrater reliability because it is a statistic that controls for chance agreement, but is more appropriate for ordinal data than kappa (Hubert, personal communication, April 1997; Liebetrau, 1983).

D.12. Limitations

This proposed study does have limitations: First, we will recruit 30 families, which is a small sample size for the quantitative component. Second, our sample is not representative of all families involved with methamphetamine abuse. We will not have information on families before they come to the attention of authorities or subsequent to intervention.

D.13 Conclusion

The proposed project focuses on the beliefs of parents and children regarding parent methamphetamine abuse. These beliefs, in turn, are contextualized by family characteristics, and by parent and child development, mental health and substance abuse. Contextualized beliefs can suggest potential risk and protective factors to be explored in future research. These data will lead to the development of an RO1 proposal to NIDA, and several peer-reviewed manuscripts. Data from the proposed study also will contribute to the development of preventive and intervention services to enhance the mental health and substance abuse attitudes in highly vulnerable children of methamphetamine abusers.

E. PROTECTION OF HUMAN SUBJECTS

E.1 Proposed Involvement of Human Subjects

The study population will consist of 30 mothers, five fathers and their children who have active DCFS cases with a history of parent methamphetamine abuse. The parents will be recruited from DCFS professionals from the RURAL Field Office of DCFS. Parents and children will be asked to participate in a home visit of approximately one hour. In session 2, occurring at the DCFS field office, parents will be asked to fill out standardized instruments describing their child's behavior and adjustment, as well as provide medical and development histories for their children; and mental health and substance abuse histories for themselves. (Total time is approximately 2 hours, 10 minutes.) In session 3, also occurring at the DCFS field office, parents will be asked to participate in a semi-structured interview on their beliefs about parent methamphetamine abuse and its effects on children. (Total time is approximately 1-1/2 hours.) In the second session, children will respond to several standardized instruments describing their trauma symptoms, language and attitudes towards substance abuse. (Total time approximately 1 hour and 15 minutes.) In the third session, children will participate in interviews focused on their beliefs about parent methamphetamine abuse. (Total time is approximately 1 hour.)

We will seek informed consent from the University of Illinois, Department of Children and Family Services, and children and parents prior to initiating any data collection. We have received permission from UIUC and DCFS IRB boards for our earlier pilot work involving interviews with children and their methamphetamine–abusing parents, and some structured testing.

E.2 Sources of Research Material

Data for the proposed study will come from four primary sources: (1) DCFS case record reviews, (2) home visits, (3) structured clinical tests/assessments, and (4) interviews. Participant names will not be used, but only a unique study identifier.

E.3 Recruitment of Subjects and Consent Procedures

All recruitment and consent procedures will be performed in accordance with guidelines of the UIUC Human Subjects Research Committee, and the Institutional Review Board of the Illinois Department of Children and Family Services, and with their approval. We have the necessary DCFS collaboration necessary to recruit families for the study and will utilize recruitment methods shown to be effective in our previous studies. Members of the research team will meet with DCFS professionals individually, and as a group, to explain the project. DCFS professionals will secure parents' permission for us to contact them about participating in the study as well as volunteer to participate themselves. The study will be explained to parents and children in detail including its purpose, nature, procedures, and risks and benefits. The provisions for confidentiality will be described. All questions will be solicited and answered in detail. Participants will be told that their participation is voluntary and that refusal to participate will not affect DCFS status in any way, and that consent, once given, may be withdrawn at any time. We are not employed by DCFS and will not report to DCFS employees regarding any individual parent's or child's participation (or lack thereof) in the study. Participants will be informed, however, that certain information (e.g., evidence of new child abuse) is mandated by law to be reported to DCFS. In our experience parents are well aware of this caveat and are not distressed by it.

E.4 Potential Risks

The risks of participation are primarily related to the participant feeling uncomfortable or upset by the interview process or testing. There is a risk of reexperiencing psychological trauma associated with self-report of stress, distress, or coping. However, in our previous work most participants enjoyed having the opportunity to talk about themselves and their experiences. Although this did not occur in our pilot work, there is a possibility that interviews may elicit some PTSD-like experiences for the participants including flashbacks, dissociative episodes, or thoughts of hurting themselves if trauma memories are elicited. The licensed clinicians doing the interview are the "psychiatric back-up" for any emergency. These licensed clinicians are familiar with such abreactions and can help subjects calm or soothe themselves if it occurs and, if appropriate, the clinicians will refer them to a mental health agency for follow-up treatment of PTSD (to the crisis phone line or the ER at Provena Behavioral Health in Urbana IL, the health care provider for most of these participants). A risk to children is that they may divulge sensitive information that could further disrupt their families and lives. A risk to parents is that they will reveal information about child maltreatment that we will report to DCFS. However, parents already will have daily contact with professional child maltreatment investigators. Another risk to parents is that they may reveal illegal behavior. Any illegal behavior they do reveal to us presumably is known as they have open DCFS cases.

E.5 Protection of Human Subjects

All participants will be told that if they are experiencing discomfort or they are uncomfortable with the interview process, it can be terminated or paused. They also will be told that it is not necessary for them to respond to every one of our questions. Interviews are paced according to the participant's response, and sensitive questions are embedded within a larger protocol that includes positive prior and subsequent activities. Participants also may respond to questions in the third person, for example, they may discuss "a child." Interviewers are experienced clinicians who are trained to determine if a participant is experiencing discomfort, and will be able to appropriately terminate or interrupt the interview, help the participants to calm or soothe themselves and, if appropriate, make an immediate referral.

All interviews and standardized test are conducted in a private space. This will help to ensure the confidentiality of the interview data. The confidentiality of the data collected will be carefully protected. In addition, we will apply for a NIDA certificate of confidentiality. All data relating to each participant will be assigned an identifying code number, and names will not be used. Audiotapes and transcriptions will be catalogued by individuals' code number and secured in locked cabinets. Names and code numbers will be locked in a single locked file, accessible only to key personnel on the project. Data prepared for entry and data stored on disks for processing and analysis will include only code numbers. Data access will be allowed only for persons associated with the study either as transcribers and coders, data entry personnel, or data analysts. Protection of the files will be maintained by permitting access only by password. Master lists of code numbers and associated subject names will be retained only until completion of the study and then destroyed.

E.6 Acceptability of Risks

This study involves both some benefit and some risk to participants. There may be a benefit to discussing difficult experiences with an experienced clinician. In addition, we will notify the guardians of children who score in the clinical range on any measure of mental health, and provide an appropriate clinical referral. This is an important benefit to children whose mental health needs may go unnoticed. The psychological risks of doing the interviews are modest, and we have strategies in place to deal with any potential negative consequences. Compensation (a toy or coupons) is modest and unlikely to be coercive.

E.7 Importance of Knowledge to Be Gained

The knowledge gained could impact on clinical practice and policy recommendations for vulnerable children whose parents abuse methamphetamine. For example, any social risk and protective factors that are identified maybe used to inform the development of prevention interventions.

References

Addams, J. (1899). A function of the social settlement. Reprinted in C. Lasch (Ed.), *The social thought of Jane Addams*. Indianapolis: Bobbs-Merrill, 1965.

Addams, J. (1902). *Democracy and social ethics*. Urbana: University of Illinois Press.

Achenbach, T., & Rescorla, L. (2001). *Manual for the Child Behaviour Checklist/ 11/2-5 and 2001 profile*. Burlington: University of Vermont Department of Child Psychiatry.

American Association of Social Workers (1929). *Social case work, generic and specific: A report of the Milford Conference*.

Austin, D., M. (2003). History of research in social work. In I. C. Colby, A. Garcia, R. G. McRoy, & L. Videka Sherman (R. L. Edwards, Ed.), *Encyclopedia of social work: 1997 supplement* (19th ed., pp. 81-94).

Bamba, S. (2008). Japanese perspectives on supporting the well-being of maltreated children in state care: The concept of ibasho [Doctoral dissertation, order no. 3314728]. Dissertations & Theses @ CIC Institutions, *ProQuest Dissertations & Theses A&I* (304605734). Retrieved from http://login.ezproxy.lib .umn.edu/login?url = http://search.proquest.com/docview/304605734?account id = 14586

Bamba, S. (2010).The experiences and perspectives of Japanese substitute caregivers and maltreated children: A cultural-developmental approach to child welfare practice. *Social Work, 55*, 127-137.

Bamba, S., & Haight, W. L. (2011). *Child welfare and development: A Japanese case study*. New York: Cambridge University Press.

Bazeley, P. (2010). Computer assisted integration of mixed methods data sources and analyses. In A. Tashakkori and C. Teddlie (Eds.), *SAGE handbook of mixed methods in social and behavioral research* (pp. 431-467). London: SAGE.

Bazeley, P. (2012). Integrative analysis strategies for mixed data sources. *American Behavioral Scientist, 56*, 814-828.

Bernard, L., D.(1977). Education for social work. *Encyclopedia of social work, 17*(1), 474-485

Bergman, M. (2008). Introduction: Whither mixed methods. In M. Bergman (Ed.), *Advances in mixed methods research: Theories and applications* (pp.1-8). London: SAGE.

Biesta, G. (2010). Pragmatism and the philosophical foundations of mixed methods research. In A. Tashakkori and C. Teddlie (Eds.), *SAGE handbook of mixed methods in social and behavioral research* (pp. 95-117). London: SAGE.

Black, J., Haight, W., & Ostler, T. (2006). Health and psychiatric issues of children of rural methamphetamine abusers and manufacturers. *Psychiatric Times, 23*(14), 18-19.

Booth, C. (1903). *Life and labour of the people in London.* London: Macmillan.

Briere, J. (1996). *Trauma symptom checklist for children.* Odessa, FL: Psychological Assessment Resources, 00253-8.

Bryman, A. (2007). Barriers to integrating quantitative and qualitative research. *Journal of Mixed Methods Research, 1,* 8–22.

Bryman, A. (2008). Why do researchers integrate/combine/mesh/blend/mix/merge/fuse quantitative and qualitative research? In M. Bergman (Ed.), *Advances in mixed methods research: Theories and applications* (pp. 87–100). London: SAGE.

Butler, E. B. (1911). *Women and the trades: Pittsburgh, 1907-1908.* New York: Charities Publication Committee.

Campbell, D. T., & Fiske, D. W. (1959). Convergent and discriminant validation by the multitrait-multimethod matrix. *Psychological Bulletin, 56*(2), 81.

Caracelli, V. J., & Greene, J. C. (1993). Data analysis strategies for mixed-method evaluation designs. *Educational Evaluation and Policy Analysis, 15,* 195–207.

Chaumba, J. (2013). The use and value of mixed methods research in social work. *Advances in Social Work, 14,* 307–333.

Cook, T., Shannon, P. J., Vinson, G., Letts, J., & Dwe, E. (2015). War trauma and torture experiences reported during public health screening of newly resettled Karen refugees: A qualitative study. *BMC International Health and Human Rights, 15.* Retrieved from http://beta.bmcinthealthhumrights.com/articles/10 .1186/s12914-015 -0046-y

Cook, T. D. (1985). Postpositivist critical multiplism. In R. L. Shotland & M.M Mark, (Eds.) *Social science and social policy* (pp. 21–62). London: SAGE.

Cowger, C. D., & Menon, G. (2001). Integrating qualitative and quantitative research methods. In B. Thyer (Ed.), *The handbook of social work research methods* (pp. 473–484). Thousand Oaks, CA: SAGE.

Creswell, J. W. (2010). Mapping the developing landscape of mixed methods research. In A. Tashakkori & C. Teddlie (Eds.), *SAGE handbook of mixed methods in social and behavioral research* (pp. 45–68). Thousand Oaks, CA: SAGE.

Creswell, J. W. (2014). *Research design: Qualitative, quantitative, and mixed methods approaches.* (4th ed.). Los Angeles: SAGE.

Creswell, J. W. (2015). *A concise introduction to mixed methods research.* Los Angeles: SAGE.

Creswell, J. W., & Garrett, A. R. (2008). The "movement" of mixed methods research and the role of educators. *South African Journal of Education, 28,* 321–333.

Creswell, J. W., Klassen, A. C., Plano Clark, V. L., & Smith, K. C. (2011) for the Office of Behavioral and Social Sciences Research. *Best practices for mixed methods research in the health sciences.* National Institutes of Health. Retrieved from http://obssr.od.nih.gov/mixed_methods_research

Creswell, J. W., & Plano Clark, V. L. (2007). *Designing and conducting mixed methods research* (1st ed.). Thousand Oaks, CA: SAGE.

Creswell, J. W., & Plano Clark, V. L. (2011). *Designing and conducting mixed methods research* (2nd ed.). Thousand Oaks, CA: SAGE.

Creswell, J. W., Plano Clark, V. L., Gutmann, M., & Hanson, W. (2003). Advanced mixed methods research design. In A. Tashakkori and C. Teddlie (Eds.), *SAGE handbook of mixed methods in social and behavioral research* (pp. 209–240). Thousand Oaks, CA: SAGE.

Crotty, M. (1998). *The foundations of social research: Meaning and perspective in the research process.* Thousand Oaks, CA: SAGE.

D'Agostino, Jr., R. B. (1998). Tutorial in biostatistics: Propensity scores methods for bias reduction in comparison of a treatment to non-randomized control group. *Statistics in Medicine, 17*, 2265-2281.

Denzin, N. K. (1978). Triangulation: A case for methodological evaluation and combination. In N. K. Denzin (Ed.), *Sociological methods* (2nd ed., pp. 339–357). New York: McGraw-Hill.

Denzin, N. K., & Lincoln, Y. S. (2000). *Handbook of qualitative methods.* Thousand Oaks, CA: SAGE.

Devine, E. (1909). Results of the Pittsburgh Survey. *The American Association Quarterly, The Third Series, 10*(1). Papers and Discussions of the 21st Annual Meeting, December 1908. Atlantic City, NJ.

Dewey, J. (1958). *Experience and nature.* Courier Corporation, Dover, DE: Dover Publications.

Dilthey, W. (1883). *Introduction to human sciences. Selected works* (I. R. Makkreel & F. Rodi, Eds., & M. Neville, Trans.). Princeton, NJ: Princeton University Press.

Dunlap, K. M. (1993). A history of research in social work education: 1915-1991. *Journal of Social Work Education, 29*, 293-301.

Epstein, I. (1988). Quantitative and qualitative methods. In R. M. Grinell (Ed.), *Social work research and evaluation* (3rd ed., pp. 18-198). Itasca, IL: Peacock.

Fanshel, D. (1980). The future of social work research: Strategies for the coming years. In D. Fanshel (Ed.). *Future of social work research* (pp. 3-18). Washington, DC: National Association of Social Workers.

Fitch, J. A. (1910). *The Pittsburgh Survey: The steel workers* (P. U. Kellog, Ed.), vol. 3. New York: Charities Publication Committee.

Flexner, A. (1915). Is social work a profession? In *Proceedings of the National Conference of Charities and Correction*, 1915 (pp. 576-590). Chicago: Hildmann.

Gambrill, E. (2003). Evidence-based practice: Implications for knowledge development and use in social work. In A. Rosen and E. K. Proctor (Eds.), *Developing practice guidelines for social work intervention: Issues, methods, and research agenda* (pp. 37-58). New York: Columbia University Press.

Gambrill, E. (2006). Evidence-based practice and policy: Choices ahead. *Research on Social Work Practice, 16*, 338-357.

Garmezy, N. (1985). Stress-resistant children: The search for protective factors. In A. Davids (Ed.), *Recent research in developmental psychopathology* (pp. 213-233). Elmsford, NY: Pergamon Press.

Garmezy, N. (1993). Children in poverty: Resilience despite risk. *Psychiatry, 56*, 127-130.

Geertz, C. (1973). *The interpretation of cultures: Selected essays.* New York: Basic Books.

Gilgun, J. F. (1999a). CASPARS: New tools for assessing client risks and strengths. *Families in Society: The Journal of Contemporary Social Services, 80*, 450-459.

Gilgun, J. F. (1999b). Methodological pluralism and qualitative family research. In M. B. Sussman, S. K. Steinmetz, & G. W. Peterson (Eds.), *Handbook of marriage and the family* (pp. 219-261). New York: Springer Science & Business Media.

Gilgun, J. F. (1999c). Mapping resilience as process among adults with childhood adversities. In E. A. Thompson, A. I. Thompson, & J. A. Futrell (Ed.), *The dynamics of resilient families* (pp. 41–70). Thousand Oaks, CA: SAGE.

Gilgun, J. F. (2004). Qualitative methods and the development of clinical assessment tools. *Qualitative Health Research, 14*, 1008–1019.

Gilgun, J. F. (2008). Lived experience, reflexivity, and research on perpetrators of interpersonal violence. *Qualitative Social Work, 7*, 181–197.

Gioia, D. (2012). Mixed methods research: Merging theory with practice. *Qualitative Social Work, 11*, 220–225.

Greene, J. C. (2005). The generative potential of mixed methods inquiry. *International Journal of Research & Method in Education, 28*, 207–211.

Greene, J. C. (2007). *Mixed methods in social inquiry*. Hoboken, NJ: Wiley.

Greene, J. C. (2008). Is mixed methods social inquiry a distinctive methodology? *Journal of Mixed Methods Research, 2*, 7–22.

Greene, J. C. (2011). *Integrated data analysis in mixed methods evaluation*. Professional Development Workshop, Claremont Graduate University, August 21, 2011.

Greene, J. C., Caracelli, V. J., & Graham, W. F. (1989). Toward a conceptual framework for mixed-method evaluation designs. *Educational Evaluation and Policy Analysis, 11*, 255-274.

Greene, J.C., & Hall, J. N. (2010). Dialectics and pragmatism. In A. Tashakkori & C. Teddlie (Eds.), *SAGE handbook of mixed methods in social and behavioral research* (pp. 119–167). Los Angeles, CA: SAGE.

Greene, J. C., Sommerfeld, P., & Haight, W. L. (2010). Mixing methods in social work research. In L. Shaw, K. Briar-Lawson, J. Orme, & R. Ruckdeschel (Eds.), *The SAGE handbook of social work research* (pp. 315–331). Thousand Oaks, CA: SAGE.

Gregory, A., Skiba, R., & Noguera, P. A. (2010). The achievement gap and the discipline gap: Two sides of the same coin? *Educational Researcher, 39*, 59–68.

Guo, S.(2008). Quantitative research. *Encyclopedia of Social Work, 20*(3), 492–496.

Haight, W. (2002). *African-American children at church: A sociocultural perspective*. New York: Cambridge University Press.

Haight, W., Black, J. & Sheridan, K. (2010). A mental health intervention for rural, foster children from methamphetamine-involved families: Experimental assessment with qualitative elaboration. *Children and Youth Services Review, 32*(10), 1446–1457.

Haight, W., Gibson, P. A., Kayama, M., Marshall, J. M., & Wilson, R. (2014). An ecological-systems inquiry into racial disproportionalities in out-of-school suspensions from youth, caregiver and educator perspectives. *Children and Youth Services Review, 46*, 128–138.

Haight, W., Jacobsen, T., Black, J., Kingery, L., Sheridan, K., & Mulder, C. (2005). "In these bleak days": Parent methamphetamine abuse and child welfare in the rural Midwest. *Children and Youth Services Review, 27*, 949–971.

Haight, W., Marshall, J., Hans, S., Black, J., & Sheridan, K. (2010). "They mess with me, I mess with them": Understanding physical aggression in rural girls and boys from methamphetamine-involved families. *Children and Youth Services Review, 32*, 1223–1234.

Haight, W., Marshall, J., & Woolman, J. (2015). The child protection clinic: A mixed methods evaluation of parent legal representation. *Child and Youth Services Review, 56,* 7-17.

Haight, W., Ostler, T., Black, J., Sheridan, K., & Kingery, L. (2007). A child's-eye view of parent methamphetamine abuse: Implications for helping foster families to succeed. *Children and Youth Services Review, 29*(1), 1-15.

Haight, W., Ostler, T., Black, J. and Kingery, L. (2009). *Children of Methamphetamine-Involved Families: The Case of Rural Illinois.* New York: Oxford University Press.

Haight, W. L., Black, J. E., Mangelsdorf, S., Giorgio, G., Tata, L., Schoppe, S. J., & Szewczyk, M. (2002). Making visits better: The perspectives of parents, foster parents, and child welfare workers. *Child Welfare-New York, 81,* 173-202.

Haight, W. L., Black, J. E., Workman, C. L., & Tata, L. (2001). Parent-child interaction during foster care visits. *Social Work, 46,* 325-338.

Haight, W. L., Carter-Black, J. D., & Sheridan, K. (2009). Mothers' experience of methamphetamine addiction: A case-based analysis of rural, midwestern women. *Children and Youth Services Review, 31,* 71-77.

Haight, W. L., Mangelsdorf, S., Black, J., Szewczyk, M., Schoppe, S., Giorgio, G., . . . Tata, L. (2005). Enhancing parent-child interaction during foster care visits: Experimental assessment of an intervention. *Child Welfare, 84,* 459-481.

Haight, W. L., & Miller, P. J. (1993). *Pretending at home: Early development in a sociocultural context.* Albany: Suny Press.

Hamington, M. (2010). Jane Addams. In E. N. Zalta (Ed.), *The Stanford Encyclopedia of Philosophy.* Retrieved from http://plato.stanford.edu/archives/fall2010/entries/addams-jane

Harrison, W. D. (1994). The inevitability of integrated methods. In E. Sherman & W. Reid (Eds.), *Qualitative research in social work* (pp.409-422). New York: Columbia University.

Hart, B., & Risley, T. R. (1995). *Meaningful differences in the everyday experience of young American children.* Baltimore, MD: Brookes.

Hart, B., & Risley, T. R. (2003). The early catastrophe: The 30 million word gap by age 3. *American Educator, 27,* 4-9.

Haworth, G. O. (1984). Social work research, practice, and paradigms. *The Social Service Review, 58,* 343-357.

Heath, S. B. (1983). *Ways with words: Language, life and work in communities and classrooms.* New York: Cambridge University Press.

Hesse-Biber, S., & Johnson, R. B. (2013). Coming at things differently: Future directions of possible engagement with mixed methods research. *Journal of Mixed Methods Research, 7,* 103-109.

Hookway, C. (2013). Pragmatism. In E. N. Zalta (Ed.), *The Stanford Encyclopedia of Philosophy.* Retrieved from http://plato.stanford.edu/archives/spr2015/entries/pragmatism

Hudson, W. W. (1982). Scientific imperatives in social work research and practice. *The Social Service Review, 56,* 246-258.

Johnson, R., Onwuegbuzie, A., & Turner, L. (2007). Toward a definition of mixed methods research. *Journal of Mixed Methods Research, 1,* 112-133.

Johnson, R. B., & Onwuegbuzie, A. J. (2004). Mixed methods research: A research paradigm whose time has come. *Educational Researcher, 33*(7), 14-26.

Jones, J. H. (1993). *Bad blood*. New York: Simon and Schuster.

Joy, P. A., & Kuehn, R. R. (2002). Conflict of interest and competency issues in law clinic practice. *Clinical Law Review, 9*, 493.

Karpf, M. J. (1931). *The scientific basis of social work: A study in family case work*. New York: Columbia University Press.

Kayama, M., Haight, W., Gibson, P. A., & Wilson, R. (2015). Use of criminal justice language in personal narratives of out-of-school suspensions: Black students, their caregivers, and educators. *Children and Youth Services Review, 51*, 26–35.

Kirk, S. A., & Reid, W. J. (2002). *Science and social work: A critical appraisal*. New York: Columbia University Press.

Kline, R. B. (2011). *Principles and Practice of Structural Equation Modeling* (3rd ed.) New York: Guilford Press.

Korang-Okrah, R. (2012). *Risk and resilience: Ghanaian (Akan) widows and property rights* [Doctoral dissertation]. University of Illinois at Urbana-Champaign.

Krentzman, A. R., Cranford, J. A., & Robinson, E. A. R. (2013). Multiple dimensions of spirituality in recovery: A lagged mediational analysis of Alcoholics Anonymous' principal theoretical mechanism of behavior change, *Substance Abuse, 34*, 20–32.

Krentzman, A. R., Higgins, M. M., Klatt, E. S., & Staller, K. (2015). Alexithymia, emotional dysregulation, and recovery from alcoholism: Therapeutic response to assessment of mood. *Qualitative Health Research, 25*, 794–805.

Krentzman, A. R., Mannella, K. A., Hassett, A. L., Barnett, N., Cranford, J. A., Brower, K. J., . . . Meyer, P.S. (2015). Feasibility, acceptability, and impact of a web-based gratitude exercise among individuals in outpatient treatment for alcohol use disorders. *The Journal of Positive Psychology*. Advance online publication. doi: 10.1080/17439760.2015.1015158

Ladd, G. (1992) Perspectives on the aims, assumptions, and activities of human science: An historical overview. In R. D. Parke & G. W. Ladd (Eds.) *Family-peer relations: Modes of linkage* (pp. 1–36). Mahwah, NJ: Erlbaum.

Leech, N. L., & Onwuegbuzie, A. J. (2009). A typology of mixed methods research designs. *Quality & Quantity, 43*, 265–275.

Lincoln, Y. S., & Guba, E. G. (1985). *Naturalist inquiry*. Beverly Hills, CA: SAGE.

Lipsey, M. W. (1990). *Design sensitivity: Statistical power for experimental research*. Newbury Park, CA: SAGE.

Losen, D. J. (2011). *Discipline policies, successful schools, and racial justice*. Boulder, CO: National Education Policy Center. Retrieved from http://nepc.colorado .edu/publication/discipline-policies

Maas, H. S. (1977). Research in Social Work. *Encyclopedia of social work, 17*(2), 1183–1193.

Macdonald, M. E. (1960). Social work research: A perspective. In N. A. Polansky (Ed.), *Social work research* (pp. 1–23). Chicago: University of Chicago Press.

Maxwell, J. A. (2004). Causal explanation, qualitative research, and scientific inquiry in education. *Educational Researcher, 33*(2), 3–11.

Maxwell, J. A. (2005). *Qualitative research design: An interactive approach*. Newbury Park, CA: SAGE.

Maxwell, J. A. (2010). Validity: How might you be wrong. *Qualitative educational research: Readings in reflexive methodology and transformative practice*. New York: Routledge.

Maxwell, J., & Mittapalli, K. (2010). Realism as a stance for mixed methods research. In A. Tashakkori & C. Teddlie (Eds.), *SAGE handbook of mixed methods in social and behavioral research* (2nd ed.). Los Angeles, CA: SAGE.

Mertens, D., Bledsoe, K., Sullivan, M. & Wilson, A. (2010). Utilization of mixed methods for transformative purposes. In A. Tashakkori & C. Teddlie (Eds.), *SAGE handbook of mixed methods in social and behavioral research* (2nd ed.). Los Angeles, CA: SAGE.

Miles, M. B., & Huberman, A. M. (1994). *Qualitative data analysis: An expanded sourcebook*. Thousand Oaks, CA: SAGE.

Miller, P. J. (1994). Narrative practices: Their role in socialization and self-construction. In U. Neisser & R. Fivush (Eds.) *The remembering self: Construction and accuracy in the self-narrative* (pp.158-179). Cambridge, UK: Cambridge University Press.

Mills, C. (1969). *Sociology and pragmatism: The higher learning in America*. New York: Oxford University Press.

Morgan, D. (2007). Paradigms lost and pragmatism regained: Methodological implications of combining qualitative and quantitative methods. *Journal of Mixed Methods Research, 1*, 48-76.

National Association of Social Workers. (2008). *Code of ethics*. Washington, DC: NASW Press.

O'Cathain, A. (2010). Assessing the quality of mixed methods research: Toward a comprehensive framework. In A. Tashakkori & C. Teddlie (Eds), *SAGE handbook of mixed methods in social and behavioral research* (pp. 531-555). Thousand Oaks, CA: SAGE.

Ochs, E., & Schieffelin, B. (1984). Language acquisition and socialization: Three developmental stories. In R. Schweder & R. LeVine (Eds.), *Culture theory: Essays on mind, self and emotion* (pp. 276-320). New York: Cambridge University Press.

Oetting, E. R., Beauvais, F., & Edwards, R. W. (1985). *The American drug and alcohol survey*. Fort Collins, CO: Rocky Mountain Behavioral Science Institute.

Onwuegbuzie, A. J., & Combs, J. P. (2010). Emergent data analysis techniques in mixed methods research: A synthesis. In A. Tashakkori & C. Teddlie (Eds), *SAGE handbook of mixed methods in social and behavioral research* (pp. 397-430). Thousand Oaks, CA: SAGE.

Onwuegbuzie, A. J., & Johnson, R. B. (2006). The validity issue in mixed research. *Research in the Schools, 13*, 48-63.

Ostler, T., Haight, W., and Black, J. (2007). Mental health outcomes and perspectives of rural children raised by parent who abuse methamphetamine. *Journal of American Academy of Child and Adolescent Psychiatry, 46*, 500-507.

Padgett, D. K. (2008). *Qualitative methods in social work research*. Thousand Oaks, CA: SAGE.

Petrosino, A., Turpin-Petrosino, C., & Buehler, J. (2003). Scared Straight and other juvenile awareness programs for preventing juvenile delinquency: A systematic review of the randomized experimental evidence. *The Annals of the American Academy of Political and Social Science, 589*, 41-62.

Piaget, J. (1962). *Play, dreams and imitation in childhood*. New York: Norton.

Polansky, N., A. (1971). Research in social work. *Encyclopedia of social work, 16*(1), 474-485.

Powell, J. (2002). The changing conditions of social work research. *British Journal of Social Work, 32*, 17–33.

Pumphrey, R. E., & Pumphrey, M. W. (1961). *The heritage of American social work.* New York: Columbia University Press.

Ragin, C. (1987. *The comparative method: Moving beyond qualitative and quantitative strategies.* Berkley, CA: University of California Press.

Reamer, F. G. (1998). *Ethical standards in social work: A critical review of the NASW code of ethics.* Washington, DC: NASW Press.

Reid, W. J. (1987). Research in social work. *Encyclopedia of Social Work, 18*(2), 474–485.

Reid, W. J. (1995). Research overview. *Encyclopedia of Social Work, 19*, 2040–2054.

Reid, W. J. (1998). Empirically-supported practice: Perennial myth or emerging reality. Distinguished Professorship Lecture, School of Social Welfare, University at Albany, State University of New York.

Richmond, M. E. (1917). *Social diagnosis.* New York: Russell Sage Foundation.

Ridenour, C., & Newman, I. (2008). *Mixed methods research: Exploring the interactive continuum.* Carbondale, IL: Southern Illinois University Press.

Rossman, G., & Wilson, B. (1985). Numbers and words: Combining quantitative and qualitative methods in a single large-scale evaluation study. *Evaluation Review, 9*, 627–643.

Rubin, D. B. (1976). Matching methods that are equal percent bias reducing: Some examples. *Biometrics, 32*, 109-120.

Rubin, A., & Babbie, E. (2016). *Essential research methods for social work* (8th ed.). Belmont, CA: Brooks/Cole, Cengage Learning.

Sackett, D. L., Straus, S. E., Richardson, W. S., Rosenberg, W., & Haynes, R. B. (2000). *Evidence-based medicine: How to practice and teach EBM* (2nd ed.). New York: Churchill Livingstone.

Schoppe-Sullivan, S., Mangelsdorf, S., Haight, W., Black, J., Sokolowski, M., Giorgio, G., & Tata, L. (2007). Maternal discourse, attachment-related risk, and current risk factors: Associations with maternal parenting behavior during foster care visits. *Journal of Applied Developmental Psychology, 28*, 149-165.

Schwandt, T. (2007). *The SAGE dictionary of qualitative inquiry* (3rd ed.). Thousand Oaks, CA: SAGE.

Shadish, W., R., Cook, T. D., & Campbell, D. T. (2002). *Experimental and quasi-experimental designs for generalized causal inference.* Boston: Houghton Mifflin.

Shannon, P. (2014) Refugees' advice to physicians: How to ask about mental health. *Family Practice.* Advance online publication. doi:10.1093/fampra/cmu017

Shannon, P., Im, H., Becher, E., Simmelink, J., Wieling, L., & O'Fallon, A. (2012). Screening for war trauma, torture and mental health symptoms among newly arrived refugees: A national survey of state refugee health coordinators. *Journal of Immigrant and Refugee Studies, 10*, 380-394. doi:10.1080/15562948.2012.674324

Shannon, P., McCleary, J., Wieling, E., Im, H., Becher, E., & O'Fallon, A. (2015). Exploring mental health screening feasibility and training of refugee health coordinators. *Journal of Immigrant & Refugee Studies, 13*, 80-102.

Shannon, P., O'Dougherty, M., & Mehta, E. (2012) Refugees' perspectives on barriers to communication about trauma histories in primary care. *Mental Health in Family Medicine, 9*, 47-55.

Shannon, P. J., Vinson, G., Cook, T., & Lennon, E. (2015) Characteristics of successful and unsuccessful mental health referrals of refugees: Perspectives of providers and ethnic leaders. *Administration and Policy in Mental Health and Mental Health Services Research, 42*(2). doi:10.1007/s10488-015-0639-8

Shannon, P. J., Vinson, G., Wieling, L., Cook, T., & Letts, J. (2014) Torture, war trauma, and mental health symptoms of newly arrived Karen refugees. *Journal of Loss and Trauma: International Perspectives on Stress and Coping.* Advance online publication. doi:10.1080/15325024.2014.965971

Shannon, P. J., Wieling, L, Becher, E., & Simmelink-McCleary, J. (2014) Exploring the mental health effects of political trauma with newly arrived refugees. *Qualitative Health Research, 25*(4), 443–457. Advance online publication. doi:10.1177/1049732314549475

Shannon, P. J., Wieling, L., Simmelink-McCleary, J., & Becher, E. (2014). Beyond stigma: Barriers to discussing mental health in refugee populations. *Journal of Loss and Trauma: International Perspectives on Stress and Coping.* Advance online publication.doi:10.1080/15325024.2014.9346291080/15325024.2014.934629

Shaw, I., Briar-Lawson, K., Orme, J., & Ruckdeschel, R. (2010). Mapping social work research: Pasts, presents and futures. *SAGE handbook of social work research.* London: SAGE.

Sheridan, K., Haight, W., & Cleeland, L. (2011). The role of grandparents in preventing aggressive and other externalizing behavior problems in children from rural, methamphetamine-involved families. *Children and Youth Services Review, 33,* 1583–91.

Shweder, R. A. (1996). Quanta and qualia: What is the 'object' of ethnographic method? In R. Jessor, A. Colby, & R. A. Shweder (Eds.), *Ethnography and human development: Context and meaning in social inquiry* (pp. 175–182). Chicago: University of Chicago Press.

Sperry, D. (2014). *Listening to all the words: Reassessing the verbal environments of young working-class and poor children* [Unpublished doctoral dissertation]. The University of Illinois at Urbana-Champaign.

Stuart, R. B. (1971). Research in social work: Social casework and social group work. *Encyclopedia of Social Work, 16*(1), 474–485.

Tashakkori, A., & Creswell, J. W. (2007). Editorial: The new era of mixed methods. *Journal of Mixed Methods Research, 1*(3), 3–7.

Tashakkori, A., & Teddlie, C. (1998). *Mixed methodology: Combining qualitative and quantitative approaches.* Thousand Oaks, CA: SAGE.

Tashakkori, A., & Teddlie, C. (2006). Validity issues in mixed methods research: Calling for an integrative framework. Paper presented at the Annual Meeting of the American Educational Research Association, San Francisco, CA, April 2006.

Tashakkori, A., & Teddlie, C. (2010). Preface. In A. Tashakkori & C. Teddlie (Eds.) *SAGE handbook of mixed methods in social and behavioral research* (pp. ix-xv) . Thousand Oaks, CA: SAGE.

Teddlie, C. & Tashakkori, A. (2010). Overview of contemporary issues in mixed methods research. *SAGE handbook of mixed methods in social and behavioral research.* Thousand Oaks, CA: SAGE.

Teddlie, C., & Tashakkori, A. (2012). Common "core" characteristics of mixed methods research: A review of critical issues and call for greater convergence. *American Behavioral Scientist, 56,* 774–788.

Teddlie, C., & Tashakkori, A. (Eds.). (2003). Major issues and controversies in the use of mixed methods in the social and behavioral sciences. *Handbook of mixed methods in social and behavioral research* (pp. 3-50). Thousand Oaks, CA: SAGE.

Teddlie, C., & Tashakkori, A. (Eds.). (2009). *Foundations of mixed methods research: Integrating quantitative and qualitative approaches in the social and behavioral sciences.* Thousand Oaks, CA: SAGE.

Tripodi, T., & Lalayants, M. (2008). Research: Overview. *Encyclopedia of social work, 20*(3), 512-520.

U.S. Department of Health and Human Services. (1979). *The Belmont report: Ethical principles and guidelines for the protection of human subjects of research.* Washington, DC: Author.

Vygotsky, L. S. (1962). *Thought and language.* Cambridge, MA: M.I.T. Press.

Watkins, D. C. (2012). Depression over the adult life course for African American men: Toward a framework for research and practice. *American Journal of Men's Health, 6,* 194-210.

Watkins, D. C., & Neighbors, H. W. (2012). Social determinants of depression and the black male experience. In H.M. Treadwell, C. Xanthos, & K.B. Holden (Eds.), *Social determinants of health among African-American men* (pp. 39-62). San Francisco, CA: Jossey-Bass.

Watkins, J. M., & Holmes, J. (2008). Educating for social work. In B.W. White, K. M. Sowers, & C. N. Dulmus (Eds.), *Comprehensive handbook of social work and social welfare* (pp. 2-36). Hoboken, NJ: Wiley.

Whipps, J. (2010). Pragmatist feminism. In E. N. Zalta (ed.), *The Stanford Encyclopedia of Philosophy.* Retrieved from http://plato.stanford.edu/archives/fall2010/entries/femapproach-pragmatism

Glossary

Abductive reasoning moves back and forth between induction and deduction—first converting observations into theories and then assessing those theories through action.

Analytic induction is a data analysis strategy in qualitative research that involves developing a conceptual framework based on the participants' perspectives rather than imposing an external conceptual framework.

Attrition is the loss of participants after a study has begun.

Cause-probing designs include experiments and quasi-experiments intended to examine causal relationships.

Classical American Pragmatism is a grouping of philosophies that were developed from the late nineteenth century through the early twentieth century. It was especially influential in the Progressive Era (1890–1915) and up until the Second World War. It focuses on gaining knowledge through and in pursuit of desired ends.

Commensurability refers to the extent to which the inferences drawn from the mixed data set (meta-inferences) reflect a mixed worldview moving back and forth from a qualitative to a quantitative lens.

Complementarity, according to Greene and colleagues (1989), refers to the use of data from different methods to generate a deeper, broader, and more comprehensive portrait of a complex phenomenon.

Completeness is a frequently cited rationale for mixing qualitative and quantitative approaches. According to Bryman (2008), completeness refers to the researcher's ability to bring together a more comprehensive account of the area of inquiry by employing both quantitative and qualitative approaches.

Concurrent transformative design is a design in which qualitative and quantitative data are collected at the same time. Priority may be given to one or the other component, or they may be equally weighted. What distinguishes this design from other concurrent designs is the focus on a specific theoretical perspective, for example, feminism or critical race theory.

Constructivism is a philosophy of learning founded on the premise that we construct our understanding of the world through acting in that world and reflecting on those experiences.

Convergent designs involve the separate collation and analysis of quantitative and qualitative data.

Convergent parallel mixed methods design is a design in which qualitative and quantitative data are collected at the same time, and equal weight is given to both components.

Correlational designs involve observation of any relations between variables.

Critical multiplism. Thomas Cook (1985) extended the concept of triangulation to all aspects of the research process including not only the use of multiple methods in a single study, but also multiple theoretical orientations and political and value perspectives, for example.

Data consolidation involves merging quantitative and qualitative data sets in preparation for integrated data analyses.

Data transformation in analyses of mixed methods research involves converting one type of data into the other to allow for simultaneous analysis of both data types together.

Deductive reasoning is a type of reasoning that goes from the general to the specific. In research, deductive reasoning involves deriving hypotheses from theory and then testing them empirically.

Development is identified by Greene and colleagues (1989) as a purpose for mixing qualitative and quantitative approaches. Development is broadly construed to include instrument design, sample selection, and data collection.

Diversity of views is a rationale for mixing methods. According to Bryman (2008), enhanced understanding of complex phenomena occurs when multiple perspectives, each with inherent insights and limitations, are considered.

Embedded mixed methods design is a design in which qualitative and quantitative data are collected at the same time. and priority may be given to either the quantitative or qualitative component.

Emic refers to the perspectives of people from the group under study.

Empirical puzzle, as defined by Thomas Cook (1985), arises when data do not converge.

Enhanced rigor through triangulation is cited by a number of scholars as a rationale for mixing methods.

Enhanced understanding is a frequently cited rationale for mixing qualitative and quantitative approaches. Bryman (2008) characterized enhancement as augmenting either quantitative or qualitative findings by gathering data using the other approach.

Epistemology is a branch of philosophy that investigates the origin, nature, methods, and limits of human knowledge, for example, how we come to know our social world.

Ethnography is the systematic study of culture from the point of view of those people living within the culture.

Etic perspectives are imposed from outside of the group.

Evidence-based practice is the use of current empirical evidence in conjunction with professional knowledge of the sociocultural context and particular client as a guide to practice and policy decisions.

Expansion, as discussed by Greene and colleagues (1989), refers to the use of different methods to assess *different* phenomena as a way of broadening the scope and reach of the study.

Experiments, as defined by John Stuart Mill, (1) manipulate the presumed cause and then observe the presumed effect, (2) observe whether or not variation in the presumed cause is related to (correlated with) the presumed effect, and (3) use various structural features of the experiment to reduce the plausibility of explanations for the observed effect other than the presumed cause.

Explanatory sequential mixed method design is a design in which quantitative data are collected and analyzed and then qualitative data are collected and analyzed.

Exploratory sequential mixed methods design is a design in which qualitative data are collected and analyzed and then quantitative data are collected and analyzed.

Extreme case analysis involves the identification of extreme or atypical cases for further analysis.

Extreme case sampling in qualitative research involves selecting participants who are unusual.

External validity is the validity of inferences about whether a causal relationship holds over variation in participants, settings, and variables.

Homogeneous sampling in qualitative research involves recruitment of participants who are similar, such as members of a distinct subgroup.

Inductive reasoning moves from the specific to the general, for example, inferring participants' worldviews from their actions and words.

Initiation, as defined by Greene (2007), is the use of data from different methods to evoke paradox, contradiction, or dissonance to gain new insights.

Inside-outside legitimation in mixed methods research refers to the extent to which the research has adequately presented the insider perspective from the qualitative component and the outsider view from the quantitative component to describe and/or explain the phenomenon of interest.

Integrated data displays in mixed methods analyses present information from qualitative and quantitative methods together.

Internal validity refers to the validity of our inferences about whether the relationship between two variables is causal in a given study.

Intersubjective, as defined by Pragmatist philosopher John Dewey, is an intersubjective world as constructed through cooperation, communication and coordination.

Knowledge, as described by Pragmatist philosopher John Dewey, is the relation between our actions and their consequences.

Lateral progress, as described by Jane Addams, refers to social advancement, not as the breakthroughs or peak performances of a few, but as social gains held in common.

Lines of action, as defined by Pragmatist philosopher John Dewey, are the various competing possible behaviors rehearsed in imagination that precede intelligent action in contrast to trial-and-error.

Maximum variation sampling in qualitative research involves selecting people who have different experiences and perspectives.

Mediating variables in quantitative research are the causal mechanisms through which an independent variable affects the dependent variable.

Member checks in qualitative research involve asking participants to confirm the researcher's interpretations of the data (e.g., interview responses). These can be completed during data collection, analysis or interpretation of results.

Mental model is the underlying framework or logic of justification for social research. Mental models are the set of assumptions, understandings, predispositions, values, and beliefs with which we approach our work. They include not only basic philosophical assumptions (ontology, epistemology, methodology), but also our values, beliefs, disciplinary understandings, practice wisdom, and life history.

Meta-inference in mixed methods research refers to inferences made from the whole study, not just the separate qualitative and quantitative components.

Methodology broadly refers to the underlying logic, worldview, and values that guide the selection of specific methods and their integration.

Methods are the specific ways we implement our research design. They include strategies for sampling, data collection, and analysis.

Mixed methods research can be broadly defined as the intentional integration of qualitative and quantitative approaches to research in order to enhance understanding of complex social phenomena.

Moderating variables in quantitative research affect the strength or direction of a relationship between independent and dependent variables.

Multiplism refers to the use of multiple methods in a single study. *See also Critical multiplism.*

Negative cases are purposely sought or spontaneously appearing data that differ from the researcher's expectations, assumptions, or working theories. They may refute or refine findings or raise new questions.

Observational designs describe, but do not manipulate, phenomena.

Ontology is a branch of philosophy concerned with the nature and relations of being, for example, the nature of the social world.

Positive psychology is the scientific study of strengths that allow individuals and groups to flourish.

Positivism is a theory that theology and metaphysics are earlier imperfect modes of knowledge and that positive knowledge is based on natural phenomena and their properties and relations as verified by the empirical sciences. It is associated with quantitative social science research traditions.

Post-positivism is similar to positivism except that it recognizes that our ability to observe the social world objectively is limited by our own social positions and human biases, and it devises a variety of increasingly sophisticated designs and methodological strategies to minimize human error including when studying human beings in naturalistic contexts.

Pragmatism focuses on gaining knowledge through and in pursuit of desired ends. Classical American pragmatism refers to a grouping of philosophies that were developed from the late nineteenth century through the early twentieth century, and were especially influential in the Progressive Era (1890–1915) and up until the Second World War.

Probabilistic sampling in quantitative research is selection of participants representative of the population to which the researchers seek to generalize. This typically is accomplished through random selection, in other words, by selecting participants by chance to represent the population using a systematic procedures (e.g., using a random numbers table or drawing names from a hat).

Procedures refer to how quantitative or qualitative data were obtained and what the participants experienced.

Propensity score matching is a statistical technique used to better equate treatment and comparison groups by matching on a composite of participant characteristics.

Purposeful sampling refers to sampling strategies used in qualitative research to recruit participants who can provide rich information.

Quasi-experimental designs are designs that share the aim of experiments to determine causal relationships. They also share many of the important structural features: the presumed cause is made to precede the effect, any covariation is noted, and plausible alternative explanations are eliminated. By definition, however, participants in quasi-experiments are not randomly assigned to groups. This creates a challenge: in quasi-experiments plausible alternative explanations for the observed outcome other than the presumed cause must be eliminated one by one using logic, design features, and measurement rather than random assignment to groups.

Random assignment refers to the assignment of experiment participants (people, families, communities) to experimental and control groups using a random numbers table or other tool, thus equating groups prior to exposure to the presumed cause (e.g., intervention). Random assignment of participants to groups means that other factors that may affect the outcome are equally likely to affect the experimental and the control group and thus cannot explain any observed differences between groups after exposure to the presumed cause.

Random selection refers to selection of participants in quantitative research by chance to represent the population using a systematic procedure (e.g., using a random numbers table or drawing names from a hat).

Reflexivity in qualitative research refers to a process whereby the researcher reflects on his or her own biases and perspectives in relation to the research.

Reliability of a measure refers to its stability.

Research designs are the plans for integrating different components of a study to address broad study aims and specific research questions.

Saturation is the point at which new participants are not providing additional information. In qualitative research sample size is determined when saturation is reached.

Sequential transformative design is a mixed methods design in which one approach (quantitative or qualitative) precedes the other, and priority may be given to either method or both methods may be equally important. The distinguishing feature of this design is its tie to a particular theoretical perspective.

Site is the place where the research is conducted.

Social justice designs add to basic mixed methods designs through the incorporation of a social justice perspective.

Structural equation modeling (SEM) is a family of statistical methods used to test conceptual or theoretical models. It can strengthen causal interpretations in correlational designs.

Thick description in qualitative research refers to an in-depth and detailed account of the behavior of interest in sociocultural and historical context necessary to elucidate its meaning.

Threats to validity are reasons why inferences and knowledge claims may be incorrect (i.e., alternative explanations or rival hypotheses).

Transactions (in nature) are described by Pragmatist philosopher John Dewey as the dynamic exchanges and interactions through which we refine and acquire knowledge.

Transactional realism refers to the theory of Pragmatist philosopher John Dewey that knowledge is at the same time real and constructed.

Triangulation refers to the use of different methods to offset the limitations of any single method and hence increase confidence in the research results.

Typology development in mixed methods research involves the analysis of one data type (qualitative or quantitative) to identify dimensions of interest and create a set of substantive categories or typology. This typology is then incorporated into the analysis of the contrasting data type.

Validity refers to the approximate truth of an inference or knowledge claim.

Validity of an instrument or measure refers to how well it actually reflects the concept that it's intended to measure.

Wait-list control group Refers to a process in which participants are randomly assigned to groups. The experimental group receives the intervention and the control group is assigned to a wait list or receives the usual intervention. If the new intervention is effective and does not cause unintended harm, then those clients on the wait list or other control group are offered it.

Warranted assertions refers to pragmatist philosopher John Dewey's characterization of the outcomes of inquiry not as absolute truth but as the result of careful observation of the relationship between actions and consequences in particular contexts that may or may not transfer to other contexts.

Warranted assertion analysis is an integrated analysis process in which the researcher repeatedly rereads the qualitative and quantitative data sets as a whole, working inductively toward claims grounded in all the data. Next, evidence for each claim is assembled. Then, the researcher iteratively refines each claim through vigorous searches for disconfirming evidence.

Weakness minimization in mixed methods research refers to the extent to which weaknesses from each approach are offset by the strengths of the other approach.

Index

Note: Page numbers in *italic* refer to glossary terms. Page numbers followed by "f" or "t" refer to figures or tables, respectively.

About the Authors

Wendy L. Haight, PhD, is professor and Gamble-Skogmo Chair in Child Welfare and Youth Policy. Professor Haight completed her undergraduate degree in Psychology at Reed College and her PhD at the University of Chicago, where she studied human development and culture through a wide interdisciplinary lens. Before joining the faculty at the University of Minnesota School of Social Work in 2011, she served on the faculty of the University of Illinois, Urbana Champaign, for sixteen years. Her research focuses on better understanding and supporting vulnerable children and families in diverse cultural contexts, especially those involved in public child welfare systems. She uses mixed methods to better understand complex social issues and then works within teams to design, implement, and evaluate tailored interventions. She is the author or coauthor of eight previous books and about fifty articles in peer-reviewed journals.

Laurel N. Bidwell, MSW, PhD, LICSW, is an assistant professor in the School of Social Work at St. Catherine University and the University of St. Thomas. She completed her MSW at Hunter College, the City University of New York, and began her career as a clinical social worker with children and families in school-, community- and hospital-based settings. In 2006 she obtained her PhD in Developmental Psychology at Teachers College, Columbia University. Before joining the faculty at St. Catherine University and the University of St. Thomas in 2014, she worked as a research associate at the University of Minnesota. Her research is an extension of her clinical practice, as it focuses on supporting the well-being of marginalized children and families. She has a particular interest in mixed methods evaluation research as a way of ensuring that programs and services are meeting the needs of highly vulnerable families, especially those involved with the child welfare system.